HOW THE
RAF & USAAF
BEAT THE
LUFTWAFFE

HOW THE RAF & USAAF BEAT THE LUFTWAFFE

KEN DELVE

Greenhill Books

How the RAF Beat the Luftwaffe
First published in 2021 by
Greenhill Books,
c/o Pen & Sword Books Ltd,
47 Church Street, Barnsley,
S. Yorkshire, S70 2AS

www.greenhillbooks.com
contact@greenhillbooks.com

ISBN: 978–1–78438–382–4

CIP data records for this title are available from the British Library

Designed and typeset by Donald Sommerville

Printed and bound in the UK by TJ Books, Padstow, Cornwall

Typeset in 10/13.6 pt ITC Giovanni

MIX
Paper from
responsible sources
FSC
www.fsc.org   FSC® C013056

Frontispiece: The tail turret of an Avro Manchester of 207 Squadron;
the rear-gunner, with his four machine-guns, was a critical part of the
bomber's defence against night fighters.

This book is dedicated to all those who served in the Allied and German air forces in World War Two.

Contents

Plates

1. Hurricane of 73 Squadron, France, winter 1939–40; Fighter Command operations room; Spitfire of 92 Squadron at Duxford, May 1940.
2. Adolph 'Sailor' Malan of 74 Squadron; Luftwaffe intelligence map of RAF Scampton; cartoon from a Fighter Command training pamphlet.
3. Spitfires of 616 Squadron approaching Rochford, 1940; re-arming a Hurricane.
4. Czech pilot of Fighter Command; Air Marshal Dowding, head of Fighter Command in 1940; Douglas Bader with pilots of 616 Squadron; Hermann Göring.
5. Messerschmitt Bf 109 fighter; Bristol Beaufighter night fighter; Pilots of 80 Squadron pose with a Spitfire at West Malling, July 1944.
6. Aircrew in the early stages of training; Whitley crew of 58 Squadron, Linton-on-Ouse 1940; Wellington crew of 149 Squadron.
7. Wellington crews at Marham, August 1940*; Handley Page Halifax heavy bomber in flight; Egmont Lippe-Weissenfeld Luftwaffe night-fighter ace.
8. The Junkers factory at Leipzig after the Bomber Command attack of 3/4 December 1943; Gp Capt John Searby, one of the first Master Bombers, seen at Wyton in August 1943.
9. Air Marshal Arthur Harris, head of Bomber Command; RAF leaders Coningham, Broadhurst and Tedder.
10. Drawing of a shot-down Lancaster by one of its crew; target photo from an attack on the Bec d'Ambes oil depot, France, 4 August 1944.
11. B-24 production line at Fort Worth; B-17 formation in flight.
12. A B-17 during an attack on the Focke-Wulf factory at Marienburg; B-24s of the 44th BG.
13. Flight and groundcrew personnel of B-17 'Thundermug' of the 305th Bomb Group, June 1944; B-17 undergoing maintenance; flak hit on a B-24.
14. Fighter ace Don Gabreski poses with his groundcrew and his P-47 Thunderbolt; Lt Stapp and Lt Manahan of the 305th FS, 353rd FG, with a P-51 Mustang; General Bill Kepner, head of VIII Fighter Command during 1943–4.

15. Adolf Galland, fighter ace in 1940 and General of Fighters later in the war; Me 262 jet fighter.
16. A heavily attacked oil facility; a Fw 190 shot down by an American fighter.

All photographs in Plates 1–10 come from the author's collection, except Plate 7 *, which is courtesy of the RAF Marham Aviation Heritage Centre; all photographs in Plates 11–16 are from the US National Archives.

Preface

'How did the RAF beat the Luftwaffe?' This is a good question and one that can trigger a great deal of debate, some of it partisan. The massive participation of the Americans from early 1943 is part of the story but some would argue that by managing not to lose, the RAF enabled the eventual victory. This present study does not aim to be definitive; for one thing, I do not believe there is ever such a book, although there are authors with a definite ego and publishers with an eye to marketing. This study looks at the main campaigns in which the RAF, and later the Western Allies, faced the Luftwaffe. It therefore ignores much of the war, even though, as a global war, every part of the conflict had influence on other parts, such as resource use, morale impact, and so on.

The period 1940 to 1942 could be defined as 'how the RAF beat the Luftwaffe' and the period 1943 to 1945 as 'how the Anglo-American air forces destroyed the Luftwaffe'. This split will no doubt be disputed and argued, but in air power terms and its ability to influence the overall progress of the war, the Luftwaffe was, by the later months of 1942 no longer a decisive strategic, or even tactical weapon, despite its ability to deliver sharp defeats when poor tactics were used by its opponents, and on the Eastern Front where the Soviets never achieved a significant degree of air superiority. The Luftwaffe was remarkably resilient, but it was on a continual slide to ultimate destruction. The main areas in which failure could be measured were:

- Defective strategic planning from the inception of the Luftwaffe; a tactical air arm wedded to the air–land concept, which by being highly successful in the first eighteen months of the war meant the German leadership failed to see the seeds of ultimate failure;
- Failure to provide decisive result over Britain in 1940 and over the Mediterranean/Desert in 1941–2;
- Failure to defend the Reich and the occupied countries against the RAF and, later, combined Allied bomber offensive;
- Trying to do too much with too little – the multi-front war.

There were numerous aspects to these failures, and this study looks at many of these, from equipment (not just aircraft), to tactics, leadership (political and military), logistics, morale, and others, which are discussed in each chapter. In broad terms the study is limited to the fighter and bomber roles, as these had the most impact on the point in question. This is not intended in any way to minimise the role of Allied air power in the maritime war, air–land support, transport, and all the other roles and theatres, such as the Far East, where RAF and Allied personnel fought long and bitter conflicts. Thus, this study focuses on the campaigns in the Western European Theatre of Operations, as this was the operational area in which the decisive elements took place.

It is obvious that the Russian war provided the Germans with a range of strategic problems from its start in 1941, increasingly so from early 1943, which impacted their air capability elsewhere; for example, the diversion of air assets to the Eastern Front. There are many who believe that US air power and tactics were decisive in the final defeat of the Luftwaffe. There is a large element of truth here regarding the actual destruction of the Luftwaffe, but that part of the story is only really true for the last year or so of the war. The previous five years of war had been ones of avoiding defeat, followed by building the capability that provided the foundations for the defeat and then destruction of the Luftwaffe. Would Bomber Command have been able to continue the night war if the day offensive had not been draining fighter assets (aircraft and crews)? If the night offensive had not been delivering increasingly powerful blows would the greater availability of fighter and flak assets have impacted the day offensive? If the German political and military leadership had not based its air strategy on the concept of air–land support to conquer territory would better air-defence aircraft and systems have been in place earlier? All these and more are inter-related and taken together led to the defeat and destruction of the much-vaunted Luftwaffe.

This present study has limited space to cover in detail all the factors and inter-relationships, any single aspect of which would be worthy of a full study.

The Mediterranean and North Africa

The reader may be surprised at the exclusion of the Mediterranean and North African theatre from this study. Other than the limitations in number of pages, the following rationale was applied for this exclusion:

Malta: The air battle for Malta ranks alongside the Battle of Britain as a tale of the fighter pilot few, although in this case the battle was far longer and far more difficult, with the logistics problem of supplying this tiny island in the Mediterranean. The RAF could most certainly have been declared the winner if the contest had only included the periods of Italian operations against the island; however, in the periods when the Luftwaffe took a more direct interest, the RAF could really only say that it 'held on'. I covered Malta, both its defensive and offensive role in my book *Malta Strikes Back* for those who want to read more about Malta and the RAF.

Western Desert: Operations by the Desert Air Force (DAF) and its associated units were a tale of early victory against the Italian Air Force, many hard knocks when the Luftwaffe arrived, and eventually parity and then air superiority, as more squadrons and better aircraft were sent to the desert war. Did the RAF beat the Luftwaffe here? Both sides continued to support the land operations, which was the primary role of air power in this theatre, until the Germans were eventually swamped with a two-front campaign. From an RAF air-power perspective, the most important contribution of the DAF was the development of air–land tactics, which proved invaluable in its subsequent Italian campaign, as well as the operations in north-west Europe after D-Day.

If space had permitted, then I would certainly have included a section on the Western Desert air war. Those who want more detail can always read my *Desert Air Force* book!

North Africa: The Allied invasion of North Africa in November 1942 was the first significant air power intervention by the Americans in terms of air–land and tactical bombing, as well as other air roles. The major lessons involved inter-allied cooperation and command, which proved trying at times, but some issues were resolved that proved valuable for the commanders and units that became part of the Italian campaign or went back to western Europe to be part of the invasion.

Sicily and Italy: By the time the Allies moved into Italy it was pretty much a one-sided air war. The Luftwaffe was still present, but it seldom had the capacity to intervene in Allied air operations or to mount its own air operations in support of the ground forces.

Acknowledgements

This book is the culmination of many years of research using a wide range of primary and secondary sources. The document primary sources have mainly been RAF and Luftwaffe (in translated versions) record books and papers, and most of those I have accessed with the assistance of the Air Historical Branch; indeed, all of the books and articles I have written over the years owe a huge debt to the work of the AHB in preserving documents, producing official histories, and enabling researchers to access this treasure trove of information. The other primary source has been the wonderful experience of meeting and chatting with so many veterans over the years, made easier by two of my careers that gave me access – my own aircrew service in the RAF and my time as editor of *FlyPast* magazine. The veterans' stories help to put the human perspective on the historical 'bones'. Finally, and like all authors, I rely on published secondary sources, either from those who were there (so in reality a primary source) and those, like me, who research and write about aviation subjects, and I freely acknowledge the excellent work of my fellow authors. Increasingly, research is made easier through careful use of the internet, although I stress the word careful, as a large percentage of what is out there may be confusing or wrong.

Over my forty years of research I have had help and support from a very large number of veterans, researchers and authors, and rather than name anyone specific here, I would like to recognise them all; I hope they continue to help me and all researchers and authors in recording and sharing aviation history. You can help share and access that research by visiting my Facebook page, Aviation History Research Centre, or my website, www.rafht.co.uk.

Chapter 1

Galland's View

Many years ago, I wrote a commentary article around a document produced by Adolf Galland in 1953 with his view of the Battle of Britain. Whilst covering the campaign quite broadly, his focus was on what went wrong, and who to blame, and many of the subjects he discussed related to the overall set of reasons why Allied air power defeated the Luftwaffe. One of Germany's greatest fighter pilots, Adolf Galland had gained his initial experience in the Spanish Civil War and by the outbreak of World War Two was flying Bf 109s. His flair as a fighter pilot saw him quickly promoted to command of JG 26 and subsequently to the post of Inspector of Fighters. This, however, brought him into contact, and conflict with Hermann Göring and many stormy scenes ensued. He was dismissed from this post in January 1945 and returned to combat flying, leading the Me 262-equipped JV 44. The 1953 report was compiled in the light of post-war knowledge, and antipathy towards the German leadership in general and Göring in particular; however, despite this it is a useful document, the main elements of which are discussed here.

> The Luftwaffe had to be used in a decisive way in the Battle of Britain as a means of conducting total air war. Its size, technical equipment and the means at its disposal precluded the Luftwaffe from fulfilling this mission. On the other hand, in the absence of the necessary experience, the possibilities, limitations, requirements, methods and forces needed for carrying out strategic air operations were not yet known. Whatever may have been the importance of the tests of German arms in the Spanish Civil War from tactical, technical and operational points of view, they did not provide the experience that was needed nor lead to the formulation of sound strategic concepts.

Galland makes the point that the Luftwaffe was less than five years old when it was 'called upon to prove its mettle in the Second World War' and that in those years the 'most powerful air force in the world at that time had been built up'. As in other areas of his account, Galland is being somewhat selective here, as the Luftwaffe's origins could be traced back to before this 'official formation' date. The effective strength of the Luftwaffe in late summer 1939 included 30 bomber *Gruppen* (He 111, Do 17, Ju 88) with

675 bombers, nine Ju 87 Stuka *Gruppen* with 200 aircraft, ten long-range fighter *Gruppen* with 300 Bf 110s, 13 single-engine fighter *Gruppen* with 400 Bf 109s, 21 long-range reconnaissance *Staffeln* with 104 aircraft, primarily Do 17s, and 30 close reconnaissance *Staffeln* with 200 aircraft, mainly He 126s. The majority of these were involved in the Polish campaign and the Polish Air Force was rapidly overwhelmed. Several additional *Gruppen* were formed during the first year of the war and according to German Quartermaster-General records total strength increased from fewer than 2,000 aircraft to around 7,000 aircraft, including over 3,000 bombers and around 2,750 fighters. German estimates gave British strength as 5,500 warplanes, but with only 3,600 of these being based in the UK and with only 200 of the 620 fighters being 'of the latest type . . . a large proportion of the British aircraft were out of date and this enabled the Luftwaffe to maintain air supremacy at this stage with about 2,500 aircraft of later types'.

Galland then comments that the balance of the German forces was not right – because there were too few fighters,

> The reason for this is to be found in the basic conception on which the new Luftwaffe had been built up; it was thought of as an attacking force. This conformed with the strategic concept much in favour at that time: that mastery of the air should be obtained in the initial operations of a war through the destruction, on the ground, of the enemy's air power. I personally believe that Germany would not have lost the war if the production of fighters had been on the same scale in 1940 or 1941 as it was in 1944.

To some extent this is the fighter pilot speaking – there are never enough fighters, but there is also a very valid point of air doctrine in terms of air superiority being the prerequisite for air operations. The concept of destroying an enemy's air power 'on the ground' was fundamentally flawed but appeared valid in the light of the Polish campaign, and indeed would do so again in the June 1941 offensive against Russia. The inherent secondary nature of the fighter implied by this doctrine was to be one of the factors limiting the effectiveness of the German fighter arm during the Battle of Britain.

German fighter production in 1940 averaged only 200 aircraft a month and it was not until early 1942, as a reaction to the Allied bomber offensive, that a significant increase in rates of production began. In common with most air arms in the 1930s, the bomber was seen in Germany as the decisive weapon and most attention was paid to the development of these offensive weapons. 'The air force is a strategic, offensive weapon' and to this effect aircraft such as the Do 17 and He 111 were developed, bombers with performance superior to the contemporary He 51 and Ar 65 fighters:

> This led to a completely erroneous conception; it was believed then, and for some time afterwards, that in daylight attacks, bombers would be able to master enemy fighters and would thus not need to be escorted. In any case, fighters would not be able to accompany bombers owing to their disparity of speed.

This false premise led the RAF's bomber force into problems in late 1939 and the USAAF's B-17s and B-24s to suffer heavy losses in 1943. The advent of high-performance fighters should have prompted changes in doctrine.

> The construction of the new Bf 109 of completely revolutionary design put the problem back again in proper perspective. The sceptics asserted that the new Bf 109 was not suitable for service use because of its very high take-off and landing speeds, which would give rise to insurmountable difficulties in handling it. Time has corrected these false conceptions and made one fact quite clear, the Bf 109 not only possessed superior features, but it caused a revolution in fighter design throughout the world.

The principal drawback of the single-engine fighters such as the Bf 109 was that of operational radius, around 200 km: 'This drawback played a decisive part in the outcome of the Battle of Britain.' With the realisation that the bombers might require fighter escort in daylight the Luftwaffe planners, at Göring's insistence, had to devise a twin-engined long-range fighter, the outcome being the Bf 110. The formation of such units in 1938 saw the third time when the day-fighter force was required to give up a cadre of its best pilots, the previous two occasions being the expansion of the bomber force and the creation of the Stuka dive-bomber force.

> The consequences of this reduction on three separate occasions of the effective strength of fighter personnel were felt in the period between 1934 and 1939. For a long time, fighter pilots were relegated to second place because they were not integrated into the operational air force. At manoeuvres, in conformity with regulations that had been drawn up governing their use, fighters were assigned the tasks of local air defence and combat for the purpose of achieving mastery in the air over front-line zones. Thus, they were not included, and this was the mistake, in the operational air forces. However, the pilots of the new long-range fighters were, according to Göring, to be the elite of the fighter personnel.

Once again, the fault lay in doctrine; the Luftwaffe had little on which to base a strategic doctrine and thus it was constrained to operate in a more tactical sense. Whilst the Spanish and Polish campaigns gave the Luftwaffe valuable combat experience, they also provided what were to prove inappropriate lessons.

The Battle of Britain

'In order to carry out the invasion, the primary need was to obtain air superiority, and, as far as this was possible, absolute mastery of the air. Hence the task of solving the crucial problem was assigned to the air force.' The German Navy, rightly, insisted on air cover, a protective umbrella, during any invasion operation – to achieve this the Luftwaffe would have to destroy the RAF; three strategic missions were therefore given to the Luftwaffe:

- The blockade of Britain, in conjunction with the Navy, by air attacks on shipping and ports.
- Softening-up for the invasion; an offensive aimed at gaining air superiority.
- Forcing Britain to surrender by waging total air war.

Galland had doubts:

> Many voices in Germany were raised in criticism of the idea of attacking the British on their own soil. The critics maintained that not even the military occupation of the British Isles would be enough to bring about the end of the war. Field Marshal Kesselring [commander of Luftflotte 1 in 1939–40 and Luftflotte 2 in 1940–3], for example, headed a section of opinion that believed that an air offensive against Britain would demonstrate the limitations and weaknesses of the air force, and that it would result in our losing the most powerful instrument of political and military pressure we possessed. Hitler decided differently; once again it was principally Göring who goaded him into making his decision.

At this stage Galland was not party to the discussions of either the Luftwaffe hierarchy or that of the Nazi leadership; he no doubt subsequently discussed the battle with some of those who had been part of the decision-making process, but the inclusion of hindsight perspective is inevitable, especially from such air leaders as Kesselring. Nevertheless, it was a confident Luftwaffe that commenced operations against Britain; its campaigns to date – Spain, Poland and France – seemed to vindicate both its equipment and its doctrine. True, the Luftwaffe had greater respect for the RAF than for some of its previous opponents and there was the problem of combat radius for the single-engine fighters, but overall the planners, and the aircrew, anticipated few major problems.

> The second phase of the German air offensive began on 24 July 1940, the aim being to rout the British fighter defences in combat with German fighters, and thus obtain the superiority necessary to ensure the effective employment of day bombers. To this end, German fighters were sent over the Channel on successive and intermittent sorties, first in group strength and then by squadrons. At first the British accepted the challenge and sent up Hurricanes and Spitfires to engage the German units. The Hurricanes were out of date and their performance was far inferior to that of the Messerschmitt fighter as regards both maximum speed in level flight and rate of climb. Though the Spitfire was more manoeuvrable in turning, its maximum speed was 20–30 km per hour less. German ammunition and armament were manifestly better than those of the British. The RAF lost the greater number of fighters. But even more important than these technical drawbacks were the outmoded tactics used by the British fighters.

The question of comparative fighter performance is one that has occupied countless words and is frequently clouded by partisan viewpoints: did the rugged nature of the Hurricane make it better able to survive being hit, was the armament of the German fighters far superior, and so on. The qualitative nature of the pilots and, as Galland points out, the tactics being employed, have also to be taken into consideration. The Luftwaffe entered the Battle with a confident, verging on cocky, attitude and hence their morale was superb. The RAF fighter pilots were still largely untried and they faced what appeared to be an invincible war machine that had swept previous opponents away. They had confronted each other over France but now came the real test.

> Normally each unit made up to three sorties per day. The physical strain on pilots was very heavy; airframes and engines also suffered from these efforts. It soon became evident that Fighter Command was not deceived by the German air attacks for it did not send up its fighters on hasty missions according to the exigencies of the moment. Radar enabled the British to alert their defences in good time and to send up fighters at the right moment to intercept the German formations and to engage them when and where they chose.

The failure of the fighters to draw the RAF to its destruction led to a change of tactics:

> In order to compel British fighters to fight again – the British Command had undoubtedly forbidden them to do so owing to German superiority – our fighters began to appear escorting several bombers, which attacked airfields, rail junctions and any other similar targets. The bombers were called *Lockvögel* [decoy birds] and the aim was achieved; the struggle for air supremacy resumed its rhythm.

This same tactic was subsequently employed by the RAF, during the Circus operations, when offensive fighter sweeps over Occupied Europe in 1941–2 failed to produce any Luftwaffe reaction and bomber forces were employed to force a response – a tactic that met with mixed results.

However, it was with Phase III, the direct attack on RAF airfields, that the Battle of Britain truly began. To the RAF, these attacks on its airfields, and associated installations such as radar sites, were critical and many post-war commentators have concluded that if the attacks had continued then the battle might have taken a different course. Galland, however, in his commentary puts forward a different view:

> The results obtained were very poor, for when attacks were made, practically all available British aircraft were in the air, engaged on defensive operations. Overall, damage caused to the ground organisation was superficial. Better results would have been obtained if more small-calibre bombs had been used, but the bombers were not equipped with suitable release apparatus. The British withdrew their fighter squadrons beyond London and used airfields close to the coast only for staging and emergency landings. Moreover, they had so many airfields that they had good chances of eluding attacks.

As with other parts of the Galland commentary, this smacks of post-war 'excuses' for the failure of the Luftwaffe campaign. Whilst it is true that the RAF had a reasonable number of airfields, the number within operating range of the combat area was limited – and all were well known to the Luftwaffe. RAF records show that a number of key airfields suffered significant damage, albeit repairs were rapid and the airfields, if not all of their facilities, were back in operation quite quickly; however, a concerted and continued attack on these key sites might have produced a different overall picture. In my own period of 'bomber' crew service in the 1980s, the view was that you could not destroy an airfield; all you could do was to 'reduce the sortie rate' by attacking key operating surfaces or infrastructure.

As the pace of operations increased the German fighters were given four main missions: direct escort, indirect or deployed escort, freelance patrols (*Freie Jagd*), and supplementary escorts to pick up and cover returning formations and provide protection to air-sea rescue services.

> Insofar as it can be said to have functioned at all, the system of escorting bombers yielded poor results. There were neither special tactical rules nor uniformity of plan; each fighter squadron carried out its missions as it thought best. Hence the quality of performance attained in these missions varied considerably. Some squadrons executed their missions in an extremely satisfactory manner, others failed miserably. It was not until late in the period of air battles that tactics were standardised.

Not surprisingly, Galland the fighter pilot was more in favour of the free-lance patrol missions than any of the others:

> It was difficult to make them [the bomber unit commanders] understand that it was better for the German fighters to stay out of sight and thus make the enemy attack before they saw the German fighters than to remain 'glued' to the formation they were escorting and thus allow the enemy to take the initiative.

This is very much the cry of the fighter pilot and was repeated by RAF and American fighter pilots when faced with similar close-escort tasks that restricted their freedom of action.

Göring had not been impressed with the performance of his fighter pilots in the battle to this point and he decided on the radical move of appointing younger men to command positions to 'increase the fighting spirit and the striking power of the German fighter force. With one or two exceptions, the physical condition of the older unit commanders was not equal to the strain of modern aerial warfare.' As the Luftwaffe continued to fail in the eyes of Hitler and Göring, accusations of cowardice did nothing to improve sagging morale.

By early September the battle was reaching its critical phase, Phase IV in Galland's commentary, with mass attacks against London.

> During these first large-scale attacks, Stuka squadrons were also used. They suffered heavy losses, particularly at the hands of British fighters. Göring blamed it on the fighters and declared that the standard of escort and protection was deplorable. But there was not one pilot who did not know that the fault was to be found in the technical shortcomings of the Stuka.

The bomber force usually comprised up to 500 bombers plus 200 Stukas, escorted by 500 single-engined and 200 twin-engined fighters, the attacking force forming up over the Pas de Calais before setting course for their target. German estimates that the RAF had only 200 fighters left were wildly inaccurate.

> The ferocious and indomitable resistance of the British air defences, particularly RAF fighter pilots whose fighting qualities commanded the greatest admiration. Numerically very inferior at this stage of the struggle, they fought desperately and without respite, and saved their country. The organisation and the direction of the British air defences, represented by Fighter Command, showed great drive and initiative.

Another issue for the German bombers was the low bomb load and hence poor overall destructive power of most of the bombers.

Galland went on to state that there were four reasons for the decision to abandon the daylight attacks:

1. Weather. The unpredictable autumn weather mitigated against large-scale daylight operations.
2. False evaluation of results. The RAF was still a potent force and German bombers and twin-engine fighters were being lost faster than they could be replaced.
3. Technical limitations of German aircraft. A number of considerations such as the inadequate range of the fighters and the poor performance of the Bf 110 and Ju 87, along with the weak defensive armament of the bombers.
4. Modification of the strategic plan. The German strategic shift towards the Mediterranean and Russia.

'However, there can be no doubt that the Luftwaffe could have continued the daylight offensive despite these constraints. The German Command could have given the orders for the offensive to be continued, and felt safe in doing so, if it had known the true extent of the exhaustion of the British air defences.' So, in Galland's view the RAF did not so much win as avoid losing, and the Germans chose not to carry on. As we shall see, this was a common theme from the Luftwaffe.

The Luftwaffe had lost a quarter of its effective strength in personnel in the three months of its all-out offensive against Britain, but the campaign was not yet over. The final phases of the Battle of Britain were the fighter-bomber attacks and the switch to night bombing of London. In a rushed conversion programme around one third of the fighter force was equipped to carry bombs – much to the chagrin of the fighter pilots as this 'gave them a sense of inferiority'. Although they attempted to carry out what they saw as fruitless missions, they were soon on the receiving end of criticism from the high command:

> The C-in-C declared with profound bitterness that the fighter arm had failed in its task of escorting bombers; he objected to the manner in which the fighter-bomber operations were carried out and added this to the fighters' previous shortcomings. The young commanders of fighter units, who were convinced that they had fulfilled their tasks during the air battles of the preceding weeks, and who had accepted severe losses without complaint, had once again to listen to grave charges being made against them.

Whilst there is a great deal of truth in what Galland says about the attitude of the Nazi leadership, and Göring in particular, it must be borne in mind that later in the war he had major disagreements with his superiors. However, as we will see in the coming chapters, many of the key 'failure points' identified by Galland became decisive in the defeat and destruction of the Luftwaffe.

Chapter 2

Readiness?
The Period to May 1940

Doctrine, Strategy and Leadership

The air strategy for the major combatants of World War Two was largely based on their experience of World War One, or the air doctrine that came from the later part of that war. Both the Germans and the British had deployed aircraft in a strategic bombing role in 1914–18, with seemingly promising results. The Germans had started with the Zeppelin force attacking the UK but by late 1916 this had proved vulnerable and the emphasis moved to heavy bombers making daylight and night attacks, with the defenders struggling to cope with the threat. The British likewise had deployed strategic bombers in 1917–18, primarily with the Independent Force in the final months. There was potential but the scale of the effort was very limited, though the principle of attacking the enemy 'at home' had been established. But the ability to 'step over' the bogged-down trenches and take the war to key points seemed to hold promise for the future.

As early as September 1916 General Hugh Trenchard, commander of the Royal Flying Corps in France, had outlined a possible doctrine for the RFC: 'Even with an unlimited number of machines for defensive purposes, it would still be impossible to prevent hostile machines from crossing the line if they were determined to do so, simply because the sky is too large to defend.' He went on to suggest that the only solution was to go onto the offensive behind the enemy's lines, compelling him to divert his own aircraft from offence to defence. However, the British heavy bombing offensive had not really got going in earnest by the end of the war (less than 5 per cent of British strength comprised true 'bombers'). In October 1918 the Independent Force consisted of 125 bombers, including many of poor performance and bomb load, and their early operations had brought little success but many problems. Trenchard, now commander of the Independent Force, decreed that attacks should concentrate on as many of the large industrial centres as were within reach, in order to affect German morale and tie down resources. His 'Trenchard Doctrine' was soon firmly established:

> The nation that would stand being bombed longest would win in the
> end . . . to win it will be necessary to pursue a relentless offensive by
> bombing the enemy's country, destroying his sources of supply of
> aircraft and engines, and breaking the morale of his people.

Bomber theory was developed in the 1920s by airpower strategists on
both sides of the Channel, and in America, with claims that the bomber
would always be decisive and unbeatable – 'the bomber will always get
through'. Perhaps the most influential of these strategic thinkers was an
Italian, General Douhet, and his writings provided the basis of many of the
air plans being laid in the capitals of Europe. The British Air Staff needed
no convincing, it was their theory that:

> The strategic air offensive is a means of direct attack on the enemy
> state with the object of depriving it of the means or will to continue
> the war. It may in itself be the instrument of victory or it may be the
> means by which victory can be won by other forces. It differs from
> all previous kinds of armed attack in that it alone can be brought to
> bear immediately, directly and destructively against the heartland
> of the enemy.

It was also the only way the RAF could survive as an independent
military arm.

British Air Power Doctrine in the 1930s

In 1923 the Steel–Bartholomew Committee's recommendations on the
Air Defence of Great Britain led to government approval of a plan for a
home-defence air strength of 52 squadrons, to include 17 fighter squadrons
'with as little delay as possible'. As a percentage of the total strength the
fighter element was poor – but this was the period when air strategists
were convinced that bombers were the way to win wars. In 1925 the
Government's interpretation of 'as soon as possible' changed to 'by 1935–6'.
Air Marshal Sir John Salmond had taken-over as Air-Officer-Commanding
Air Defence of Great Britain in January that year and he had firm views on
air defence, which in his view – and his experience from World War One
– included searchlights and anti-aircraft guns. It is worth noting that the
'active defence' planned for the UK, and to be in place by 1939, comprised
2,232 heavy anti-aircraft guns, 4,700 searchlights and 50 squadrons of
fighter aircraft. However, on the outbreak of war there were only 695 heavy
and 253 light anti-aircraft guns and 2,700 searchlights.

Trenchard put forward a significant memo in May 1928. It opened in an
attacking style citing: 'an unwillingness on the part of the other services to

accept the contention of the Air Staff that in future wars air attacks would most certainly be carried out against the vital centres of commerce and of the manufacture of munitions of war of every sort no matter where these centres were situated'. He went on to declare that the RAF doctrine was 'to break down the enemy means of resistance by attacks on objectives selected as most likely to achieve this end'. It was better to attack military targets at 'source' (the factories) rather than in the field, it would have greater effect for less effort, and would include 'persuading' workers to stop working; further, that 'The Hague Convention allows for military targets, including production centres, what is illegitimate, as being contrary to the dictates of humanity, is the indiscriminate bombing of a city for the sole purpose of terrorising the civilian population.' The heads of the other services replied in kind, the Chief of the Imperial General Staff commenting that: 'It is ridiculous to contend that the dropping of bombs has reached such a stage of accuracy as to ensure that the bombs would hit only the so-called military targets.'

In 1929 and again in 1933 the government slipped the programme back, the latter revision taking it to 1939–40. This reluctance did not change until 1934, a year after Hitler had come to power in Germany, when there was a realisation that continuing peace in Europe was by no means a certainty.

A Foreign Office appraisal of 1933 stated that Germany: 'controlled by a frenzied nationalism and resolved to assert her rights to full equality, will proceed to the building of formidable armaments on land and especially in the air'. A Chiefs of Staff review in October the same year agreed, but saw the danger as longer term and, anyway, there was a need to re-arm comprehensively to ensure the security of Britain's world-wide commitments. The 'one-power' standard, aimed for many years at France, now looked inappropriate. The government suggested that the military draw up their expansion plans and present them for consideration. The Defence Requirements Committee sat from November to February. Its report gave priority to the RAF establishment of a home defence force strong enough to counter any attack (it is important to appreciate here that home defence included an offensive bombing force as a central element).

The failure of Chamberlain's Air Pact, whereby the states of Europe would promise not to drop bombs on each other's territory, gave a further impetus to expansion plans. July 1934 brought Expansion Scheme A under which the RAF would be ready for war by March 1939; it provided the basis for a deterrent force plus the foundation of a training establishment as the basis for further expansion; this last was probably the single most important decision taken during this period, and one that was to prove critical to success.

With Germany identified as the most likely opponent, there was a need to develop aircraft with the range and performance to attack targets in the Ruhr and Rhineland. Acceptance of the requirement was one thing, paying for the re-equipment quite another; the funding was simply inadequate for the preferred solutions to be put into effect. The net result of this was a policy of numbers not quality, the idea being that the latter would follow in due course when more money became available and superior aircraft types were in production. The problem is illustrated by comparing the cost of twelve Hart light bombers (£245,000 to acquire and £83,000 a year to run) to the cost of ten Virginia heavy bombers (£375,000 to acquire and £139,000 a year to run). With a revised estimate of German expansion and capability, the RAF scheme was re-examined and in May 1935 Expansion Scheme C gave a: 'programme of requirements in which financial considerations were to be secondary to the attainment of the earliest possible security'. Two months later the Air Staff outlined a strategic plan: 'Provided a sufficient weight of air attack could be brought to bear on the Rhineland–Ruhr–Saar area, Germany's armament industry would be paralysed, which would in turn preclude her from maintaining an army in the field,' thus maintaining the doctrine of attack to defend.

In 1935 the major elements of the offensive bombing force comprised squadrons of Heyfords and Virginias. Even the latest 'hot ship', the Fairey Hendon night bomber, a great advance in technology as the first all-metal low-wing monoplane bomber to enter squadron service (November 1936) only had a top speed of 155 mph and a bomb load of 1,660 lb. Of the 350 aircraft on show at the King's Jubilee Review in July 1935 *all* were obsolete biplanes and the fastest of them, the Gauntlet fighter at 231 mph, had not yet reached the squadrons! However, 1935 was to prove the watershed year as aircraft manufacturers came to grips with new technology and presented a variety of advanced types for consideration. The political will was slowly changing and whereas two years previously little progress could have been made there was now a realisation that the situation had become serious. Re-armament was behind schedule, although revised Expansion Schemes appeared at regular intervals, including Scheme F which saw the bomber element as an offensive rather than counter-offensive (part of home defence) weapon, 'to make it a principal weapon for winning the war on the continent of Europe'. Dated February 1936 this scheme included provision for 68 bomber squadrons, with 990 aircraft, scheduled for completion by March 1939. Expansion not only included aircraft but also infrastructure, especially airfields. Britain thus started a truly massive airfield-building programme in the mid-1930s, which included a shift of axis to have bomber bases in Lincolnshire and Yorkshire now that Germany was the likely enemy. This programme, which came to final fruition in 1943–4, was a tremendous achievement; the fact that the RAF and its American partners never really ran out of usable airfields was its vindication. By December 1944 the RAF had around 1,000 active airfields in the British Isles (see my 'Military Airfields of Britain' series, which in eight regional volumes covers them all).

July 1936 brought a major change of structure with the formation of new commands, including Bomber Command and Fighter Command, the two most closely connected with this study. There was another rash of Expansion Schemes during 1937, the most important one being Scheme H; this was the highpoint of suggested bomber strength, proposing 90 squadrons with a strength of 1,659 aircraft. However, continued problems of translating paper plans into reality caused a re-think. The aircraft were simply not available. For years the aircraft manufacturers had struggled against official indifference and a paucity of orders for aircraft, and no impetus for new ideas and types. This situation could not be reversed overnight: it would take time for new designs to come to fruition, and even longer for them to be produced in quantity. However, the increase in orders did enable aircraft and engine manufacturers, including Rolls-Royce, not only to stay in business but also to expand; true, they were initially producing outdated equipment, but they were building manufacturing capacity and a trained workforce.

There had also been a gradual conversion amongst the Air Staff towards the concept of fewer but more powerful bombers, the genesis of the 'all heavy bomber' philosophy which was to become central to Bomber Command planning. Figures supporting this conclusion showed that a squadron of twelve light bombers could deliver 6,000 lb whereas a squadron of ten of the new heavy bombers (to Specification B1/35) could deliver 20,000 lb. The death-knell of the light bomber had been sounded by Sir John Ellington (Chief of the Air Staff, [CAS]) at the end of 1935, who ruled that the medium bomber would in future be the backbone of the bomber force. The go-ahead was given and Specification B.12/36 was put forward for a four-engined aircraft of 100 ft wingspan (maximum figure stated because of hangar door size), 47 000 lb all-up weight, 230 mph cruise and a range of 1,500 miles. The aircraft was also to have the latest navigation equipment, and three gun turrets including a four-gun tail turret. It was a huge advance on anything yet proposed, but it would be some years before it was ready.

In the meantime, the expansion must go ahead with whatever was available. The 90-squadron plan was questioned by Sir Thomas Inskip, Minister for the Co-ordination of Defence, on the grounds of cost and from a conviction that the strategic concept was wrong, and the RAF should adopt a more defensive doctrine comprising a greater percentage of fighters, balanced only by light bombers and medium bombers. The Air Staff were dismayed; they held to the offensive doctrine but had to accept a cut in the proposed size of the bomber force (Scheme K coming into effect in 1938 with a plan for 77 bomber squadrons, and a larger percentage of fighters in the overall total plan.) The New Aircraft park at the 1936 Hendon show displayed such revelations as the Spitfire, Hurricane, Battle, Blenheim and Wellington (although they were all some way from entry to squadron service), it was a marked contrast from the situation in 1935 at Mildenhall. What was needed now was time to get sufficient numbers of the new types into squadron service and for enough aircrew to be trained.

The starting point for the planners was the doctrine of independent bombing of Germany to achieve victory, or at the very least to disrupt German ability to support a field army. It was a tall order. The original Joint Planning Committee assumptions made in 1934 (and which proved to be remarkably accurate) suggested a three-phase campaign:

1. Countering the all-out German air offensive, by attacking Luftwaffe installations.
2. Countering the German land offensive, by attacking ground forces.
3. A war-winning air offensive against German industry and transport.

The need to attack the Luftwaffe, especially its bomber formations, was stressed in view of the degree of destruction it was anticipated this 'German air menace' could inflict. This general outline was taken up by the Joint Planning Committee in October 1936:

The offensive employment of our own and allied bombers is the only measure which could affect the issue during the first weeks of the war. The three classes of objectives are:
1. Demoralise the German people, by methods similar to those we foresee the Germans themselves using against us; their Government might be forced to desist from this type of attack.
2. Discover and attack some target, the security of which was regarded by Germany as vital to her survival during the limited period within which she hoped to gain a decision over us; she would be forced to divert her air attacks on to our own aerodromes and maintenance organisation.
3. Inflict direct casualties upon the German bombing aircraft, either in the air or upon the ground, or upon their maintenance.

Unfortunately, the paper went on to explain, none of these categories was particularly suitable for attack by the British bomber force, mainly because of the superior German air striking power and the vulnerability of Britain to air attack. Britain would, therefore, have to adopt a defensive air strategy to reduce the scale of the German air attack to survivable limits. By 1937 this general philosophy had been translated into 'Planning for a War with Germany', the blueprint for the war. The Air Targets Intelligence sub-committee, formed in 1936, was now issuing appreciations of certain industrial and military targets, although the data upon which they based their assessments were very limited. There was also an over-simplification of the effect of aerial bombardment, a failing that was to persist for many years. Towards the end of 1937 these initial summaries started being issued as definite plans, the Western Air (WA) Plans. On 13 December 1937 Bomber Command was instructed to commence detailed planning for WA 1, WA 4 and WA 5, planning to be complete by 1 April 1938. The time-scale was extended because of the sheer amount of work to be done, and the re-organisation of Bomber Command that took place in the first half of 1938.

At the end of 1937 Air Marshal Ludlow-Hewitt, who had been appointed C-in-C Bomber Command, said that Bomber Command was: 'entirely unprepared for war, unable to operate except in fair weather, and extremely vulnerable in the air and on the ground'. Ludlow-Hewitt therefore ordered a re-organisation to reflect the requirements of these offensive plans – to put aircraft in the right locations to suit their part in the overall strategy, plus a desire to combine aircraft of the same type within a single group. The intention was that Bomber Command would be an independent strategic weapon undertaking an offensive to paralyse the Ruhr, and especially the coking plants and power stations. This would 'prevent Germany waging war on a large scale in less than three months'. They estimated that in 3,000 sorties, with 176 losses, the Command could knock-out 26 coking plants and 19 power stations; the effect of this would be to bring total disruption to the industries of the Ruhr. Thus, for little effort, the bombers would have a decisive effect on the war, which of course proved to be both impossible to achieve as well as being a strategic nonsense, the start of what Harris would later decry as 'panacea targets'.

The rapid expansion had proved difficult, squadrons splitting to form new squadrons and thus reducing the overall experience level and efficiency. The training organisation was still in its infancy. A Bomber Command Operational Training Instruction of 1937 stated:

> During the process of expansion and re-arming, and pending the completion of the new scheme in the Flying Training Schools, it will

be necessary for squadrons not only to convert their new pilots to service types, but also to consolidate and complete the flying and ground training given to pilots and air observers that form part of the Training School Syllabus.

The net effect of this was that the experienced crews on the squadrons spent much of their time teaching the new crews; there was little time left to develop tactics or improve standards.

> The RAF was probably the first to overcome the purely financial limits to its expansion, and its rate of growth was higher than that of the other Services. At frequent intervals between 1934 and 1939 the Air Staff assessed the German position more or less accurately and uttered warnings more or less audibly. The effect of the warnings on the Government was to make it aware of the crucial importance of the air arm. Indeed, as time went on, the dangers of air attack and the overwhelming importance of air defence appeared if anything greater than the war was to prove them to be. The priority was becoming more pronounced as the crisis over Czechoslovakia approached, and at the time of Munich, all obstacles to air defences were swept away and nothing but industrial capacity limited the rate of rearmament in the air.   (Michael Postan, *British War Production*)

Whereas in Germany, finance and raw material availability was limited, as well as there being a tactical air rather than a strategic air doctrine, in Britain, even when the financial taps had been eased open, there was a problem of just what to produce. Indeed, by early 1938 it was no longer a question of what the country could (or would) afford but rather a question of what industry could turn out, along with who would fly the aircraft and service them. In April 1938 approval was given for Scheme L, which would require 12,000 aircraft within a two-year period!

The 'bomber first' mentality that had dominated the Expansion Plans of the early 1930s did not change until Scheme M, which was approved in November 1938 (after the Munich Crisis), with an effective date for completion of March 1942. This scheme envisaged 163 squadrons to be based in the UK, of which 64 were to be fighter squadrons (14 of these being Auxiliary Air Force), each with an establishment of 16 aircraft. This was of course only a paper air force.

The increase in fighter to bomber percentage was slow in coming, and it was not until November 1938 that the target was set at 2:1 in favour of fighters, a ratio that was still inadequate in terms of the change in the nature of air war, although the combatants had yet to appreciate that. Even

RAF Expansion Schemes 1934–1938				
Scheme	Approved	Squadrons	Fighter Squadrons	Fighter Squadron Establishment
A	18 Jul 34	84	28+5	12
C	21 May 35	123	35+5	12
F	25 Feb 36	124	30+5	14
H	14 Jan 37	145	34+9	14
J	22 Dec 37	154	38+9	14
K	14 Mar 38	145	38+9	14
L	27 Apr 38	141	38+9	16
M	7 Nov 38	163	50+14	16

Notes:
Approved: Date the Scheme was approved by the Cabinet. *Squadrons:* Total home-based squadrons. *Fighter Squadrons*: Regular + Auxiliary squadrons.

that 2:1 ratio had been opposed by such RAF luminaries as Lord Trenchard, a bomber advocate.

Meanwhile, fighter development for the RAF verged on the ridiculous. The agile biplane armed with two machine guns dominated ideas in the 1920s and most of the 1930s, and the RAF's main fighter of the late 1930s, the delightful Gloster Gauntlet, followed that pattern and the latest fighter, the Gloster Gladiator, which entered service in early 1937, had as its main claim to improvement an increase in the number of guns to four! The specification that eventually led to the new generation of fighters was F7/30 for a 'Single-Seater Day and Night Fighter'. This specification was dated October 1931 and the General Requirements paragraph included statements such as 'a satisfactory fighting view is essential', and that designers 'should consider the advantages offered in this respect by the low wing monoplane or pusher'. The main requirements for the aircraft were:

a. Highest possible rate of climb.
b. Highest possible speed at 15,000 ft.
c. Fighting view.
d. Capability of easy and rapid production in quantity.
e. Ease of maintenance.

This was a lengthy document and amongst the key provisions was that the 'aircraft must have a high degree of manoeuvrability'. By the time of F10/35 this requirement had been toned down as being 'not required'. The aircraft was to have provision for four 0.303 in. Vickers guns and a total of 2,000 rounds of ammunition, with a minimum supply of 400 rounds per gun, as well as being able to carry four 20 lb bombs. It stated that two of the guns were to be in the cockpit, with interrupter gear if required, and the other two in cockpit or wing. There was no requirement for an enclosed cockpit and the pilot's view was a prime concern: 'The pilot's view is to conform as closely as possible to that obtainable in "pusher" aircraft.' Virtually all of these requirements could be said to apply to an aircraft that suited the later months of World War One, such as the Sopwith Camel or Bristol Fighter but with (slightly) improved performance. If the manufacturers had followed these requirements to the letter, then the Spitfire and Hurricane might never have been born.

Whilst the basic provisions of F7/30 could be said to describe an agile, manoeuvrable fighter, those of F5/34 (dated 16 November 1934) tipped the balance to what is best described as a bomber destroyer. The introduction to this specification stated:

> The speed excess of a modern fighter over that of a contemporary bomber has so reduced the chance of repeated attacks by the same fighters(s) that it becomes essential to obtain decisive results in the short space of time offered for one attack only. This specification is issued to govern the production of a day fighter in which speed in overtaking the enemy at 15,000 ft, combined with rapid climb to this height, is of primary importance. In conjunction with this performance the maximum hitting power must be aimed at, and 8 machine guns are considered advisable.

No mention here of manoeuvrability: what was needed was to catch the enemy bomber and hit it hard in a single attack. All of this was encapsulated in F10/35 but with added provisions under 'Handling' that emphasised the requirement for the fighter to be 'a steady gun platform' in which a 'high degree of manoeuvrability at high speeds is not required'.

From its first flight on 6 November 1935 the Hawker Hurricane showed every indication of being a winner; true, it did not have the agility, and some would argue beauty, of the older biplanes but it looked the part of a modern fighter – and it had eight guns. An order for 600 was promptly placed and two years later the first Hurricanes entered squadron service, going to 111 Squadron at Northolt to replace Gauntlets; by summer 1939 the number of squadrons had increased to twelve and the Hurricane was the most significant fighter in the order of battle. By that time, it had been joined by the Supermarine Spitfire, which had first flown five months after the Hurricane but had been slightly slower in production development, the first machines not joining 19 Squadron at Duxford until August 1938. The Spitfire, too, was an immediate hit with those who saw and certainly with those who flew it. Undoubtedly both types had teething troubles, and both were lacking what would soon be considered as essential operational equipment, but they were nevertheless an indication of massive progress.

Squadron equipment remained a focus of concern during the first months of the war. Although the focus was on getting as many Hurricanes and Spitfires into service as quickly as possible it was still policy to form squadrons with whatever equipment was available; for example, 263 Squadron formed at Filton in October 1939 with the Gloster Gladiator, a type with which they were to achieve a measure of fame in spring 1940 over Norway. The squadron diarist was one of those who recorded useful snippets for later historians:

> 25 November 1939: 'Owing to the outstanding success and capabilities of the Squadron they have been ordered to take-over the air safety of the western part of England. They are the only squadron detailed for this area, which speaks very highly of its standard considering that it was formed seven weeks ago and 18 of the pilots were straight from Flying Training Schools.'

Is this sarcasm or genuine pride?

> 22 January 1940, summary of a report on gun harmonisation and air firing: 'The experiments conducted have shown conclusively that guns installed in Gladiator aircraft have not the spread of bullets that has been previously calculated, and it is estimated that gun spread is approximately one foot per 100 yards up to a range of 300 yards. It is understood that experiments were conducted by the Air Fighting Development Unit in determining bullet spread by means of photographing tracer ammunition. It is suggested for consideration that the trajectory of tracer ammunition is not so accurate as ball ammunition.'

The interesting points from these extracts are the fact that the Gladiator was still a front-line fighter, and that its armament was still not operationally fit, and that Fighter Command was stretched thin and able to provide only a single squadron of biplane fighters to cover a large geographic area.

In February 1940 a memo was issued stating the 'decision to re-arm nine fighter squadrons from Blenheims, in the following order of priority: with Hurricanes (601, 229, 245, 145 Squadrons), with Spitfires (64, 222, 92, 234 Squadrons) and with Defiants (141 Squadron). This is to be complete as near to 31 March 1940 as possible' (SOM 109/40 dated 13 February 1940).

The fact that the RAF had unsuitable aircraft such as the Blenheim and Defiant in its day-fighter inventory was yet another indication of outdated tactical concepts, plus the 'as many squadrons as possible' aim.

Guns and Gunnery

The role of the fighter is to shoot down enemy aircraft; to do that it must have effective weapons, a suitable platform (the aircraft) and pilots and aircrew able to take advantage of both. In the RAF there was an ongoing debate early in the war about fighter armament: machine-guns versus cannon. The standard RAF fighter, and indeed bomber gun, was the 0.303 in. Browning. In the 1930s the Air Fighting Committee undertook a number of trials into fighter armament: a July 1935 paper concluded that the provision of eight guns (of 0.303 in. calibre) would: 'provide a means of obtaining a decisive result in the minimum of time while at the same time increasing the chances of obtaining this result at longer ranges'. A paper the previous year had investigated the use of larger calibre guns, primarily 20 mm Hispano cannon and concluded that the heavier weight of the cannon – one 20 mm cannon plus 60 rounds of ammunition weighed the same as four Brownings and 300 rounds of ammunition – was a disadvantage and when this was added to the cannon's aiming problems and slower rate of fire that the rifle-calibre Browning was better.

In May 1935 Air Cdre Verney, Director of Technical Development, wrote to the Air Ministry to clarify a number of points concerning the new fighter, one of which concerned the armament:

> As I understand it the view of the Air Staff is that the fighter's opportunities will be so fleeting that nothing but the maximum rate of fire in a minimum time is worth having. While agreeing with this, I feel sure that the trend of weapon development must be to increase the range of attack. My suggestion is for a single-seater fighter with 8 guns in the no allowance position either in the wings or fuselage, plus the COW [Coventry Ordnance Works] gun in the fuselage. Such a fighter could attack from the rear at a range of 100 to 500 yards using its COW gun. When the range had closed sufficiently the machine guns will be used.

In June 1935 a trial took place at Shoeburyness with eight 0.303 in. guns being aimed at a metal aircraft target positioned tail-on to the guns. Assuming a two-second sight-on burst (256 rounds) 109 hits were recorded, including fourteen though the seats. The same set-up with a 20 mm cannon allowed for only 17 rounds fired in the same period, although the resultant holes were much larger. The engine-mount system for cannon was considered a problem and it was concluded that if four such guns could be wing-mounted this would prove to be effective.

Several enhancements to fighter weaponry were made in late 1939; for example, reflector sights were fitted in September and October and by December most of the Brownings had been modified to the improved Mk II standard. Such changes were often the result of analysis by the Fighter Command Armament Section, who also looked at the question of gun harmonisation.

> At the start of the war all guns on Hurricanes and Spitfires were harmonised to give both a lateral and a vertical dispersion. Later the guns of some aircraft were harmonised to give a circular dispersion. On 19 December 1939 one squadron (No. 111) harmonised its guns to give a rectangular dispersion of 12 ft by 8 ft at 250 yards. Later, after experimentation with nine squadrons, it was decided that all Hurricanes and Spitfires in the Command should harmonise their guns in accordance with the pattern of the British Air Force in France, whereby all guns converged on a point at 250 yards.
>
> (Fighter Command Diary)

Harmonisation, and the range at which a pilot should open fire, caused much debate and whilst the instructions for the former were laid down – although not always followed – the latter was more a matter of personal choice, as we shall see later.

It was also important to have an effective gunsight and, whilst early production aircraft had a simple ring-and-bead sight, provision had been made for a reflector sight; the RAF evaluated several such sights and in May 1938 chose the GM2 for its new fighters. Gunsights continued to be developed throughout the war and various fighter marks had different sights, although most were variations on the basic reflector design. Fighter exponents such as Bob Stanford Tuck, 'Sailor' Malan and Douglas Bader were often in disagreement; at one meeting with Sholto Douglas, Bader had a shouting match with Tuck, insisting that eight Brownings were perfectly adequate, whilst Tuck argued vehemently for cannon.

John Ellacombe, a pilot with 151 Squadron:

> The number of times we fired at Heinkels and Dorniers and saw all our shells exploding, most of them were armour-piercing high explosive, and you would see them exploding on the wings and not bursting in the plane. It was very frustrating. Later on, when we got 20 mm cannon and we saw that exploding, we realised what we had missed.

Cannon-armed Spitfire IBs entered service with 19 Squadron in spring 1940. Typical of the combat reports relating to the new guns was that for 16 August:

> A Flight of 19 Squadron was sent to intercept a raid near Clacton and joined combat with Bf 110s. Although three were claimed for no loss the cannons performed badly and only two pilots had no stoppages and all were handicapped by no tracer. Pilot commented that 'when the 20 mm guns were fired accurately the effects on the Bf 110s were most gratifying'.   (AHB Narrative)

However, at this juncture the CO's view (Sqn Ldr R. Pinkham) was that his men would have scored far more kills if they had been flying standard eight-gun aircraft.

However, it was becoming clear that the 0.303 in. guns were ineffective against some German bomber types, with their increasing amounts of armour protection. There were numerous instances of fighters using up all their ammunition with no apparent result and it was apparent that the heavier punch of the cannon was the way forward, though it would be some time before an effective armament combination was universally in use.

German Air Power Doctrine in the 1930s

In Germany the situation was very different in the 1920s and 1930s; until Hitler came to power in 1933 there had been little development of aviation. The Germans were limited in their military preparations by the constraints of the Versailles Treaty, which banned them from creating an air force. The 1922 Treaty of Rapallo enabled a secret aviation programme to start, using facilities in the Soviet Union. Companies such as Junkers, Heinkel and Dornier were coming to the fore and by 1926 there was also a military training and experimental unit at Lipetsk. This was all useful but limited, and of course gave the Russians access to German ideas and equipment. The Locarno Treaty of 1926 and the Paris Air Agreement eased the restrictions on Germany and allowed for the construction of civil aircraft, albeit with limitations and monitoring. This did at least enable designers to put aerodynamic theories into practice, and it would of course be easy to turn good civil aircraft into transports and bombers.

The German Army was limited to 100,000 men and any thought of military aviation was tied to the needs of the Army. There was a great boost in 'recreational' glider flying and schools were established in many areas. This not only provided good training for future pilots but also aviation skills in designing and building airframes. A major restriction remained the inability to work on the types of aero engines that would be needed for military aircraft. The Luftwaffe became official in March 1935 as an independent arm within the Armed Forces (Wehrmacht). The Chief of Staff of the Luftwaffe, General Walther Wever, a World War One fighter ace, was a strategic thinker and supporter of the strategic bomber, albeit not completely aligned with the thoughts of Douhet. He outlined his tenets of air strategy as:

- To destroy the enemy air force by bombing its bases and aircraft factories and defeating enemy air forces attacking German targets;
- To prevent the movement of large enemy ground forces to the decisive areas by destroying railways and roads, particularly bridges and tunnels, which are indispensable for the movement and supply of forces;
- To support the operations of the army formations, independent of railways (armoured forces and motorised forces) by impeding the enemy advance and participating directly in ground operations;
- To support naval operations by attacking naval bases, protecting Germany's naval bases and participating directly in naval battles;
- To paralyse the enemy armed forces by stopping production in the armament factories.

There was nothing startling here or very different from the way the RAF was thinking, except for point three which gave more prominence to air–land operations rather than strategic air. Wever had pressed hard for the creation of a strategic bombing force but any such plans were constrained by economics; there was a limit to what could be achieved in a short period of time, and for Hitler there were many areas that needed attention. With the potential for war in the later 1930s, despite Hitler's incredibly astute reading of the weakness of Western political leaders, re-armament had to focus on what was most needed in the short term. Aircraft development should be linked to strategy, the definition of how many you need of each type/role to achieve the strategic aim. That requires leadership and decisions based on both the need and the reality. In autumn 1936 Hitler inaugurated a four-year plan to reorganise the German economy, to provide a greater self-sufficiency for war. However, he was faced with a difficult economic situation in which Germany struggled to find the hard currency required to pay for its imports of strategic materials, such as oil, iron ore (for steel production), rubber, copper and aluminium, all of which were vital to the aviation industry. Indeed, the expansion of the Luftwaffe was limited by the lack of such resources. This had an impact on both the size and composition of the Luftwaffe in the immediate pre-war period and early war years. Would a bigger Luftwaffe that also included strategic bombers have been a war-winning weapon over Britain in 1940?

It could have gone that way if General Wever had not been killed in an aircraft crash in 1936. He had supported Junkers and Dornier and pushed them to develop their Ju 89 and Do 19 projects for the 'Ural Bomber' contract; both carried four engines with long-range and a reasonable bomb load, and prototypes for both existed in 1936. True there were problems, especially with the engines, but the potential was there. However, with the death of Wever this came to naught and the prototypes were destroyed; it was some time before the Germans looked again for a strategic bomber. Instead, the requirement was for light and medium bombers, with the ability to dive-bomb as a key requirement, something that was to haunt subsequent German bomber development. Ernst Udet was largely responsible for the focus on dive-bombers, and the development of the Ju 87 was in large part down to his driving of the programme, especially after threats to close it down in summer 1936. The Ju 87, best known as the Stuka, had shown early promise and went into series production to become a key weapon in the Luftwaffe air-support arsenal.

Two key aspects determined the direction of Luftwaffe aircraft development: the lack of time and money to build a strategic bombing force (a big bomber costs much more than a fighter) and the fact that the Luftwaffe was seen by the General Staff as a supporting adjunct to the Army. When Hitler came to power, the military 'work-arounds', such as supporting the growth of sport flying, the pact with Russia, and the development of civil types were all put under review, and he set about dismantling or ignoring the treaty restrictions. Civil types such as the Ju 52 were immediately given modifications that would enable them to act as bombers, albeit not very effectively. First flown in October 1930, the aircraft had several cutting-edge design elements and was used by Junkers to test ideas that would later be employed in its series of bombers. It served as a civil airliner with several airlines and eventually became the backbone of the Luftwaffe's transport fleet and remained in production to 1945.

> Between the years 1933 and 1939 the main effort lay in rationalising the existing aircraft plants, the geographical enlargement of which was upon a small scale only. Rationalisation took the form of rendering most of the existing plants fully autonomous and whilst, in some cases such as that of Heinkel at Rostock, this took the form of concentrating at one site all the means of production from component construction and erection to final assembly of the aircraft,

in other cases such as the state-controlled concerns of Junkers and Arado, autonomy took the form of a number of factories grouped around a main assembly plant, each manufacturing and assembling a single major component. In 1938, in order to increase the output of certain major operational aircraft types, General Udet, as the then Generalluftzeugmeister [Director-General of Equipment] instituted a system of sub-contracting within the aircraft industry whereby a given type was handled by several different firms. The first aircraft type, the production of which was 'farmed out' in this way was the Ju 88 to be followed later by the Me 109 and still later by the Fw 190 all of which, in the later stages of the war, were being constructed by 'alien firms'.   (Air Intelligence Section [ADIK] 3/9/1945, Interrogation of Generaldirektor Karl Frydag, a senior production bureaucrat)

One of the oft-quoted reasons for the ultimate failure of the German war effort is the lack of a strategic bombing capability in the Luftwaffe. The composition of the Luftwaffe, as with any element of the armed forces, was based on the perceived doctrine and the ability to meet the equipment needs of that doctrine. The German focus on bombers as an arm of land force operations led to the successes in the early years of the war; air–land integration was far superior to Germany's enemies, with aircraft, training and tactics all focused accordingly. The Blitzkrieg could not have happened without this air–land integration. If the war had ended with the collapse of Britain in 1940/41, history would have recorded that this doctrine was war-winning, and the Germans had got it right. Of course that did not happen, and, as the war progressed, the air doctrine disparity between the Germans and the Allies started to have a major impact. One of the key elements of this disparity was the role of the heavy bomber.

In an interview in 1945, Field Marshal Kesselring, commented on 'Luftwaffe policy and the question of a German four-engine bomber'. In his role as Chief of the Luftwaffe General Staff in 1936–7 he had been responsible for halting development of such an aircraft, so in part this post-war commentary concluded:

There was no other decision, so it was not my fault . . . Even if the role of the Luftwaffe had been viewed as a strategic one, and a well thought out production programme devised to cover it, by 1939 there would still have been no strategic Luftwaffe of any real significance.

This was primarily based on issues such as lack of raw materials, the restrictions of the secret re-arming programme, and sheer time – the Luftwaffe was being created out of nothing.

For this reason, it was too much to expect Germany to possess a strategic air force as early as 1940 or 1941. Even if suitable aircraft had been available, we should certainly not have had them, or trained crews to fly them, in the numbers necessary for a successful and decisive air operation. It is even questionable whether output could have kept pace with losses. With the prevailing shortage of raw materials, the production of bombers in any adequate numbers could only have been achieved at the expense of other aircraft types.

All these are valid points, of course, and, as the Allies found, the number of aircraft needed to have such decisive impact was far greater than the pre-war theorists postulated. The more important question, is timing; when would an 'adequate' force of strategic bombers have been decisive?

The importance of dive-bombing in German ideas was shown in the 1935 requirement for a new medium bomber. Designed for a range of 2,000 miles, speed of 250 mph, crew of three or four, bomb load of 1,500–2,000 lb, *and* astonishingly the ability to dive at 20 to 30 degrees, the Junkers Ju 88 first flew on 21 December 1936. Reaching a speed of 360 mph, the 'Schnellbomber' looked to have great promise and Göring was delighted. But, as development continued, the performance came down to around 280 mph, still reasonable for the time and, having other problems, the type did not enter service until September 1939. This was still a short timeframe from design to entry into service, although production of the Ju 88 remained slow for some time. It was without doubt a major success, and RAF pilots frequently bemoaned the fact that it was fast and could get away, and it was tough, seemingly able to take a lot of hits and yet keep on flying. It was indeed an excellent and adaptable aircraft; the problem turned out to be that it stayed in service too long, as there was no replacement due to the failure of Luftwaffe aircraft procurement.

In respect to fighters, the Luftwaffe had gone down a different route to the RAF, with the Bf 109 having a mixed armament of cannon and machine guns.

'The German Air Force held and steadily improved the lead it had obtained over Great Britain' (Churchill, *The Second World War*). As Werner Baumbach said in *Broken Swastika, The Defeat of the Luftwaffe*, this 'is to be ascribed less to the strategic foresight of the men at the head of the armed force than the outstanding achievements of [Germany's] scientists, inventors and technicians. Germany's activities in civil aeronautics showed the way to the technical conquest of the air.' There is a large degree of truth in this, and indeed, as we shall see, German inventiveness continued to make up for blunders in other areas, but it was just as well for the Allies that the Germans were always under constraints and subject to political inter-ference and mis-guidance. The British too ended up relying on scientists and industry to make up for the feet-dragging and legacy ideas of some in the RAF leadership.

According to Air Vice-Marshal Sir Thomas Elmhirst in a 1946 lecture:

> The GAF [German Air Force] went into the war an exceedingly strong, well trained and equipped tactical air force as a support to an army for a European land war. Göring may have had other ideas, but Hitler and the Supreme Command Staff had not. The GAF had no 'functional' commands [unlike the RAF's Fighter, Bomber and Coastal formed in 1936] for studying the use of air fighting in home defence. In fact, they had no night fighters [but at the time neither did the RAF]. It had no Command for operating with the Navy, no shipping 'strike' force; Göring and the Admiralty never got on. It had no Bomber Command planning the strategic use of bombers. In general, it was an unbalanced force to meet opposition.
>
> (Lecture, 24 October 1946)

Leadership

The discussion around leadership and its influence on the outcome revolves around two main areas, political leadership (or interference) and military leadership, which can be divided into strategic command leadership and operational (squadron-level leadership). According to Air Vice-Marshal Elmhirst:

> There was little of either tradition or experience on which Göring and Udet could build up the GAF. It had been formed in the 1914–18 war as an Army support force, and the majority of the best flying personnel in that war and of age who would have been leaders in 1939 had been killed. Also, full conversion to the Nazi doctrine was necessary to ensure high appointment in 1939. The two leaders I have mentioned were an odd couple to build a firm foundation, and their experience was unlikely to be sufficient to plan and build up a balanced force and lay down a policy for its operations in a world-wide campaign.

Hermann Göring, an early supporter of Hitler and, with his World War One record as a fighter ace, a man with military credentials as well as Nazi ideology, was made Minister of Civil Aviation and C-in-C of the new Luftwaffe. As we shall see, this appointment eventually proved to be a contributing factor in the downfall of the Luftwaffe. He set about creating a High Command for the Luftwaffe, drafting in many of his old contacts but in the absence of enough of those he had to bring in officers with no air experience. There was no Luftwaffe staff college that could analyse the lessons of 1914–18 and developments in air power or produce a school of thought that looked ahead. The Army General Staff was focused on land warfare and where it considered air power at all it was only as an adjunct to the needs of the Army.

This lack of a staff college was made worse by the skewed political basis of the Nazi organisation, where the military needs of the Luftwaffe were subsumed into the political machinations, especially those of Göring. As Commander-in-Chief, Göring was wary of any influence or 'attempts at meddling' by the Army or Navy in his policy, although he, for obvious reasons, would accept interference from Hitler. This combination was to be a factor in the ultimate failure of the Luftwaffe.

The death of Wever was a tragedy for the Luftwaffe; he was replaced by Albert Kesselring.

> I did not need to explore new ways but could carry on from where he left off. This helped to establish quickly an atmosphere of trust between myself, the General Staff departments and the numerous inspectorates. With the loyal support of exceptionally competent officers my work was made a pleasure.   (Kesselring, *Memoirs*)

This was to some extent a surprising appointment as Kesselring was not an airman, having served in the artillery in World War One. He remained in the Army after the war and joined the General Staff, being discharged from the Army in 1933 to become head of the Department of Administration at the Air Ministry where he was involved in laying the foundations for the Luftwaffe (and his own subsequent career). His Army background was perhaps a major reason why he was more inclined to the development of tactical aircraft rather than strategic bombers. In this he was followed by General Hans-Jürgen Stumpff, another leader with no air experience but a General Staff background. Stumpff stayed in the role until January 1939, by which time the shape and equipment of the Luftwaffe had been fixed, seemingly correctly, based on the experience of the Spanish Civil War, and certainly in line with what the Army wanted. The problems that this caused as the war progressed were not to become clear until late 1940 or early 1941.

However, the Luftwaffe initially appeared to be a very effective weapon, in its first combats in the 1936–9 war in Spain and the opening couple of years of the Second World War. There were several reasons for this, including its image as a *corps d'élite*, for which Göring could take some credit, both in establishing the mindset and structure, and ensuring that the German treasury provided the required funds, which meant taking advantage of his position with Hitler to influence the budget allocations.

Stumpff was succeeded by General Hans Jeschonnek, a pilot with a World War One record, albeit brief. In the middle 1930s he was in effect a protégé of Wever, holding appointments with a bomber *Geschwader* and in training and experimental work, which made him a most suitable occupant of the post. However, his political credentials, despite being a fervent supporter of Hitler, were not strong, although he initially had the backing of Göring and all seemed well.

So, as the war was about to start, the Luftwaffe leaders were committed to an air–land strategy in which close support of the Army was the primary task. In spring 1939 Jeschonnek had delivered a significant speech at a staff course:

> We must realise that all states are really on the same technical level and there is no such thing as a permanent lead. But the development of air tactics is so recent that in that field conclusions can be reached which, translated into action, could mean actual superiority over the enemy. The duty of the General Staff is to indicate to the technicians the requirements they must meet, but its most important task is to make best possible use of what the technicians give them, to extract the maximum out of men and machines at the lowest possible cost. The further development of air power must take economy as its motto, economy with material even more than with money.

The man in charge of the technical side was another World War One ace, Ernst Udet, who had served under Göring. After the war he became a well-known barnstorming pilot. At the urging of Göring he joined the Nazi Party in 1933 and one of his first tasks was to evaluate two Curtis Hawk II biplanes, which Udet used for dive-bombing trials and which helped firm up his conviction that dive-bombing was the way forward. For the next few years he was a key exponent of dive-bombing and a great supporter of the Ju 87, as we have seen. In 1936 he took command of the technical development organisation (T-Amt) and was later Director-General of Equipment.

Building up the RAF

But what had been happening in the RAF's leadership? Having survived post-war attempts to dissolve it out of existence, the RAF developed its doctrine and its leaders in the theatres of Empire, primarily Mesopotamia and the North-West Frontier provinces of India. Many of those who went on to hold command positions served in these areas and got to know each other.

Sir Edward Ellington was Chief of the Air Staff in the key period May 1933 to September 1937; trained as an artillery officer, Ellington qualified as a pilot in 1912 but never saw combat service, holding instead a series of staff appointments, albeit some of those being connected with the Western Front. In the 1920s he held a number of RAF overseas commands, such as RAF Middle East and RAF India. By the time he became CAS in May 1933, his experience and background were not at all suited to the state of air power and its likely development and employment in Europe. Sir Cyril Newall took over in September 1937 and held the post to October 1940. He had served operationally with the RFC in World War One, including with the Independent Force, which was to provide the RAF with its core air strategy for the next twenty years, and in which he became a 'Trenchard man'. His inter-war career was a mix of staff appointments at home and abroad, but with bombing the main focus. He was the Air Member for Supply and Organization from 1935 to 1937, before becoming CAS. His appointment was something of a surprise, with Hugh Dowding, more experienced and more senior, the favoured candidate. Some see the hand of Trenchard, 'father of the RAF', in this decision, and indeed those who are not great supporters of 'Boom' Trenchard point to the adverse influence he wielded in the 1930s, even when he had no official role.

Opinion on Newall's effectiveness as CAS is mixed; whilst he initially supported the focus on bombers in the re-armament program, with Expansion Schemes from the early 1930s limiting the growth of the fighter force in order to produce bombers and more bombers, he proved a bit more flexible when Sir Thomas Inskip, Minister for Defence Coordination, pushed for an increase in fighters.

In 1938 Newall threw himself behind two decisions that were to have a major positive impact for the RAF: the increase in aircraft production, including shadow factories, and the creation of a dedicated repair organisation. The Air Ministry and the aviation industry had launched a production expansion plan in 1936:

> Some of the new capacity was in the nature of 'shadow schemes', i.e. conceived as contributions to the war potential. But this conception had to be modified with the further expansion of the air programmes. 'Shadow' factories had now to be reckoned as additions to peacetime capacity, and still further capacity had to be laid down. In the course of this continuous piling up of factory buildings and plant, shortages of machine tools and delays in construction were bound to occur here and there, but the factory programme as a whole was as yet well within the powers of the building industry and of the machine-tool

industry in this country and abroad, and it was in fact being fulfilled more or less according to expectations. So generous had been the Air Ministry under Lord Swinton to schemes of forward planning and so expansive were the policies of the firms themselves that the industry was now if anything over-provided with buildings and plant.   (Postan, *British War Production*)

Raw materials and labour were a more challenging issue, but at least with factory space, the British were reasonably placed to continue to grow (and disperse) their aircraft and equipment production capability, which was to prove essential in the early years of the war. Of equal import was the 1938 decision to put aircraft production under the newly created post of Air Member for Development and Production, headed by AVM Sir Wilfred Freeman, assisted by Ernest Lemon, a railway (!) engineer, as Director-General of Production (DGP). The AMDP was involved in negotiating between the Air Ministry and industry and ended up advising on technical matters and assuming the general planning of production. A key decision was to develop an extensive subcontracting structure, a concept that the Air Staff had viewed with distrust:

> The production of aircraft was so complicated that it could not be entrusted to firms without previous experience of aircraft production and could not therefore be distributed among the various engineering and allied trades. The future expansion of aircraft production was to come from additional plant under the direct management of the 'parent' firms.

The DGP had a different view and suggested that 'parent' firms should entrust to subcontractors at least 35 per cent of the outstanding orders in order to meet the overall production targets. With minor variations on the themes of expansion or parent firm capacity, shadow factories and subcontracting, the British aviation industry was able to meet the needs of the late 1930s and the early war years. This aspect of the air war is often overlooked but without such moves as this, the RAF would not have had the equipment it needed. In the first half of 1939, the number of aircraft delivered exceeded the planned number each month.

In July 1938, AVM Arthur Tedder became Director-General for Research in the Air Ministry; he was without doubt one of the key air power 'thinkers' in the RAF throughout the war, and had early on recognised the need to 'win the war as well as this battle'; this was a discussion in May 1940 with Sir Wilfred Freeman, when he was with the Ministry of Aircraft Production: 'We must keep on looking to the future. We must keep working on new equipment and if we break up technical teams now it will be difficult to get them together again.' This was to be a key success factor for the RAF and a key failure point for the Germans. Tedder did not last long in this position, as he found it hard to work with Lord Beaverbrook after he became Minister for Aircraft Production in Churchill's government. MAP's loss proved to be a major gain for the RAF, as Tedder went to join Middle East Command; his subsequent leadership in the theatre and his development of the application of air power alongside the likes of Coningham proved invaluable to the RAF.

Maintaining the principle of looking ahead whilst you are losing is difficult and it is true that the numbers game was not ignored, and obsolete or obsolescent types continued to enter service, but the fundamental under-standing that the RAF still had to keep developing was there. The likes of Freeman and Beaverbrook had their disagreements, and many thought Beaverbrook an arrogant and difficult character, but they still combined to produce what was needed. When Freeman left his position in late 1940, he wrote to Beaverbrook praising

> the energy, courage and decision with which you tackled the difficult problem of aircraft production. Without the ever-increasing flow of aircraft from the storage units, for which you have been entirely responsible, our pilots could never have won such resounding victories. It has been a great privilege and an abiding lesson to serve under you and if at any future date I can serve you again in any capacity, I shall indeed be grateful for the opportunity.

To which he received the reply: 'You more than any other man, gave the RAF the machines whose superior quality won the vital battles of this summer.'

The German aircraft industry was not so structured or prepared, although British estimates of aircraft production before the outbreak of the war suggested monthly figures higher than those for the RAF; for example, an average of 700 a month against an RAF average of 400–500, although post war data suggested the actual German figure was closer to 600–700 until late 1939. The British were also estimating total Luftwaffe strength at around 4,000 aircraft by mid-1939. The combination of the enemy supposedly having greater numbers, higher production, and more modern types helped fuel the British assumption that the country was totally unprepared to face the devastating power of German air attack – a perception that Hitler and the Luftwaffe were very keen to promote.

A top secret Luftwaffe memo dated 2 May 1939 discussed the 'Air Situation in Europe':

The Luftwaffe is at the present time superior to any single air force in Europe. This is true in respect to the quantity and quality of aircraft and equipment as well as to organisation, training and tactical and operational preparedness for aerial warfare. Even in the event of hostilities with the combined British and French air forces the Luftwaffe is still to be regarded as superior for the year of 1939.

It went on to say that a key factor was the obsolescence of the aircraft potential enemies operated, which was certainly true of the French Air Force, but becoming less so for the RAF:

In this age of technical development, it must be taken into consideration that highly industrialised countries will be able to develop technically perfect defensive weapon to ward off dangerous offensive weapons after they have had the opportunity to start up necessary industries. It remains to be seen, however, whether such weapons can be produced in the necessary quantities at the proper time. With the air forces approaching technical parity the advantage of tactical and operational preparedness for war assumes special importance.

I wonder if some in the Luftwaffe looked back on this later in the war and wished they had paid more attention to its perceptive content.

Pilots and Training

To expand an air force requires infrastructure, equipment and people. The RAF made several decisions as early as the 1920s that would provide a firm foundation for the massive expansion it would later make. One of Trenchard's greatest legacies for the RAF was the setting up of the RAF Apprentices Scheme. Founded in 1920 and based initially at Cranwell until its permanent home at Halton was ready, No. 1 School of Technical Training took boys between 15 and 17½ and put them through a three-year technical course; having survived the 'Halton Grinder' the newly minted technicians became 'Halton Brats'. The graduates of the school, and others that were subsequently founded, gave the RAF a cadre of superbly trained engineers who proved invaluable. The decision to form the Royal Auxiliary Air Force was part of Trenchard's attempts to circumvent the lack of political will for military expenditure in the 1920s; the Order in Council authorising its formation was signed in October 1924 and the first units established the following year. It was a 'flying club with a military flavour', and as pilots had to pay for their own licence (a cost of £96, or at least £5,000 in today's terms), it was inevitably something of a wealthy man's flying club. The Auxiliaries had to fly a minimum number of hours each quarter and to attend a two-week annual camp for more concentrated training, including in tactics and gunnery. The Auxiliary Air Force supplied a cadre of trained and motivated pilots who provided a major boost to the RAF's front-line capability.

On 13 August 1939, the Spitfires of 611 Squadron arrived at Duxford for their annual training camp and it was here, their designated war station, that they received notification, on 26 August, of their call-up. This was one of twenty RAuxAF squadrons that were embodied into the full-time RAF on the outbreak of war, some fourteen of which served in the Battle of Britain.

Max Aitken was one of those who signed up and joined 601 Squadron at Hendon:

> My companions there were, as you would expect, a pretty wild and high-spirited gathering many of whom I knew. They were the sort of young men who had not quite been expelled from their schools, whom mothers warned their daughters against – in vain – who stayed up far too late at parties and then, when everyone else was half dead with fatigue, went on to other parties. *(Aitken Papers)*

To many in 2019, this sounds like the type of person you do not want, but for the situation they, and the RAF, were to face in 1940, they were ideal.

The other cadre of aircrew, especially pilots, was provided by the RAF Volunteer Reserve (RAFVR), which was formed in July 1936 to supplement the RAuxAF; the main difference was that the RAF paid for their training, and again it was an 'easy' way to get volunteers trained without actually having to take them into the RAF full-time – yet. This source of aircrew provided a pool of nearly 6,500 pilots, 1,600 observers, and nearly 2,000 wireless operators at the outbreak of war. The system continued in use after the outbreak of war, with the RAFVR training aircrew who then remained in civilian occupations until called forward for formal aircrew training. Between them, these two schemes were crucial to the early survival and growth of the RAF.

The pre-war RAF pilots were well trained and many had a large number of flying hours, although with the late re-equipment with monoplane fighters, this was often on the old biplanes; even a retracting undercarriage was a new feature, and many learned the hard way that you had to put the gear down. Mike Croskell joined 213 Squadron in December 1939; his CO quickly discerned that Mike had never flown a type with retractable undercarriage and flaps, so he was sent for a rapid course at Aston Down on the Harvard to learn about such things, returning to the squadron for his introduction to the Hurricane. With the Phoney War prevailing, pilots such as this were given breathing space to learn their new machines, and this period from late 1939 to spring 1940 was crucial to the RAF's fighter squadrons, but it was also a period when the Luftwaffe pilots were gaining combat experience.

As the conflict with Germany looked ever more likely, one of the most important decision taken by the British authorities was to disperse their training overseas, in part because of lack of facilities and airspace for the expected scale of the training need, and in part because of the threat from enemy air action. The most significant of the schemes was the British Commonwealth Air Training Plan (BCATP), which primarily used Australia, Canada, South Africa and New Zealand, and produced nearly 132,000 aircrew – a total that could never have been achieved if training had been concentrated in the UK. Equally important of course was the large number of young men from those nations who became aircrew, but a big part of the total was British personnel who spent months learning their trade in peaceful conditions. When approached in September 1939, Canadian Prime Minister William Mackenzie King stated that the plan would be 'the most essential military action that Canada could undertake'. The final agreement was signed on 17 December 1939 and agreed the cost sharing and the percentage of trainees that each country would produce, with Canada having the biggest share, both because of its size, its more convenient location (closer to the UK to get trained aircrew into service) and its logistics and production resources, not least being its proximity to the USA.

According to one set of statistics, the BCATP produced:

RCAF aircrew	72,835
RAF aircrew	42,110 (inc. French, Czechs, etc.)
RAAF aircrew	9,606
RNZAF aircrew	7,002
Fleet Air Arm	5,296

Pilots followed the standard elementary phase of around 50 hours flying on types such as the Fairchild Cornell and the Tiger Moth, followed by service flying training with 75–100 hours on Harvards, for pilots destined for single-engine types, and twins such as the Anson and Oxford for the multi-engine types. The length of training and number of flying hours, and even syllabus content varied at different stages of the war, depending on demand and priorities. Non-pilot aircrew had their own specialist schools of appropriate durations and syllabus structure and type. Of the total aircrew trained, just under 50,000 were pilots.

Although out of chronological sequence here, it is appropriate to make brief mention of the other overseas training schemes that provided aircrew for the RAF. From May 1940 the Rhodesian Air Training Group (RATG), under AVM Meredith, was also producing aircrew under the Empire Air Training Scheme (EATS), and by the end of the scheme had produced almost 17,000 aircrew. The building of infrastructure and the support of the programme was an incredible achievement for the small nation. The USA also played a role from 1941 with the Towers Scheme and the Arnold Scheme; the former was run by the US Navy and was much smaller than the USAAF Arnold Scheme; nearly 8,000 trainees entered the latter, though almost 50 per cent were 'washed out' (failed to complete the training).

Pre-war – Luftwaffe

The Germans had used subterfuge to help build a clandestine air force, with many civilian aircraft clearly having a potential for conversion to military use and with the pact with Russia that enabled training to take place. However, there was also an 'air-mindedness' in Germany, with flourishing gliding schools that helped build basic flying skills and airmanship.

> When Hitler became Chancellor in 1933, he appointed Goring to take charge of civil aviation and air raid precautions, which had previously been under the Ministry of Transport. Goring's first act was to centralise all flying clubs under the Deutsche Luftsportverband (DLV). The members of this new body wore uniform and the full-time flying training of members soon began on a large scale and included instruction in formation flying and other exercises which seemed inappropriate to normal civil or commercial flying training. Within this organisation the seeds of the future German Air Force were sown. Meanwhile, the Lufthansa schools (DVS) were considerably expanded, pupils and instructors were put into uniform, and several public airfields were taken over by the DVS for its own use. By September 1935, the GAF was sufficiently well trained to show its prowess in several air exercises, in the largest of which 24 squadrons took part.   (RAF report on GAF, April 1943)

The Luftwaffe training scheme in the later 1930s was good, with the same basic structure as that used by the RAF, with elementary and advanced schools and a comprehensive syllabus with a good number of flying hours, for pilots 200–250 hours. The candidates were of high calibre and there was no shortage of young men wanting to become pilots. Having qualified, they then went to an operational training school (*Ergänzungsgruppe*) whilst awaiting posting to a unit. The Luftwaffe had high accident rates and operational rates were low, with an in-commission rate of only 49 per cent for bombers, rising to 70 per cent for fighters. The only quick way to solve the issue and improve in-commission rates was a drastic reduction in flying and training time. Despite this, by August 1938 the Luftwaffe still had only two-thirds of its authorised crew strength and over 40 per cent of crews were not considered fully operational. Out of 3,714 authorised crews, only 1,432 were fully operational, the bomber force being particularly poor (1,409 authorised crews but only 378 fully operational).

Inexperience and Indecision

Young pilots with few hours, little tactical exposure and no tactical experience were especially vulnerable. Air combat, especially fighter to fighter, often went from cruising around to adrenalin rush and then to 'where did everyone go' in a handful of minutes, and that was if you saw the enemy and were not just shot down by the one that sneaked up on you.

Bob Foster was with 605 Squadron:

> For the first few occasions you don't really know what is going on half the time. I fired at quite a lot of stuff but didn't register anything that I know of, because I didn't hang around in the danger zone. If you did, it was the last thing you would do. Everything was over so quickly.

David Crook was a pilot with 609 Squadron, which was involved in flying protective sorties over the Dunkirk area:

> We shot a number of Huns down and lost four of our pilots. Desmond was also killed near Frinton-on-Sea; he lost his way back in bad weather and ran out of petrol and was killed in trying to make a forced landing. I think there is no doubt that some of these losses were due to inexperience and lack of caution. None of us had ever been in action before, and everybody's idea was to go all out for the first Hun that appeared. This policy does not pay when you are fighting a cunning and crafty foe, and the Germans frequently used to send over a decoy aircraft with a number of fighters hovering in the sun some thousands of feet above, who would come down like a ton of bricks on anybody attacking the decoy. This ruse almost certainly accounted for one pilot, Presser, and possibly one or two others – the last anybody saw of Presser was when he was diving down to attack a Junkers 88, and there were definitely some Messerschmitts above.　(Flt Lt David Crook DFC, *Spitfire Pilot*)

This neatly summarises one of the problems faced by the RAF pilots – they had no experience and were having to gain it 'on the job' and at no small cost. The important thing was to learn the lessons and apply them; some of this hard-earned wisdom was transmitted through official and unofficial channels and brought about various changes, not least the harmonisation of guns at 250 rather than 400 yards. Other lessons of the 'Hun in the sun' and a host of others were applied by those with experience, passed on by flight commanders – and eventually at training schools – but many a new pilot in the forthcoming Battle of Britain still had to find out for himself; with luck the lesson came as a warning, without luck it was a parachute trip or a final crash. The pre-war training system had done little to prepare fighter and bomber crews for the real world of air war. The exercises, the bombing ranges, the 'air combat' training were all of little use. But the RAF learned quickly that operational training was a vital element, and soon established specialist training units, something the Luftwaffe failed to do to quite the same extent.

Tactics

The pre-war prescribed Fighter Command attacks comprised six basic attack formations designed with slow and poorly armed bombers as the target, with the prime concern being that whenever possible 'fighters should attack enemy bomber formations in equal numbers by astern and quarter attacks from the same level'. It looked neat and worked well on exercises in the 1920s and 1930s, but it was totally inappropriate to air combat by 1940.

> Fighter Command adhered to the orthodox methods of attack, i.e. in vic formation if possible, or in line astern, from the rear, either above or below. The Command did not approve of beam attacks, which called for accurate sharpshooting in the fractional time when the beam of the enemy was exposed. Nor for similar reasons did it approve of the deflection shot.   (Fighter Command Diary)

The RAF fighter tactics at the start of war were soon proved to be deficient. The Fighting Area Attacks were pretty much based on fighters lining up to take shots at unescorted bombers. The three main attacks, as directed in 1938, were:

- No. 1 Attack was a succession of single aircraft attacking a single bomber from astern, with Sections stepped down in line astern behind the target. The Section Leader opens fire at 400 yards and maintains his fire on the target at this range until he decides to break away, with the procedure then followed by his Number 2 and Number 3.
- No. 2 Attack was pretty much the same except that the Sections were not stepped down but fanned out to rear and flanks of the bomber.

- No. 3 Attack was an attack by a vic Section of 3 against a vic of three bombers, with the normal plan being for two Sections abreast to engage two groups of bombers, one Section breaking left after completing the attack and the other breaking right.

There were numerous other set attacks for single-engine and turret fighters but these three encapsulate the major problems the fighters were to encounter when the shooting war started.

Bob Doe: 'I knew the basics of deflection shooting. It's the shooting that matters in a dog-fight, rather than the flying.'

> Another thing which browned us off were the faults which had shown up in our machines [autumn 1940, Spitfire I, 74 Squadron]. The peacetime pilots must have really goofed off – we had to ask if they ever fired their guns way up in the icy cold. Did they ever test the bloody things to see if they'd work? On one of our first high-altitude battles we, 74, had only nine machine-guns fire out of 96. The oil had frozen, locking breech mechanisms solid. Now all guns were lubed with refrigerator oil, then wiped almost dry.
>
> (Sqn Ldr 'Spud' Spurdle, *Blue Arena*)

The standard flight of three fighters was so rigid in its procedures that there was little opportunity for aircraft to cover each other, even though in theory one was a 'weaver' to keep an eye on the tails of the others. The Germans referred to the formation as '*Idiotenreihen*', which roughly meant 'rows of idiots'. The overall squadron formation was four such vics. Billy Drake: 'We had been taught about Fighting Area tactics, able to fly in close formation and going that way into battle. Our idea was to fly in vics of three, and nobody was really looking after each other.'

Bob Foster:

> We flew in tight formation still, with weavers at the back – and old Jack [Jack Fleming] was a weaver. He saw some 109s and was alerting the squadron. He didn't see the other 109s behind him. The weavers often got caught, and as a tactic, it was no good at all, left over from pre-war thinking. With hindsight, I think we stuck to our tight formations for far too long. Despite all the casualties, we still flew these tight vics of three.

The Germans meanwhile had adopted new tactics, not being hide-bound by tradition in the same way as the RAF; in the Spanish Civil War they employed the '*Schwarm*' formation of four aircraft, essentially a fluid four that provided great flexibility. The tactic has been ascribed to Werner Mölders, an ace in Spain and again in early World War Two.

Did the RAF pay attention to the air warfare lessons from the Spanish Civil War? In general, it seems not. There was a view that the Republican air force was not a real opponent and so anything that happened to them would not happen to the RAF. The RAF's leaders were 'old school' and wedded to both their fighter and bomber concepts and tactics.

On the outbreak of war in September 1939 the Luftwaffe employed its air–land tactics to the campaign in Poland; despite valiant efforts by the, on paper, strong Polish forces, the German tactics, training and experience proved devastating. Much of the Polish Air Force was destroyed on the ground, another lesson that future opponents should have heeded. Those Polish pilots who escaped and made their way to France and Britain became some of the RAF's most effective fighter and bomber crews. But few lessons were learned on either side; the rapid collapse of Poland left Britain and France at war with Germany but seemingly with little idea of what to do next.

Chapter 3

France and the Battle of Britain

On the outbreak of war, the RAF knew that its German opponents had modern aircraft and that many of the aircrew had combat experience from the Spanish Civil War. Nevertheless, the RAF had a proud tradition and with the arrival of modern fighters such as the Hurricane and Spitfire, pre-war RAF pilots had developed a confidence in their machines and morale was good. An example might be Billy Drake, a Hurricane pilot in 1940: 'We were flying an aeroplane with a sound engine that seemed to go on for ever, with eight machine guns that should be very lethal, a gun-sight that worked, and we personally were as good as aviators as anybody we would meet on the enemy side.' Pilots generally were eager to get into battle. The fighters had to wait but for the bombers the war started immediately.

Under the terms of the alliance with the French, an expeditionary force was to be despatched to France, and this included an air element, the Fighter Command contribution being six Hurricane squadrons, although this was later raised to ten. When war came on 3 September 1939 the Command duly sent the first four Hurricane squadrons to France. In France there was little to do except carry on training, patrol up and down the border and take in a spot of French culture, as well as attempt to co-operate with the French. The first success came on 2 November, but for Air Marshal Dowding, head of Fighter Command, the downside was the call for two more squadrons that same month, although the Gladiator-equipped 607 and 615 squadrons were sent, both moving to Merville on 15 November – and both eventually re-equipping in France with Hurricanes in the spring of 1940. The so-called 'Phoney War' lasted for six months. One advantage of the Phoney War was the time it gave the RAF to press ahead with its re-equipment and growth plans, which saw more Hurricane and Spitfire squadrons entering service, and improved radar and reporting systems being introduced. The Luftwaffe made no such significant steps in the same period. Did Hitler really believe that the western allies would now look for peace? He had gambled again and seemingly won; after all, why did the mighty, on paper, French Army not march into a virtually undefended Germany, when surely this was the best way to help the Polish ally and end the war?

After a period of six months of virtual inactivity, the Germans invaded Denmark and Norway in April with yet another rapid, well planned and well executed operation. This again demonstrated that militarily they could do almost as they wished. The RAF played some role in the Norwegian campaign with a few ineffective and costly bombing raids, and a stout but pointless involvement around Narvik. There were no real lessons learned, as it was all over too quickly. The loss of the Scandinavian countries presented the RAF with a new challenge; German bombers from Norway could reach Scotland and northern England, which meant that the fighter defences had to remain dispersed.

The rapid success in Scandinavia was followed by the Blitzkrieg attack on France via the Low Countries in 10 May 1940.

> With the lessons of the two previous campaigns [Spain and Poland] available, the overwhelming air force worked perfectly as a support force to the German Army in the advance into Holland, Belgium and France. The Germans deployed a total strength of some 3,500 combat and 500 transport aircraft, while the Allies numbered between them some 250 Hurricanes and a similar number of French and Belgian fighters in North France and the Low Countries. Further, Allied armies were woefully deficient in AA guns. The tactics were the same, sweep the opposing airfields clear, attack communications, and then bomb in front of the advancing Army.   (Elmhirst lecture)

The comment on the lack of anti-aircraft capability is enlightening, but perhaps not surprising, as the Allies did not have the same air–land integration concept as the Germans, hence the lack of an appreciation of the criticality of layered and comprehensive anti-aircraft capability.

> In the meantime, with the beginning of the campaign against Holland, Belgium and France on the 10 May 1940, the Luftwaffe became involved in a new series of attacks. The objects of these attacks, based on previous battle experience were:
> 1. The destruction of the enemy's air forces and their sources of supply.
> 2. Indirect and direct support of the Army.
> 3. Attacks on enemy harbours and shipping.
>
> These tasks were entrusted to Luftflotten 2 and 3. Out of a strength of 5,142 aircraft, the Luftwaffe had 3,824 serviceable aircraft available at that time. (Out of this average of 3,824 serviceable aircraft there were 591 reconnaissance aircraft, 1,120 bombers, 342 Stukas, 42 ground attack aircraft, 248 twin-engine fighters, 1,016 single-engine fighters, 401 transport aircraft and 154 seaplanes). Compared with this, the allies (including the Belgian and Dutch Air

Forces) had 6,000 aircraft, of which 3,000 were at continental bases. Right at the outset of the campaign the full weight of the German air offensive simultaneously hammered the ground organisations of the Netherlands, Belgium and Northern France. The Dutch and Belgian Air Forces were destroyed, and the Franco-British air forces were hard hit and forced to use bases in the rear.   (Survey by 8th Abteilung, September 1944 [numbers given are as per the original document though the aircraft type figures do not add to the total of 3,824])

Whilst the number of aircraft is one indicator of potential strength, it comes down to how many are of appropriate quality (modern and effective), how many are serviceable, and how good is the equipment and the aircrew. All those factors played a significant role in the air campaigns. An early example of numbers being only numbers is the Battle of France, with slightly different data to that above: Luftwaffe nominal strength was around 2,800 aircraft (1,600 bombers and 1,200 fighters), some few hundred having been lost in the campaign against Poland. French strength stood at 1,500+ in service and a similar number in 'reserve'; however, the reality was that many were obsolete types and serviceability was a miserable 30 per cent of the in-service number. The RAF contributed a few hundred aircraft to the battle. So, on paper, the two sides were close to balance, although tipped in numbers towards the Germans. In addition, the lack of serviceability and the maintenance and logistics support was a key failure of the French establishment. Aircraft that cannot fly, or cannot be repaired if they have flown, are just a statistic and have no combat value.

The German fighter aircraft now concentrated in the West were far superior to the French in numbers and quality. The British Air Force in France comprised ten fighter squadrons of Hurricanes which could be spared from vital Home Defence and 19 squadrons of other types. Neither the French nor the British air authorities had equipped themselves with dive bombers, which at this time, as in Poland, became prominent, and were to play an important part in the demoralisation of the French infantry. The strength of the German Air Force at this time, taken as a whole, was about three to one. Although these were heavy odds at which to fight the brave and efficient German foe, I rested upon the conclusion that in our own air, over our own country and its waters, we would beat the German Air Force.   (Churchill, *History of the Second World War*)

After the vacillations of Chamberlain, Britain now had a leader who was the right man at the right time. Winston Churchill became Prime Minister on 10 May 1940. As a war leader he was at times as interfering as Hitler, especially when frustrated by the lack of success by land commanders. However, he was a great supporter of air power, which is why he is important to this study; he frequently defended the RAF against proposals from the Army or Navy; he was particularly supportive of Bomber Command, as he saw this as the only way, for a long while, to hit back at Germany. With a different national leader Bomber Command might never have been given the chance to prove itself. Furthermore, his ability to build a strong relationship with President Roosevelt not only enabled the RAF to get its hands on American aircraft and have access to training facilities, but also helped the Prime Minister persuade the Americans to follow the 'Germany First' strategy that was essential to the defeat of Germany. But all of that was yet to come. In the dark days of 1940, there were more pressing issues, one of which was getting the right equipment for the RAF.

> During these weeks of intense struggle and ceaseless anxiety Lord Beaverbrook rendered signal service. At all costs the fighter squadrons must be replenished with trustworthy machines. This was no time for red tape and circumlocution. All his remarkable qualities fitted the need. I was glad to be able sometimes to lean on him. He did not fail. This was his hour. His personal force and genius, combined with so much persuasion and contrivance, swept aside many obstacles. Everything in the supply pipeline was drawn forward to the battle. New or repaired aeroplanes streamed to the delighted squadrons in numbers they had never known before. All the services of maintenance and repair were driven to an intense degree.   (Churchill, *Second World War*)

The situation was actually more complex than this and the formation of the Ministry of Aircraft Production (MAP) set the dogmatic and prickly Beaverbrook on a collision course with the Air Ministry, as it cut across areas that in the past had been the sole mandate of the Air Ministry and, in its view, its expert knowledge of what the RAF needed. With Churchill's backing, Beaverbrook was able to establish MAP's control far and wide, including deciding what types would be ordered, and to control the production schedules whilst endeavouring to meet the Air Staff needs. MAP also took control of dispersal of production, supply, repair and requisitioning – the aim at this critical period was to get the maximum number of aircraft in the shortest possible time. Distinguished fighter pilot Alan Deere recalled: 'The miracles worked by Lord Beaverbrook at the MAP were being felt at squadron level where replacement aircraft arrived virtually the same day as the demand was sent.' Without doubt, if this had been left to the 'established' pre-war processes of the Air Ministry, the RAF would have not been as well served as it was under the new arrangement. Not all historians are supporters of the 'Beaverbrook miracle', but the numbers prove the effectiveness of MAP, and if Beaverbrook used his political connections to get things done, then that was no bad thing. This was, therefore, another of the building blocks for the RAF in avoiding defeat and then moving on to victory over the Luftwaffe.

Battle of France

The Battle of France was a strategic pivot for the RAF. The deployment of light bombers (Battles and Blenheims) in a desperate attempt to stem the German Blitzkrieg demonstrated, at a high cost in aircrew, the failure of equipment and tactics, and whilst the fighters (Hurricanes) did rather better, there was little to be happy about.

The massacre of the light bombers proved two things, the undaunted and undoubted courage of the RAF aircrew, and the harsh reality that in the face of fighter opposition, and intense anti-aircraft fire, such daylight operations were impossibly costly. The Hurricane squadrons, along with some French fighter units, did their best to shield some of the bomber attacks but on occasions the fighters failed to rendezvous with bombers or having done so were dragged into engagements with enemy fighters thus leaving the bombers vulnerable to other fighters. All this was new to the RAF in terms of threats, tactics, the pace of air combat, and a range of other elements.

Engagements with fighters and bombers, attempts to support Allied bombers, the effective German flak, all provided a rapid series of lessons for commanders and pilots. Some of the pre-war breed stuck rigidly to the rules and tactics that had been drummed into them; others started to recognise that they were being out-classed, out-gunned and out-numbered. Furthermore, it was discovered that the standard harmonisation on the guns of 400 yards was no good against fighters and that 250 yards 'achieved far more lethal results'. But every lesson learned cost a few more aircraft and pilots, though some caught on quicker than others and those who didn't were usually not around for very long. The period 16–26 May saw ever more Fighter Command squadrons being dragged into the conflict in France, but on a rotational basis of up to three squadrons a day, a useful way to broaden the experience level, but unfortunately each squadron seemed to have to learn the lessons for itself and so the same mistakes and losses occurred. However, many future tactical leaders had their baptism of fire in this period; those who survived and paid attention learnt quickly and were determined that old tactics and ideas had to change. The RAF 'system' rapidly developed an ability to promote the right type of people to the important roles of flight commander and squadron commander, and later wing leaders. The right wartime leader is a different beast to the right peacetime leader, and this mindset change in the RAF was another important factor. It did not always work of course, but below the senior command level it was less about politics and more about getting the job done.

The decisive point for the RAF came with the refusal to send any more fighter squadrons to France, despite severe pressure from the French and Churchill. This was one of Dowding's more important decisions; a weaker leader might have given in to political pressure. Of the 261 Hurricanes sent to France, 195 never came back. If those extra fighter squadrons had been sent who knows what effect that may have had on the outcome of the Battle of Britain. Many of the RAF pilots involved believed that a few more squadrons would make all the difference and why didn't 'they' send across more of the chaps, even a few Spitfires. This, however, was total anathema to Dowding who, by the middle of May, was fighting against a French request for ten more squadrons; he said: 'The Hurricane tap is now full on and you will not be able to resist the pressure to send Hurricanes to France until I have been bled white.' Churchill was under pressure to prop up the rapidly collapsing French, who within days of the invasion were already saying the battle was lost and that only more RAF aircraft, fighters and bombers, could help prevent defeat. To have thrown almost every RAF asset into the battle, as the French wanted, would not have made any real difference; it would have led to the destruction of the RAF and the defeat of Britain.

On 4 June Dowding sent a short message to squadrons that had been involved in the fighting over France:

> My Dear Fighter Boys. I don't send out many congratulatory letters and signals, but I feel that I must take this occasion, when the intensive fighting in Northern France is for the time being over, to tell you how proud I am of you and of the way in which you have fought since the 'Blitzkrieg' started. I wish I could have spent my time visiting you and hearing your accounts of the fighting, but I have occupied myself in working for you in other ways. I want you to know that my thoughts are always with you, and that it is you and your fighting spirit which will crack the morale of the German Air Force and preserve our Country through the trials which yet lie ahead. Good luck to you.

Paris was occupied on 14 June and scarcely a week later an armistice was signed between France and Germany. In Churchill's famous words, 'The Battle of France is over, the Battle of Britain is about to begin.' In the meantime, the 'Battle' of Dunkirk had been fought; over a period of nine days the evacuation of allied troops had been carried out in the face of intense air attack. Despite popular belief amongst the troops waiting on the beaches, the RAF was present and trying to hold off the waves of attacking German bombers. With an average of 300 sorties a day from the UK it was a great strain on Fighter Command and yet another source of concern for Dowding as just over 100 Spitfires and Hurricanes were lost, along with another slice of experienced pre-war-trained pilots. The net result of the campaign in France was the loss of almost 1,000 aircraft, roughly half of which were fighters.

The RAF fighters could have taken some comfort from a later German assessment:

> Of all the enemy air forces operating in 1940, the British Air Force was the most formidable in battle. Encounters of German units with British Spitfire and Hurricane formations during the Western campaign, and above all along the Channel at the time of the British retreat to Dunkirk, had been the hardest so far. In supporting the BEF, and their French ally in France, the British had brought only parts of their Royal Air Force into operation.
>
> (Lecture by Hauptmann Otto Bechtle, Berlin-Gatow, 2 February 1944)

How much of this was a true realisation of the new enemy and how much was a look-back from 1944 is of course debatable.

How Did the Aircraft Compare?

> In the quality of the fighter aircraft there was little to choose. The Germans were faster, with a better rate of climb; ours more manoeuvrable, better armed. Their airmen, well aware of their great numbers, were also proud victors of Poland, Norway, the Low Countries, France; ours had supreme confidence in themselves as individuals and that determination which the British race displays in fullest measure when in supreme adversity.
>
> (Churchill, Second World War)

Plt Off Maurice Stephens was in France with 3 Squadron in May 1940 and met with some success:

> Suddenly we spotted about 60 tiny black dots in the sky, flying west like a swarm of midges. The next moment we among them – Stukas, with an escort of about twenty 109s. I got one lined up in my gunsight, and opened fire from about 50 yards. After a short burst he

> blew up in an orange ball of flame, followed by a terrifying clatter as my Hurricane flew through the debris . . . Just then, from out of the cloud a few hundred yards away, emerged a Dornier 17. I gave him a short burst from short range, hitting the starboard engine which started smoking. I had the satisfaction of seeing the pilot belly land the aircraft in a ploughed field.

So, despite some pilots saying that the Brownings were ineffective, it was clearly not just a case of weight of lead but also where you put it and at what range!

Mike Crosskill:

> I was confident that in a scrap with a Bf 109, the Hurricane could always out-turn it. What the 109 used to do was stick the nose down good and hard, and dive down. Until we got the new carburettor, we could not really follow them. They knew that if we were chasing them and they did a steep dive they would get away from us.

The 109s had a fuel-injector that allowed this type of manoeuvre, whereas the simple float carbs in the RAF fighters would starve the engine of fuel and it would cough and splutter, and even stop. The problem persisted throughout the battle; some pilots mastered the roll and follow manoeuvre, others just let the enemy go. A temporary solution was eventually fitted – 'Miss Shilling's Orifice' – named after the female engineer who came up with the idea.

When a German aircraft was damaged or shot down in the Battle of Britain the pilot invariably claimed it was caused by a Spitfire – it seemed an embarrassment to be shot down by a Hurricane. Despite the experience of the French campaign when most German fighters only faced RAF Hurricanes and honours were generally even, with some statistics even suggesting the Hurricane had the edge in terms of kill ratio, there was a perception amongst German pilots that the Hurricane was inferior. The RAF fighter to fear was the Spitfire, even though combats with Spitfires had been limited as none were based in France. The RAF did nothing to counter this, indeed it went out if its way to promote the Spitfire as the deadliest fighter in combat.

The Real Test

In July 1940 the Germans estimated that Fighter Command strength stood at 50 squadrons equipped with 900 fighters, of which 675 were serviceable – 40 per cent of these being Spitfires and the rest Hurricanes. This intelligence assessment was remarkably accurate, as on 10 July the Command's statistics were 54 squadrons equipped with 864 aircraft, of which 656 were serviceable, a good recovery from the low point of the previous month. The percentages of types were in error as Spitfires made up 35 per cent of the total, Hurricanes 50 per cent and the remainder comprised Blenheims and Defiants, both having been ignored in the German assessment. The importance of the figures is their use by the Germans to assess the remaining strength of Fighter Command in the light of Luftwaffe claims after each day's combat. By combining this with an assessment of British fighter production capacity the planners could arrive at an operational availability figure and thus work out the combat effectiveness of Fighter Command. However, as we shall see, it did not work quite as simply as that! An RAF estimate of GAF strength in France and the Low Countries gave the following breakdown:

Long-range bombers	1,200
Dive-bombers	280+
Single-engine fighters	760
Twin-engine fighters	220
Long-range reconnaissance	50
Short-range reconnaissance	90

In addition to these were 190 aircraft in Norway (130 long-range bombers, 30 twin-engine fighters and 30 long-range reconnaissance types). Together this gave a total of 2,790 combat aircraft and it was estimated that the bomber force had 69 per cent serviceability whilst the fighter force had an impressive 95 per cent serviceability. German records (from 6th Abteilung [Department of the Luftwaffe Quartermaster-General]) show that the estimates were reasonably accurate in terms of the total but that the breakdown was in error:

Bombers	981
Stukas	336
Single-engine fighters	839
Twin-engine fighters	282

These figures are for serviceable aircraft. The Germans then anticipated superiority of numbers, better tactical dispositions and greater experience:

> The Command hoped that it would not require more than four days to smash the enemy fighter defences in southern England. Once this goal was reached, the offensive was to be extended northwards, sector by sector across the line King's Lynn to Leicester until all England was covered by day attack. At the beginning of the daylight

attack, the principle of giving bomber formations the minimum necessary fighter escort so as to leave the majority of fighters free to pursue their real task of destroying the enemy in open combat was generally accepted.   (Bechtle)

On 4 July, Hitler had determined four goals for the Luftwaffe:

- Destroy the RAF (in other words, gain air superiority to enable sea and land operations)
- Destroy the RAF supply system
- Destroy British aircraft production
- Damage the Royal Navy to prevent it intervening in the invasion

This was all very sound strategy, and in the case of the first three the same as the RAF and later Allied air strategy over Europe, especially from 1942.

> The range of our aircraft has deprived England of her exclusively insular character. For the first time in history the country is a battle-field, from Dover to the Shetlands and the Humber to the Mersey. The employment of bomber and fighter squadrons in the decisive battles in the West and the destructive onslaught on the enemy's supply and transport in the Western campaign are inseparably associated with the idea of the German Luftwaffe. A very large number of aerodromes, benefiting from greatly improved ground organisation and protected by excellent AA defences, provide our bomber, fighter, reconnaissance and transport squadrons with concentration areas for the air war against Great Britain. Our proximity to the English coast which our victories have won for us places all parts of the country within reach.   (Baumbach, *Broken Swastika*)

This was all true, if a little jingoistic. Baumbach also went on to state that there were two key aspects, gaining air superiority and 'cutting off the island from its source of supply'.

The challenge came in turning strategy into operational impact. This the Germans failed to do. The central tenet of the application of air power is 'selection and maintenance of the aim'; this is one of the main reasons to have an independent air arm that is not assigned to either sea or land. A quite reasonable and appropriate aim for the Luftwaffe was the first goal stated by Hitler, destruction of the RAF. As with all such attempts at achieving air superiority, it was a matter of sticking with it and accepting the losses, and hoping the other side was losing more, until a tipping point was reached at which the enemy was no longer able to continue, which for the Germans should have been destruction of fighters on the ground and in the air, and destruction of the control network, through constant pressure. For this to be successful, intelligence was required on where the enemy fighter force and its support infrastructure was based, an estimate of its strength, its weak points, and its ability to absorb damage. Instead there were weaknesses in the German intelligence services. True, at the outbreak of war they had a good idea, and excellent target maps and photos, of RAF airfields, but they had little strategic appreciation of the options the RAF had to re-deploy its fighter units.

The whole question of intelligence-gathering, analysis and dissemination is massive and ranges from air reconnaissance to signals intelligence and human intelligence (agents, partisans, PoW interrogation, and so on). Both sides had such organisations, but the Allies proved to be better and more consistent, especially as the war progressed, in part because the Germans faced challenges in the Occupied Countries (for example, resistance workers later provided key details of the V-weapon sites), but also in the field of signals intelligence, in clear language or code, and then making use of that information.

The RAF's Y Service had the dual function of intercepting signals and working out where they came from, using direction finding (D/F). If the intercepts were encrypted, they were sent to Bletchley Park, home of the Government Code and Cypher School. The work done at Bletchley, and the intelligence it provided, was critical to the British and Allied war effort, though this study does not have the space to do more than recognise the vital role of such intelligence work.

And what was the RAF strategy at this time? That is still a good question, and one that commanders at the time might have been hard-pressed to answer. The collapse of France had a major impact on the strategic air position; it gave the Luftwaffe numerous well-equipped airfields within fighter range of south-east England, as well as providing bomber bases within reach of almost the whole of Britain. For the RAF, it meant the defensive situation had changed, with insufficient airfields in the now most vulnerable sector. However, to commanders with a more offensive spirit, it also brought the enemy airfields within range – but by now Fighter Command was focused on defence, and Bomber Command was looking at Germany.

What if the RAF had taken a more offensive view at this time? What if the fighter and bomber commanders had worked together, in a fashion similar to that of the Luftwaffe, and seen the opportunity here to destroy the Luftwaffe on the ground in France? Some commentators have seen this as a strategic leadership failure by the British air commanders.

Lessons Learned?

Losses in combat had meant a new breed of pilots had started to arrive on the RAF squadrons and the experienced pilots were sharing their knowledge. According to Billy Drake:

> They sent virtually every fighter pilot who survived the Battle of France to go and teach RAF squadrons new tactics, which we had learned in the battle. We taught them what we knew about air warfare, which was still fairly basic. I taught them what the Hurricane was all about, what you could do with the aircraft, and if attacked by a 109 how to evade him.

The RAF at last recognised the need to learn its trade all over again in the crucible of modern air war, and it introduced specialist units such as the Air Fighting Development Unit (AFDU). The task of such units, often involving squadron pilots in aircraft evaluations, was to look at aircraft, weapons and tactics. The lessons were then passed on to the operational units, although it took some time for the process to become effective. The AFDU was formed in July 1940 and the importance of this unit cannot be overstated; it was staffed by experienced pilots whose task was to evaluate new aircraft, both in terms of handling and performance and, in most cases, in tactical trials against other aircraft, allied and enemy. What is less certain is what effect the reports actually had in terms of changes being made or useful information being relayed to the operational units or appropriate training units.

The Central Gunnery School (CGS) had formed at Warmwell in November 1939 as the centre of excellence for air gunnery to improve standards and provide specialist training. This was a good development, and various courses were developed and implemented in the early years of war that saw major improvements in the understanding and application of air-to-air gunnery. However, there was no substitute for experience, and whilst 'cine gunning' a drogue or another aircraft was useful the real experience came in the multi-aircraft combat arena.

The Battle of Britain started with Luftwaffe attacks on coastal shipping. The first major battle took place on 8 July when Fighter Command scrambled five squadrons to intercept a large enemy force attacking a convoy in the Channel; the fight eventually involved over 100 aircraft. Convoy attacks of this type, varying in intensity and sometimes limited to small numbers of unescorted raiders using cloud cover, was the pattern of the battle for the first few weeks. Most activity centred on shipping off Dover. During July the average number of defensive sorties was 500–600 a day, the highest rate occurring on 28 July when 794 sorties were flown, during which the

RAF claimed ten aircraft for the loss of five of its own. Day-fighter strength grew during July, enabling the Command to field 49 Hurricane and Spitfire squadrons by early August; the number of Spitfire units remained at 18 but an additional four Hurricane units were now in the line. The battle to 'decide the war' was now under way.

Doctrine, Politics and Leadership

> The German air assault on Britain is a tale of divided counsels, conflicting purposes, and never fully accomplished plans. Three or four times in these months the enemy abandoned a method of attack which was causing us severe stress and turned to something new. But all these stages overlapped one another; each one merged into the next!   (Churchill, *Second World War*)

Air Chief Marshal Hugh 'Stuffy' Dowding was an experienced officer, having served with operational squadrons in World War One, including as commanding officer of 16 Squadron. To improve squadron training and morale he introduced a bombing contest. This was brought to a hasty conclusion when the one and only bomb ended up in a canal next to the airfield! During his time as CO, the squadron operated in the support roles of bomber, recce and artillery observation. By 1916 he was commander of 9th Wing for the Battle of the Somme, his first contact with Trenchard. Post-war he held various staff appointments, including that of Air Member for Supply and Research, with a remit to help shape the future of the RAF. Some have argued he did well and laid the foundation for future success, with his support of radar, others that he did little to push a new generation of aircraft and aerial guns. In 1936 he was appointed head of the newly formed Fighter Command. His appointment to Fighter Command was not without its critics, and he had 'enemies', or at least lukewarm supporters, above and below him. One of these was Trafford Leigh-Mallory, who was destined to cause controversy during the Battle of Britain from his post as commander of No. 12 Group. The reasons why Leigh-Mallory did not support his commander can be traced to his ambition and the fact that Dowding appointed Keith Park to command No. 11 Group, which would take centre stage in the forthcoming battle; this also led to antipathy between the two key operational commanders. It also did not help that the Assistant Chief of Air Staff (ACAS), AVM William Sholto Douglas, was a supporter of Leigh-Mallory.

There can be little doubt that Dowding played a significant role in the Battle of Britain through his strategic direction and leadership, although there were some issues with his aloof command style. Decisions such as rotating squadrons between the operational groups helped keep No. 11 Group at least at minimal operational effectiveness. Squadrons would be rotated when losses or other factors determined that they should spend some time in a quieter sector but remain in being as squadrons whilst they came back up to strength. Dowding also defined three categories of squadron:

A: Based in or close to No. 11 Group and kept up to strength by drafting in new pilots;

B: Outside the No. 11 Group area and sent into the Group as a whole squadron;

C: Those that had suffered so heavily that they needed to be rebuilt around their remaining core, or potentially the pilots sent to other squadrons.

It Is Only Effective if You Shoot Him Down!

Getting the aircraft in the right place to take a shot was the start point of a successful engagement. And this is where Radio Direction Finding (RDF, now of course known as radar) was important. The famous 1960s film *Battle of Britain* summed this up in a great scene with Dowding saying he was 'trusting in God and praying for radar'. Most historians have agreed that a major factor in the RAF's victory in the Battle of Britain was Britain's radar network.

In the early 1930s the British Air Defence Plan was based upon that employed during the First World War and comprised an Aircraft Fighting Zone 150 miles long, from Duxford and around London to Devizes in Wiltshire. This was divided into ten sections, each 15 miles wide, defended by one or more dedicated day-fighter squadrons, with associated searchlights and anti-aircraft guns. There was an additional ring of searchlights and guns around London. The outward edge of the Aircraft Zone was positioned 35 miles from the coast, a distance based upon the time it would take the fighter to climb to 14,000 ft. Initial detection of raiders depended upon visual sighting by the Observer Corps, plus a limited number of 'acoustic mirror devices'. Each HQ received information from the observation units and displayed raids on a plotting table, thus allowing the overall picture of the air situation to be seen by the controller.

The weak link remained that of detection – it was a big sky so how did you find the enemy? This was borne out in the July 1934 annual air exercise, when at least half of the day-bomber formations reached their targets without being intercepted by fighters – proof that fighters were a waste of resources as the bomber would always win through? If the fighters could not find bomber formations in good weather by day, what chance would they have at night? Not that this was of any concern at the time.

At the first meeting of the Committee for Scientific Survey of Air Defence, in January 1935, the problems highlighted by the previous year's exercise were discussed, as were the prospects of any scientific breakthrough that might provide an answer. The committee members consulted Robert Watson-Watt, head of the radio research branch of the National Physical Laboratory, as to the feasibility of using radio waves. A month later he presented his thoughts on how to use such radio waves to detect aircraft, the principle being to 'bounce' the waves off the aircraft and pick up the echo. Within a matter of weeks an experiment had been arranged using the BBC's transmitter at Daventry. The idea was for an aircraft to fly through the centre of the transmitting beam while Watson-Watt and his colleagues attempted to detect its presence on a cathode-ray oscilloscope. It worked as planned, the passage of the aircraft causing a blip on the equipment. All that was needed now was high-level support for development of the technique, and that came from Air Marshal Hugh Dowding, the Air Member for Research and Development.

In September 1935 the Air Defence Sub-Committee acquired Treasury funding for a chain of RDF stations along the east coast; a remarkable achievement so early in the development of the technique. The next three years saw several technical developments of the equipment, many individuals making invaluable contributions to the work. Since the initial proving of the RDF principle in 1935, progress had been rapid, although many problems remained. By mid-1937 three stations were in operation, at Bawdsey, Canewdon and Dover, along with an experimental filter station at Bawdsey. The development of the last of these added a new dimension to the system by providing, as the term implied, a filtering of the mass of information from the various sources so that the controllers could be provided with a simpler, more accurate air picture on which to base their operations. The earlier problem of track discrimination had virtually been solved, but height prediction remained a significant issue.

The system's first major test came in the 1938 Home Defence exercises, and in general terms it appeared to work well, some 75 per cent of attempted interceptions (day and night) proving successful. New RDF stations (code-named Chain Home – CH, and Chain Home Low – CHL) were constructed in a plan to create unbroken coverage around the east and southern coasts of Britain. At the same time an extensive programme for the construction of Command, Group and Sector operations rooms was under way. By September 1939 twenty CH stations were operational, with detection ranges in excess of 100 miles. The additional system of CHL was also well under way. A post-war Fighter Command report summarised its importance:

> How valuable this system was to be, was proved in the Battle of Britain, for without its help the courage and determination of the pilots and the devotion and hard work of the ground staff would have been to little avail. This system of radar allied with the reports by sight and sound of the Royal [from 1941] Observer Corps developed rapidly through the war.

Fighter Comparison, Summer 1940

One Fighter Command document addressed 'manoeuvrability in air fighting':

> The attached notes concerning the relative manoeuvrability of Spitfire versus Hurricane are forwarded for the information of pilots. They are the result of combat tests by experienced pilots and the principles will apply against hostile aircraft of similar performance. It was found that the Hurricane will easily out-turn the Spitfire in a simple tail chase and bring guns to bear in two or three turns. A tail chase is therefore of advantage to the Hurricane, but fatal to the Spitfire. The correct tactics for the Spitfire against the Hurricane (or any hostile aircraft with better turning circle but lower speed) are as follows:
>
> Approach in such a way that the guns are brought to bear as soon as it is within range, if possible, by a surprise attack from above. Maintain the attack only as long as the sights are on. If the attack is not decisive, and sights cannot be kept on owing to the turn of the other aircraft, break off instantly. If the aircraft turns away and tries to escape, the Spitfire has the immediate and decisive advantage, provided the pilot does not lose sight of the enemy. If the slower aeroplane with better turning circle is flown by a very skilful pilot, it is difficult for the pilot of the Spitfire to get the sights on for more than a moment, and make an effective attack, unless he can use the element of surprise by making the enemy pilot lose sight of him. The Spitfire pilot can, however, retain the initiative and sooner or later bring off a decisive attack by exercising patience in attaining the most favourable position well above the enemy. It is considered that higher speed is much more valuable than smaller turning circle, provided the sacrifice of quick turning is not out of proportion to the gain in speed. Other factors being equal, the aircraft with the

greater speed has the advantage both strategically and tactically, over that with the better turning circle. It is considered that a combat between two fighter pilots of great experience and equal skill, one in the Spitfire and the other in a slower but more 'manoeuvrable' type would result in a victory for the pilot of the Spitfire.

In May 1940 the British had the opportunity of carrying-out comparative tests with a captured Bf 109E, courtesy of the French. Plt Off Adolf 'Sailor' Malan, plus Spitfire, was detached from 74 Squadron for this task. The general conclusion following the trials was that the Spitfire was superior to the 109 in most areas of performance; tactical advice included such comments as 'Another effective form of evasion with the Spitfire was found to be a steep, climbing spiral at 120 mph; in this manoeuvre the Spitfire gained rapidly on the Me 109, eventually allowing the pilot to execute a half roll on to the tail of his opponent.' These tests also contributed to the decision to harmonise fighters' guns at 250 yards instead of the previous 400 yards.

Interestingly, but not surprisingly, German trials of a Bf 109 against a captured Spitfire suggested that the latter was generally inferior; the great fighter pilot Werner Mölders commented that

It handles well, is light on the controls, faultless in the turn and has a performance approximately that of the Me 109. As a fighting aircraft, however, it is miserable. A sudden push forward on the stick will cause the motor to cut . . . in a rapidly changing air combat situation the motor is either over-speeding or else is not being used to the full.

Survivability was another important aspect, including the safety of the pilot. Major considerations included bullet-proof (armoured) glass for windscreens, armour for the cockpit and protection for the fuel tanks, which later involved self-sealing tanks to prevent fumes igniting. In addition to the purely practical benefit of protecting the aircraft and pilot was the morale effect of knowing that there was at least some protection against enemy fire.

In general terms the Spitfire was no better and no worse than its contemporaries in respect of self-protection, although it is usually stated that the Hurricane was able to take more punishment. Cannon strikes could punch major holes in the metal structure of the Spitfire and depending on the location of the strike it could be either catastrophic or barely noticeable; the fuel tanks were always an area for concern but more devastating was damage to the control surfaces that made the aircraft unflyable. It is usually considered that to cause critical damage to an aircraft you need to keep the sight on for a minimum of two seconds (a figure we still used in the Tornado!), but if you went for the cockpit you could 'neutralise' the aircraft in half a second by hitting the most critical system of all, the pilot. To hold a manoeuvring aircraft in your sights for two seconds is not easy but it is true that most pilots were reluctant to shoot at the cockpit; if the pilot was hit as part of the general spraying of his aircraft with gunfire so be it – but generally he was not directly targeted, at least at this stage of the war or in this theatre.

The use of armour plate behind the pilot was a way of countering part of this random fire as it was still considered that most attacks would be from the stern and there was little that could be done to defend against a lateral attack, whilst the engine provided good protection from a frontal shot. However, the engine was also one of the most vulnerable systems in any aircraft and though the Merlin was rugged and reliable it was still prone to damage, a single bullet with a lucky hit was all it took. The tell-tale stream of glycol from a punctured cooling system, or a plume of grey-to-black smoke from a critically damaged engine invariably spelt the end of the aircraft.

In terms of visibility the Spitfire was far better than its first main opponent, the Bf 109, which had far too much 'ironwork' in the canopy and was probably the worst of all the early fighters in this respect. Jeffrey Quill took time away from his test-pilot duties to fly operational sorties in the Battle of Britain and in his autobiography he stated that this experience showed up

> . . . one or two glaring defects which needed urgent action . . . The Spitfire was fitted with a thick, armoured-glass panel at the centre of its windscreen, but the side panels were of curved Perspex and the optical distortion from these made long-distance visual scanning extremely difficult. I was determined to have the design altered, and indeed I succeeded in getting optically true glass into the side panels by 1941.   (Jeffrey Quill, *Spitfire, A Test Pilot's Story*)

The Hurricane had quite a bit of ironwork in the canopy so was not as good as the Spitfire, but it was better than the 109.

Many people assume that lookout is simply a matter of looking out of the cockpit, but it actually requires specific techniques of scanning and eye manipulation.

> I always knew, or at least was given the advice and followed it, to look at each sector – not just a glance around looking everywhere,

you know, up and behind, not giving myself time to recognise anything. But look at a sector and decide whether there was or there wasn't anything there. Then I'd look at another sector and do the same thing. I found that the best policy if you really wanted to look at something.   ('Rosie' Mackie, quoted in Avery & Shores, *Spitfire Leader*)

Combat experience had quickly shown the need to improve the rear view and whilst the 'rear view mirror' was of great benefit it was not the whole answer. Problems with the rear view were another lesson that Jeffrey Quill took away from his Battle of Britain operations with 65 Squadron:

> Also necessary was an improvement in direct rearwards vision. I did not quite see how this could be achieved in the short term, although probably something could be done in the way of further bulging of the canopy [it was]. In the longer term I believed that a big change must be made to the lines of the rear fuselage and the shape of the canopy. This would take time but in the immediate future I could try to draw attention to the urgency of the need.   (Quill)

Fighter pilots had to learn to swivel their heads, and usually wore scarves to help 'lubricate' the neck, and needed to be taught the principle of actually looking for aircraft. Once again, knowledge of the problem and its solution, coupled with training, was an absolute must. Sadly all this was in short supply in the early part of the war.

In the fight the only important performance considerations are can you 'defend and survive' or 'attack and kill', with the requirement to defend or attack switching in moments. Ignoring for now the training, experience, confidence and luck elements, the core of this is the aircraft's ability to turn better than the other guy or to out-climb, out-dive or simply have a better speed range in order to close or escape. In respect to climb and dive the Spitfire was average, and in the early years of the war the engine limitations in negative g meant that it was often poorly placed against the Bf 109. In most of the tactical scenarios of the Battle of Britain the Spitfires were at a disadvantage, often still climbing to height when they came upon the enemy.

Guns and Gunnery

Having got into position, it then came down to aiming, weapon effect and a measure of luck. Unless you are dead astern and close to the enemy there is invariably an element of deflection in any shot; if you aim at the aircraft, by the time the bullets get there the target has moved on. Sounds simple, but with manoeuvring aircraft it is a skill that must be learned and practised.

Billy Drake:

> There were two theories about how guns should be aimed. One was to harmonise all eight machine guns to meet at a point, and that was the way I liked it, to get the maximum number of bullets if you aimed straight, at a point 250 yards away. The other way, known as the 'Dowding Spread', was for those who were not as good a shot, where the guns were harmonised at 400 yards but spreading the bullets. The first method was favoured by those who were good shots. Johnny Johnson and myself had been brought up by our fathers to shoot at birds, and we understood deflection shooting.

Others, especially some of the Polish and Czech pilots, believed in getting in very close, so the chance of bullets missing was reduced, although the risk of self-damage (from bits of the enemy) or return fire was higher. Having fired at and hit the enemy, the next consideration was 'did it cause critical damage'? To hit the enemy and not destroy him, or at least put him out of the fight, was no better than not hitting him at all. We have already looked at fighter armament and the RAF pre-war debate over machine gun versus cannon, and this theme will come up again a number of times. However, the RAF reports from the battle of France had not indicated any serious concerns with fighter weaponry. There was more, and justified, concern about tactics, both to score success and to avoid getting shot down.

The reality is that in the early part of the battle there was little option other than to scramble aircraft when the enemy was detected and sector control had determined the squadrons in the best place to get airborne to intercept. It was a struggle for survival, get something up and get stuck in. In an ideal world the defenders would position for height and sun, but rarely did that ideal happen for the RAF at this period.

'They came out of the sun at lightning speed and it was all over in a split second. I realised the aeroplane was finished, and pulled the pin on the Sutton harness, got to my feet and then bang, I was out in space.' Bill Green's Hurricane had been bounced when his squadron was orbiting over Deal and he thought he had been doing a good job of searching the sky! Like many other pilots, he had been less than two weeks in the battle. One of the notable scenes in the 1969 *Battle of Britain* film concerned the arrival of a new pilot on a Spitfire squadron; the grizzled CO asks how many hours he has on Spits, to which he replies '10½ Sir', to which he gets the quick response, 'Well let's make it 11 before Jerry has you for breakfast.' The pilots sitting around dispersal, mutter cynically and make machine-gun noises. There follows a quick air-combat lesson with the experienced pilot running rings around the youngster, who offers the classic line after one bounce from the sun, 'I thought you might come out of the sun' to which the retort was, 'Don't just think, look, search for the bastards.' A few minutes of film but a wealth of truism in terms of the period.

Edward Wells was one of an increasing band of New Zealanders who arrived in the UK as pilots from the RNZAF, although his qualification had been gained on the likes of the Vickers Vincent biplane, a lumbering antiquated type that was suitable for RAF inter-war colonial policing but not as a route to modern monoplane fighter operations. 'Hawkeye' Wells, his nickname based on his marksmanship with 12-bore shotguns, was sent to No. 7 OTU at Hawarden for fighter conversion:

> I gazed in awe and excitement at the rather battered collection of Mark 1 Spitfires which we were to fly. Various lectures on the technical features of these aircraft, plus some rather airy-fairy talks on what were alleged to be the enemy's tactics in the air and what was supposed to the be the best way of dealing with them, filled the next few days. To us at that time, these talks were pure gospel and we drank in every word, as our lecturers were young pilots with operational experience.

Despite this, he thought that more time could have been spent on 'how to operate the aircraft properly, which is a very much more exacting requirement than just to be able to fly them'.

Johnny Kent also went to Hawarden for conversion to the Hurricane and, in theory, an introduction to tactics:

> When I met the instructors hardly any of them had been on operations and mine had not served in a squadron for over three years. Fortunately, the Flight Commander, Bill Kain, had been in France with 73 Squadron and really knew what the score was. He rather apologetically explained that the rules required both Mac and I to be given a dual check before being allowed to fly Hurricanes. As he was pushed for time and short of instructors, he felt that the best thing to do was for us to check out one another in a Miles Master. This took about fifteen minutes and then we transferred ourselves into a couple of Hurricanes and went off on a 'dog-fighting' exercise. Everything was confused during this period and the training syllabus was very sketchy – it consisted mostly of formation flying and dog-fighting exercises. I kept after Bill Kain about air firing, explaining that I had never fired eight guns and I wanted to find out what they sounded like – and what effect they had on the aircraft. Finally, in desperation, he allowed me one shot. My target was a spit of sand

in the Dee Estuary and, on my first attack, I got a neat group with a half-second burst, but on my second dive the guns failed to fire. I tried several more times, but just nothing happened so, in a bit of a temper, I returned to the airfield and told Bill Kain what I thought of an installation which could produce stoppages in all eight guns at once. Bill then explained that there had been no stoppage – that was all the ammunition they could spare me! I knew that both the country and the air force were in a pretty bad way, but this brought home to me just how desperate the situation was. It did not matter so much in my particular case as I had done so much front-gun firing before, although it was with only two guns, but many of the new boys never fired their guns at all until they went into action for the first time – a sobering thought when one considers the task before them.   (Johnny Kent, *One of the Few*)

Some, like Billy Drake, had over 100 hours on the Hurricane when he first went into combat, others were like Peter Ayhurst, who was 18 years old and had the princely total of 3½ hours on type when he went into battle. Even those who had some time on type had, in many cases, never fired the guns!

Bob Foster:

I finished training at Sutton Bridge by 18 July having done about 40–50 hours. We did a lot of formation flying in simulated attacks, useless when it came to fighting but that was the way it went. My instructor, Basil Smallwood, had spent a week flying patrols in France and was now instructing on Hurricanes.

Foster was lucky that his first posting took him north to Edinburgh where he gained another forty hours' flying experience in a quiet area before joining the battle; one of his course colleagues went to Kenley and was dead within a few weeks.

In August 1940 Johnnie Johnson was posted to 19 Squadron at Duxford with a total of 205 hours in his logbook, of which twenty-three were on Spitfires. The promised extra training was not forthcoming as the squadron was having problems with its new cannon armament: 'I don't know how we shall find time to train you chaps. We've simply got to get these things working first.' The idea that any necessary advanced training could be carried out on-squadron was totally flawed, especially at a time when the squadrons were hard-pressed to maintain operational status. Most flight and squadron commanders did the best they could and tried to shield new boys from operations until they had built up a few more hours and had flown a few mock combats. Sadly, for many a bright young pilot his first combat experience was his last. The situation varied from unit to unit and depended to a large degree on the attitude of the squadron commander, and to a lesser extent the flight commanders or even senior (experienced) pilots.

> We had a great deal of respect for 'Crash' Curry [Sqn Ldr John Harvey Curry, DFC]. He set about really putting us through our paces with 'tail-chasing'. A small formation of say four aircraft went off and he would do all sorts of attacks on us, 'out of the sun', 'up and under' and really gave us a hard time. He was a magnificent pilot; nobody could touch him – he had his own 'Flying Circus' in Texas before the war. He did not approve of the RAF gunsight and had his own built into his aircraft. He was out 'polishing' his Spitfire almost every day until it gleamed, and no airman was allowed to go near it.
>
> (Jerry Jarrold, 80 Squadron)

> In the afternoon we were on patrol when I experienced the first really serious result of the squadron's losses and lack of leadership. There were a number of small formations of 109s high above us and over the south coast and every now and then one or two of them would start to dive towards us, but I always turned to meet them head-on and they would break off their attack. On this occasion, after a number of these abortive passes had been made, I found that several of my pilots had broken formation and were heading for home. It was clearly a case of what was called '109-itis' and it was apparent that these pilots had lost all confidence in their ability to cope with the German fighters. I knew that this confidence had to be restored as rapidly as possible and the place to do it was in a combat area and not when on a so-called rest. When we had returned to our airfield I had all the pilots in and gave them a really good talking to and announced that if I had any more people breaking away – and by doing so exposing not only themselves to attack but the rest of the squadron – I would not wait for the Germans to shoot down the offender but would do it myself. They all looked a bit glum and there was little doubt that they loathed my guts – I didn't care as I felt that they needed a bit of straight talking.   (Johnny Kent, *One of the Few*)

One of the most frequent comments made by fighter pilots involved in this, and indeed other, air battles, was the sudden change from a sky full of aircraft to being on your own. Bob 'Spud' Spurdle neatly expresses this in his autobiography *The Blue Arena*:

I rechecked that my gun's safety catch was off. The gun-sight graticule glowed clearly, and I lowered my seat a notch. Malan [Sqn Ldr A. G. Malan, CO of 74 Squadron] curved to meet the Huns head on and all at once we were into them. Yellow spinners, stiff square-tipped wings with sparkles of light flickering. I tried to follow my leader around but, being fascinated by the enemy aircraft, somehow lost him. I couldn't find a single Jerry. Twisting and turning, I couldn't see a damned aircraft! Nothing! The sky was clean and bare. Far off, white contrails curved lazily this way and that. But I couldn't watch them. Where had everyone gone? It was no use horsing around up here, twisting from side to side, looking up, back and around, frantic with disappointment. I dived for the deck – orders were to go straight back if separated and there was no fight in one's vicinity.

On the way back he latched on to another Spitfire – Malan's – and compounded his error. 'He looked at me and shook his fist. Automatically I lowered my undercarriage, Malan just turned away and slowly shook his head.' The hand gesture normally meant lower the undercarriage but, in this case, Malan was obviously just venting his feelings, as he did again back at Biggin Hill. 'Spud' Spurdle went on to have a fine combat career, ending up as CO of 80 Squadron with a DFC and Bar. Some of the young men survived and learned, but some did not.

Maintaining squadron integrity was an important aspect of morale, as a squadron number carried with it the history, achievements and personalities of that squadron, and on such things are morale built and maintained. The Luftwaffe did not, in general, follow this type of rotation policy and units were kept up to strength by the posting in of new pilots, as indeed was the case with RAF Bomber Command. In such circumstances, losses and constant new faces had an impact on morale, especially if senior leaders kept on saying that you were winning, and the battle was won when the reality looked very different in the squadrons. 'Sailor' Malan of 74 Squadron was, according to Alan Deere, 'the best fighter tactician and leader produced by the RAF in World War Two'. This was a sentiment echoed by many, including 'Dizzy' Allen: 'I doubt if there was a more successful squadron commander in 1940 than Malan. He was a crack shot, a brilliant aerobatic pilot, but, above all, was utterly determined.' Malan was thirty years old during the Battle, though Dowding had once stated that 'only exceptionally should officers over twenty-six years of age be posted to command fighter squadrons.'

And What About the Luftwaffe?

At a conference at Karinhall on 19 August 1940, Göring had this to say concerning leadership:

> Until further notice, the main task of Luftflotten 2 and 3 will be to inflict the utmost damage possible on the enemy fighter forces. With this are to be combined attacks on the ground organisation of the enemy bombers, conducted however in such a manner as to avoid all unnecessary losses. The difficulties inherent in such a great task make it essential that while avoiding any rigid plan, the whole operation must be planned and carried through with the utmost care. This can only be possible if unit commanders at all levels are of the best type. I have therefore ordered that in future, unit commanders are to be appointed regardless of rank and exclusively from among the most suitable and capable officers. Where possible such officers should be appointed from their own unit. Immediate steps are to be taken by *Luftflotten*, *Korps* and *Gruppen* to test the suitability of all subordinate unit commanders, with a view to effecting exchanges and removals where necessary. Not only unsuitable, but also inexperienced officers, whose lack of experience may lead to unnecessary losses, must be replaced. Otherwise suitable but inexperienced officers must serve under a really seasoned commander until such time as the latter is prepared to recommend their promotion. The protection of returning bombers and fighters over the Channel must be assured by specially designated fighter formations. The same applies to the defence of our own ground organisations Young pilots not considered sufficiently experienced to fly over England could usefully carry out this latter task under the leadership of veteran pilots. The training of these young pilots and the importance of adequate supervision during their first operations are matters which cannot be too strongly emphasised.

This was all excellent and accurate; sadly, for the his aircrew, neither Göring nor the Luftwaffe training system really adhered to this, and as unbounded success turned to failure over England, accusations of cowardice and bad leadership became common.

Hauptmann Bechtle's 1944 lecture stated:

> In the first few days of the air war [over England] it became apparent that the numerous dogged British fighter pilots who were supplemented by formations of volunteers from nations conquered by Germany made operations by bombers and Stukas so difficult

that it was necessary to have an escort of two or even three times the strength of the formation which was being escorted.

Park outlined his tactics to Dowding:

> The general plan adopted was to engage the enemy high-fighter screen with pairs of Spitfire squadrons from Hornchurch and Biggin Hill half-way between London and the coast, and so enable Hurricane squadrons from London Sectors to attack bomber formations and their close escort before they reached the line of fighter aerodromes East and South of London. The remaining squadrons from London Sectors which could not be despatched in time to intercept the first wave of the attack by climbing in pairs, formed a third and inner screen by patrolling along the lines of aerodromes East and South of London. The fighter squadrons from Debden, Tangmere and some-times Northolt, were employed in wings of three or in pairs to form a screen South-East of London to intercept a third wave of the attack coming inland, also to mop up retreating formations of the earlier waves. The Spitfire squadrons were re-disposed so as to concentrate three squadrons at both Hornchurch and Biggin Hill. The primary role of these squadrons was to engage and drive back the enemy high-fighter screen, and so protect the Hurricane squadrons, whose task was to attack close escorts, and then the bomber formations, all of which flew at much lower altitude.

This sounded good and sensible, but the reality seldom matched this until the later stages of the battle; most of the time the reality was that those who found the enemy went into the attack as best they could.

'Getting struck in' was very much an RAF view, and one soon recognised by the German bomber crews: 'One thing was plain, the RAF fully realised how critical the situation was, and the English fighters had no hesitation in going bald-headed for our bomber squadrons' (Baumbach). Indeed, the bombers were the threat and so the bombers had to be the primary target – make them drop early, shoot them down, chase them away – such a result meant that the mission was a failure. The success of pilots such as 'Cobber' Kain of 73 Squadron, the RAF's first ace of the war, was a morale booster to other RAF fighter pilots; indeed, the Hurricane squadrons appear to have come out of this initial phase of the conflict with a success ratio of 2:1.

> If we saw something we went for it. We never felt at a disadvantage if we were flying Hurricanes. It depended entirely on where we were, what position we were in the sky, where the enemy formation was. Our idea was, if we were in a certain place, and we saw a formation

of Germans, we went for that. Morale was high. The fact that we lost companions meant nothing, really. It was just an accepted fact that, as long as it wasn't oneself that was shot down, the fact that Joe Soap was shot down was hard luck. We were young and we were doing a job of work, and that job was warfare.   (Billy Drake)

The comment 'we were young' is an important one; throughout history the fact that young people in uniform believe themselves to be invulnerable – it will always be the other guy – has been at the root of why losses alone seldom meant that units collapsed. Leadership also played a vital role in the 'press on' attitude of a squadron and its pilots, as did the unstinting loyalty and support of the groundcrew back at base.

A pamphlet that was published in late 1940 or early 1941 by No. 13 Group. The 'Forget-me-Nots for Fighters' contained 'pearls of wisdom' from the experiences of the Battle of Britain and used cartoons to illustrate the points made. The booklet was issued during AVM Saul's tenure as Air-Officer-Commanding, and in his introduction he states:

This book is the outcome of discussion amongst the Training Staff on the best and simplest way to bring to the notice of new Fighter Pilots certain salient points in air fighting, which it is essential that they should master before taking their places as operational pilots in Fighter Squadrons. The various points illustrated are by no means comprehensive, and it must be clearly understood that only the main points which a new Fighter Pilot should know before going into action are included. These have been compiled on the advice and guidance of many well-known and proved Fighter Pilots, who have willingly co-operated in placing their knowledge and experience at the disposal of their younger brother pilots.

In selecting the motto of the Three Musketeers – 'all for one and one for all' – to put at the head of this Foreword, I have done so because it expresses what should be the creed to every Fighter Pilot. Never forget that you are an essential cog in the wheel, and if you break or fail it will let down your brother pilots, and the grimness of war allows for no such weakness. Air fighting is a combination of skill and courage, which, allied with confidence and experience, makes the Fighter Pilot master of his trade.

August–September 1940: The Real Test

Much of what has been discussed above relates to the six weeks that were the heart of the Battle of Britain, from Eagle Day to the last major daylight raids.

The middle of August brought the first crisis point for the RAF; intensive attacks had damaged all the main fighter airfields in No. 11 Group, although the work of the repair teams cannot be praised too highly in getting airfields back into operation, helped by the fact that the Hurricane and Spitfire did not require much in the way of an operating surface.

> 13 August 1940 saw the opening of the air offensive against England, carried out by Luftflotten 2, 3 and 5 from bases in France, Belgium, Holland and Norway. The Luftwaffe had, at that date, 4,632 aircraft, of which 3,306 were serviceable. (Of the 3,306 serviceable aircraft there were 390 reconnaissance, 981 bombers, 336 Stukas, 34 ground attack, 282 twin-engined fighters, 839 single-engined fighters, 288 transport aircraft, and 156 seaplanes). The strength of the British air defences had remained unimpaired by the campaign in the West. The RAF had over 675 fighters, 860 bombers and 402 reconnaissance aircraft available in July 1940.　(8th Abteilung survey)

There was great variation in the RAF's daily sortie rates for August, from as few as 288 to a high of 974. The latter took place on 15 August in response to the Luftwaffe's concerted attacks on the RAF's airfields under the so-called *Adler Tag* ('Eagle Day') plan. This new strategy to destroy Fighter Command's combat potential consisted of a series of attacks on radar installations and fighter airfields and was launched on 12 August. The first raids were on Hawkinge, Manston and Lympne, the last being hit twice with the result that by the end of the second attack, the airfield was pockmarked with craters and there was barely a clear space on which to land. Hawkinge was hit at around 1700, with Ju 88s destroying two hangars, plus workshops and other buildings, as well as leaving the airfield surface badly damaged. Overnight the craters were filled, the unexploded bombs dealt with and the airfield was declared operational again within twenty-four hours. It was a similar story at Manston, with 65 Squadron's Spitfires taking off as the bombs fell. This pattern of airfield attacks continued to the end of the first week of September but, with a few notable exceptions, there appears to have been little overall co-ordination of the strategy.

Churchill was visiting Uxbridge (No. 11 Group) on 16 August to watch the battle and was there when everything that the group had was up in the air, often facing massive odds. The pressure continued and casualties were high, with Fighter Command losing a quarter of its fighter pilots in just a few weeks, with survivors worn out from intensive operations and the stress of combat, and with a stream of new and inexperienced faces appearing, in many cases for a very short period of time. Nevertheless, the Germans were also losing experienced aircrew at a far higher rate than they had expected. As the RAF was clearly still resilient, the attacks on airfields were stepped up. The crisis intensified and the RAF infrastructure was close to collapse, when a 'happy accident' brought a change of strategy. The Luftwaffe's ultimate failure was that of not maintaining the aim of achieving air superiority; they let the RAF off the hook and enabled the fighter squadrons to recover.

The later weeks of the battle saw the combat debut of the Spitfire II, the first unit, 611 Squadron at Digby having re-equipped in August, with three further squadrons in September. In addition to various modifications that the RAF had been requesting, and in many cases was retrofitting to the existing Mark Is, the new variant had a Merlin XII engine and a pressurised water-glycol cooling system. When Miroslav Liskutin joined 145 Squadron at Catterick it was equipped with Spitfire Mk IIs. His view was that the Mk II was an

> ... excellent aircraft for all aspects of flying and particularly for aerobatics. This variant seemed to be the best in its class, although there was a limit of 20 seconds for inverted flying. The danger of inadvertently exceeding the limit was minimal as the engine always picked up promptly and there were no detectable signs of damage. For air firing purposes the Spitfire was undoubtedly an excellent gun platform. The only disadvantage came from the distribution of weapons along the wing, which called for a harmonising pattern at a given distance. As a rule, these harmonising patterns were planned for an impact grouping at 250 yards or 300 yards, creating a circle of 3 feet in diameter. Different harmonisation patterns were used for special purposes. Minor variations were allowed to individual pilots who requested it.   (Miroslav Liskutin, *Challenge in the Air*)

The Brownings had 300 rounds per gun, enough for 17 seconds of fire, and the cannon had 60 rounds per gun, enough for eight seconds; Liskutin's comment on the latter weapon was 'The destructive potential of these weapons with their standard ammunition gave us the confidence of being equal or superior to the Luftwaffe fighters.' Many pilots liked to keep a few rounds back for the run to home in case they were intercepted or given a golden opportunity of a quick shot; this was particularly true later when the Spitfires were roving over enemy territory on the offensive. However, as there was no round counter in the cockpit it was always an estimate of how much ammunition was left, based on a mental calculation of how many seconds of firing so far – and in combat that was a hard calculation to keep going.

Not Going According to Plan

By mid-August it was clear to the Luftwaffe that the fight against the RAF was not going as well as predicted; during a conference at Karinhall on 15 August 1940 Göring had this to say:

> The fighter escort defences of our Stuka formations must be re-adjusted, as the enemy is concentrating his fighters against our Stuka operations. It appears necessary to allocate three fighter *Gruppen* to each Stuka *Gruppe*, one of these fighter *Gruppen* to remain with the Stukas, and dive with them to the attack; the second to fly ahead over the target at medium altitude and engage the fighter defences; the third to protect the whole attack from above.

And at a conference on 19 August:

> To sum up: we have reached the decisive period of the air war against England. The vital task is to turn all means at our disposal to the defeat of the enemy air force. Our first aim is the destruction of the enemy's fighters. If they no longer take to the air, we shall attack them on the ground, or force them into battle by directing bomber attacks against targets within range of our fighters. At the same time, and on a growing scale, we must continue our activities against the ground organisation of the enemy bomber units. Surprise attacks on the aircraft industry must be made day and night. Once the enemy air force has been annihilated, our attacks will be directed as ordered against other vital targets.

Amongst the individual points he had made were:

> Until further notice, the main task of Luftflotten 2 and 3 will be to inflict the utmost damage possible on the enemy fighter forces. With this are to be combined attacks on the ground organisation of the enemy bombers, conducted, however, in such a manner as to avoid all unnecessary losses. I will return later to the question of operations against the enemy aircraft industry. As long as the enemy fighter defences retain their present strength, attacks on aircraft factories must be carried out under the cover of weather conditions permitting surprise raids by solitary aircraft. We must succeed in seriously disrupting the material supplies of the enemy air force, by the destruction of the relatively small number of aircraft engine and aluminium plants. These attacks on the enemy aircraft industry are of particular importance and should also be carried out by night. Should it, however, not be possible to locate an industrial

target because of poor visibility or bad weather conditions, some other worthwhile target must be attacked. There can no longer be any restriction on the choice of targets. To myself I reserve only the right to order attacks on London or Liverpool.

This could have been a Bomber Command memo of 1942!

On 20 August 1940, Göring ordered his units to 'continue the fight against the British Air Force until further notice with the aim of weakening British fighter strength. The enemy is to be forced by ceaseless attacks to bring his fighter formations into operation.' This undoubtedly correct tactic was, unfortunately for the Germans, not followed through and whilst airfield attacks continued into early September, the bombing of London on 24/25 August and the British retaliatory raid on Berlin, changed the nature of the battle, with Hitler declaring that he would destroy the British capital. For the next few weeks, London was to be the focus of numerous large-scale German attacks, and the battle took on a new significance.

On the night of 24/25 August, Luftwaffe bombs landed on the East End of London, in the Cripplegate area. The planned objective had been the Thameshaven oil terminal near Tilbury, but the attackers had mistaken their target. Up to this time, both sides had taken great pains to avoid bombing cities, the 'plan' being to attack only military or war-industry targets, even though the Germans had, in the Spanish Civil War and the Poland and France campaigns, attacked cities. In part this was through concern that Bomber Command, a strong element in the RAF, was far more capable of strategic bombing than the Luftwaffe. In response to the German attacks on London, Churchill ordered an attack on Berlin, which was carried out on the night of 25/26 August. After a few more stray bombs hit London, the RAF went to Berlin again. The war, and the Battle of Britain, had taken a new course; Nazi politics and Hitler's ego turned sensible strategy into a war-losing scenario. But the RAF was not yet out of the woods.

Send Help . . . Please

The geographical positioning of the three southern Groups, 10, 11 and 12, meant that, in theory at least, each could support the others, which primarily meant 10 and 12 supporting Park's No. 11 Group, as this was where the real battle was fought. The command structure meant that at group level all commanders were equal and that any request for help was just that, a request, which could be ignored, or answered in the way that the group commander thought best.

AVM Quintin Brand of 10 Group is the Battle of Britain commander most ignored, and yet he played an important role. He had been a day and night fighter pilot and squadron commander in World War One, and held a number of appointments in the inter-war period, especially at the Royal Aircraft Establishment at Farnborough, but he held no key staff posts, which may have shielded him from some of the old-fashioned and rigid mindset of the RAF's home-based staffs. Appointed to command the new No. 10 Group in 1940, he shared Park's ideas on fighter deployment and throughout the Battle he both defended his own area and supported Park whenever requests were made. Like Park, he was shuffled sideways after the battle, taking command of No. 20 Group, before being retired in November 1943. It is likely that he was another victim of the Sholto Douglas/Leigh-Mallory clear-out of those who did not share their views.

Which brings us to AOC No. 12 Group, Trafford Leigh-Mallory. Comment has already been made on 'LM', but the main point here is his lack of support for Park amid the tribulations of No. 11 Group. Each of the group commanders was equal, but what was the 'boss', Dowding, doing to make them co-operate? The short answer appears to be nothing at all. The greatest tactical controversy of the Battle of Britain was the Big Wing; it was controversial at the time and has remained so amongst historians ever since. The essence of the argument was that it was better to shoot down fifty bombers after they have hit their targets than twenty before. The concept has been credited to Douglas Bader with the support of Leigh-Mallory. The opposing view was that of Keith Park in No. 11 Group, who, by the nature of geography, had little opportunity to assemble such wings even if he had supported the concept. In the 1969 *Battle of Britain* film the controversy has some great dialogue, with LM offering the 'get 50 after the target' line, to which Park retorts that those targets are his airfields and that 12 Group was not getting fifty, it was not even getting five. Park was supported by Dowding, Leigh-Mallory was supported by Sholto Douglas, thus reinforcing one of the leadership conflicts alluded to earlier.

Tom Neil, a pilot with 249 Squadron for much of the battle:

> All we saw of 12 Group's contribution to engagements was a vast formation of Hurricanes in the (discredited) vics of three, streaming comfortably over our heads in pursuit of an enemy who had long since disappeared in the direction of France.

Numerous documents issued by No. 11 Group during this period show Keith Park's ire at what he perceived to be a lack of co-operation from his counterpart in No. 12 Group, whereas No. 10 Group, on the other hand, received nothing but praise. Typical of these is the 'No. 11 Group Instructions to Controllers' dated 27 August 1940:

Thanks to the friendly co-operation afforded by No. 10 Group, they are always prepared to detail two to four squadrons to engage from the West mass attacks approaching the Portsmouth area. Up to date, No. 12 Group, on the other hand, have not shown the same desire to co-operate by despatching their squadrons to the places requested. The result of this attitude has been that on two occasions recently when 12 Group offered assistance and were requested by us to patrol our aerodromes, their squadrons did not, in fact, patrol over our aerodromes. On both these occasions our aerodromes were heavily bombed, because our own patrols were not strong enough to turn all the enemy back before they reached their objective.

To clarify its own position, Fighter Command issued an instruction, dated 24 October, concerning the 'reinforcement of No. 11 Group by No. 12 Group':

As a result of recent discussions the following principles are laid down. No. 11 Group must always give No. 12 Group the maximum possible notice of probable intention to call on him [AOC No. 12 Group] for assistance. It will be seldom that No. 11 Group can diagnose from preliminary symptoms that the first attack will be on a scale so large as to necessitate assistance being called from No. 12 Group. It may, however, often happen that the first raid has been met in strength by No. 11 Group and the assistance of No. 12 Group is required when it is seen that further raids are building up over the Straits of Dover. No. 11 Group must remember 12 Group's requirements with regard to warning, and, even if it is doubtful whether assistance will be required, warning should be given to enable 12 Group to bring units to readiness and stand-by. No. 12 Group should not send less reinforcement than the amount asked for if it is in a position to meet the requirements, but he may send more at his discretion.

Should Dowding have played a more decisive role in this 'battle' between his two main group commanders? The answer is, of course, that he should have brought them together and resolved the problem, but that was not his style. Having created an operational command structure that went from the Fighter Command operations room with its view of the whole battle, to the group operations rooms, with oversight of their part of the battle, to the sector control rooms that fought the hour-by-hour battle, he was inclined to let this 'Dowding system' run its own elements in its own way.

The Big Wing's major effect appears to have been on morale, friend and foe. Hard-pressed squadrons that suddenly saw a wing of three or more squadrons appear could feel a definite morale boost. For the Luftwaffe pilots, fighter and bomber, the effect was the exact opposite: where were all these RAF fighters coming from? Especially when their leaders had done the numbers, based on claims, and declared that the RAF had been destroyed. Douglas Bader always maintained that those who defamed the Big Wing did so because they did not understand and did not ask the right questions: 'The 12 Group Wing, properly exploited, could have provided the spearhead against the enemy formations, creating havoc among them and given 11 Group's pilots time to gain height and position to continue the destruction' (Bader Papers).

Fighter Availability

Great play has been made by some historians of wastage rates and supply of fighters and whilst it is true that during the height of the battle, the situation did deteriorate, it never became critical. The weekly situation in respect of wastage rates along with output from manufacturers and, a significant element in the equation, aircraft repaired by support units and returned to service, were highlighted in an RAF analysis. The low point occurred in the first week of September when the wastage rate was 270 aircraft, 112 of which were Spitfires, against an ASU (Aircraft Storage Unit) stock of 86 Hurricanes and 39 Spitfires. A 1945 Air Historical Branch (AHB) study summarised the position:

> Wastage in aircraft during the fighting in July and early August was more than offset by output. Less than 300 aircraft were lost in the period 20 July to 10 August whereas just over 500 were produced or repaired. But as soon as heavy fighting began, wastage leapt ahead of output and remained practically twice as high until the second week in September. It is apparent that the two weeks from 25 August to 7 September constituted the crisis of the battle as far as aircraft supply was concerned. There is only one inference to be drawn: that despite the great labours of all those concerned with the supply and production of aircraft, a disastrous situation would shortly have been reached if the Germans had maintained the scale of their attacks.

On 6 October Churchill asked the Secretary of State for Air for 'figures of total losses of Hurricanes and Spitfires during the months of August and September'. The following day he received the reply shown in this table:

Reason for loss	August 1940			September 1940		
	Hurricane	Spitfire	Total	Hurricane	Spitfire	Total
Enemy Action	238	143	381	228	134	362
Accidents	15	11	26	15	8	23
Total	253	154	407	243	142	385

On the subject of serviceability, another important aspect of the RAF's efficiency was the dedication of squadron groundcrew, as Alan Deere recalled:

> On-the-spot repairs of damaged aircraft were carried out by our own groundcrews, who were magnificent. All night long, lights burned in the shuttered hangars as the fitters, electricians, armourers and riggers worked unceasingly to put the maximum number on the line for the next day's operations. All day they worked too, not even ceasing when the airfield was threatened with attack. A grand body of men without whose efforts victory would not have been possible.

The period 24 August–6 September 1940 seriously drained the strength of Fighter Command. Losses of Hurricanes and Spitfires were around 470 destroyed or seriously damaged.

More Pilots Needed

The biggest problem was pilots, with only 200 or so coming out of training each month, and there were questions on the quality of some of that output. Out of a total strength of some 1,000 pilots, 103 had been killed; 128 were seriously injured and, for now at least, out of the battle. 'Their places could only be filled by 260 new, ardent, but inexperienced pilots drawn from training units, in many cases before their full courses were complete' (Churchill, *Second World War*).The only option, and one that was to become increasingly desperate once the Battle of Britain commenced, was to find pilots from somewhere else. The RAF structure (what in later years we came to call 'the two-wing master race' as a reference to pilot aircrew wings versus other aircrew flying badges) was based on most non-technical ground posts being filled by pilots. On paper this amounted to hundreds of pilots who could have gone back to the front line, but despite the call for this to happen there was little impact, with some sources suggesting that fewer than thirty pilots were released. As we will see later in this section, the Luftwaffe went through the same process for the same reasons in 1944. Statistics for the last week of August 1940 (from the Fighter Command Diary) show the intense nature of the Battle at this period:

Aircraft Losses 25–31 August 1940		
Date	German Losses (all types, over UK)	RAF Fighter Losses	RAF Pilots Saved
25 August	55	13	4
26 August	47	15	11
27 August	5	0	0
28 August	28	14	7
29 August	11	9	7
30 August	62	25	15
31 August	88	37	25
Totals	296	113	69

The column that shows RAF pilots saved is also very significant, especially as lack of pilots was one of the critical factors. The advantage of operating over home territory was the chance that a pilot who crash-landed or baled out might be in a fit state to return to the battle immediately or after a period of recovery. The Luftwaffe crews who came down over Britain were lost to the war. The North Sea and Channel were a different matter and crews who came down in the Channel might be rescued – or could drown. The Luftwaffe had a reasonably effective air–sea rescue organisation whereas the RAF had none. In the period 10 July–11 August, the RAF lost (killed) 69 pilots over the North Sea/Channel (58 in the latter). How many of those might have been rescued and returned to duty? Of course, some did get rescued, usually by small craft or naval vessels.

Dowding put out the call for pilots, with the Fleet Air Arm allowing volunteers to move across, albeit not many chose to do so, and thirty pilots were strong-armed from the Fairey Battle squadrons. Both sources needed some training for their new role, but that training, under pressure of need, was minimal. The RAF's training system was turning out a steady stream of all types of aircrew, and the service as a whole was starting to benefit from its foresight in this area, which in subsequent years was to be one of the key, and under-recognised, factors in the RAF's success.

You cannot train people that you do not have, which brings us to another of the 'how the RAF won' aspects – quite simply, the supply of volunteers from the Commonwealth, Empire and Allied nations. Without this manpower, the RAF would have run out of people!

The Battle of Britain saw pilots from various countries come to join the fight, including American volunteers who defied their own country's neutrality laws to join the fight for freedom. However, as far as the Battle of Britain was concerned, there were two particularly important groups, both of whom brought experience – and a fanatical hatred of the German enemy. The Czech and Polish squadrons of Fighter Command (and Bomber Command in due course) were slow in forming, as the RAF at first did not know what to do with these foreigners – some 35,000 Polish military personnel (3,500 airmen) had made their way to Britain. In July 1940 two squadrons were formed, 302 and 303, under RAF leadership, whilst other Polish pilots ended up in RAF squadrons. The two Hurricane-equipped Polish squadrons entered the battle on 31 August and made an immediate impression for aggressiveness and effectiveness. The tap was on and the deployment of Poles and the Czechs (310 and 312 (fighter) Squadrons and like the Poles also in other squadrons) increased. The top-scoring squadron in the Battle of Britain was a Czech squadron, and the top Czech ace, Sgt Joseph František, notched up 28 kills (11 having been in Poland and France) before he died in a flying accident. In terms of number of pilots in the battle, the Poles, with 145, were second behind Great Britain (2,344). Only slightly behind the Poles were the New Zealanders, with 126 and a reputation of daring and good shooting, with Canada on 98. Both these nations went on to provide vary large numbers of aircrew across all the RAF's commands, of which more later. The point here is that some 600 or so of the just under 3,000 fighter pilots in the battle were not from Great Britain, a significant percentage when numbers were short. The use of national shoulder flashes on uniforms meant that if you looked around squadrons (especially bomber and maritime) you would see a diverse set of nations, all with the same aim of flying with the RAF and defeating the enemy.

The AHB summary concluded:

> During August 304 pilots had become casualties; during the fortnight 25 August to 7 September 125 pilots were killed and 133 wounded. This casualty rate, plus the small number of pilots posted to instructional work, represented wastage of some 400 pilots a month. Output from OTUs in August, however, was 260 pilots, the Command, in short, was wasting away.

With an establishment of twenty-four pilots per squadron, the Command should have had 1,200 pilots on strength at the end of August, but it was 201 short of this. Added to which a further 160 were classified as non-operational, the majority 'because they had not reached a sufficiently high standard of training. There was, therefore, an average deficiency of six or seven operational pilots in each squadron.' It was this deficiency, plus the difficulty of replacing tired squadrons by complete and rested squadrons –

a tactic that had been employed earlier in the battle – that led Dowding to introduce his Stabilisation Scheme. Under this squadrons were categorised A, B or C:

A class squadrons – No. 11 Group plus the Duxford and Middle Wallop sectors.
B class squadrons – mainly No. 10 and the rest of No. 12 Groups.
C class squadrons – mainly No. 13 Group.

The idea was to keep the A class squadrons at 19–20 operational pilots by drawing on the C class squadrons. The B class units, and there were only five of these when the scheme was introduced, were potential replacements for any A class unit that had to be withdrawn from the battle.

> The implication [of this scheme] is that pilot casualties so far exceeded output during this critical fortnight that almost half of the squadrons in Fighter Command had to be reduced to a semi-operational state in order to devote their best energies to producing pilots for the squadrons that were actively engaging the enemy. Insofar as the battle was largely confined to south-east England, the scheme was practicable and prudent. But it starkly reveals how dangerous was the pilot position.   (AHB)

For the period 10 July–31 October the Command lost an average of four pilots a day killed in action (KIA), with an average of 28.9 per week.

September 1940: The Decisive Weeks

> The battle against the British Air Force was continued on the lines of this directive without a decision being obtained. Recognising this fact, the German High Command decided in September to switch the main weight of the air offensive to London, the heart of the enemy power. Incomparably greater success than hitherto could be anticipated from this policy. For, while the main objective of wearing down the British fighter forces was not abandoned, economic war from the air could be embarked upon with full fury, and the morale of the civilian population subjected at the same time to a heavy strain. The few daylight attacks by strong bomber formations (200–300 bombers of all types were over the target every time) achieved good results against dock and supply installations along the Thames. Major conflagrations caused extensive devastation.   (Bechtle)

In a speech on 4 September 1940, Hitler decreed that he would wipe out British cities. To certain Luftwaffe leaders this seemed an ideal way of forcing the 'few remaining' RAF fighters to take to the air and be destroyed. By late

Left: A Hurricane of 73 Squadron being re-armed in France, winter 1939–40. The intensive operations that followed the German assault of May 1940 provided RAF fighter pilots with their first experience of modern air combat, where they found out weaknesses in their aircraft and tactics.

Left: The Fighter Command operations room structure turned raid data from radar and other sources into the battle planning and execution to meet each raid. By the time the Battle of Britain started, the system had been tried and tested.

Below: Spitfire of 92 Squadron at Duxford, May 1940: Blue Section (from left) of Plt Off Bob Holland, Fg Off Bob Stanford Tuck, Plt Off Alan Wright. Stanford Tuck was one of many who learnt quickly and became both an effective fighter pilot and fighter leader.

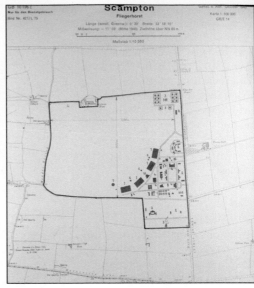

Above: Luftwaffe intelligence on RAF bases was pretty good and they had comprehensive target folders on most RAF airfields, such as this plan of Scampton. However, overall RAF intelligence, especially aerial reconnaissance and signals intelligence, was far more comprehensive.

Above left: Pilots such as 'Sailor' Malan, here with 74 Squadron, were great tacticians and leaders. He was also one of a number of pilots to take part in evaluation trials comparing RAF types and captured German aircraft, which provided very useful performance and tactics data.

Left: Extract from a pamphlet issued to Fighter Command pilots; cartoons were used to get the message about the main threats across, in this case to keep a vigilant lookout at all times.

Spitfires of 616 Squadron approaching Rochford, 1940. The Spitfire was seen by the Germans as their main opponent, even though in the Battle of Britain Hurricanes bore the brunt of the fighting.

Re-arming the guns on a Hurricane. The pre-war debate on fighter weapons saw the RAF favour eight rifle-calibre machine guns, which would give more allowance for inaccurate aiming than cannons. By the middle of the Battle of Britain this rationale was being challenged.

Czech (Sgt Bohumir Furst of 310 Sqn pictured) and Polish pilots proved invaluable. Indeed, throughout the war the RAF relied on overseas aircrew for all of its commands, but especially Fighter and Bomber Command.

Architect of victory; as the head of Fighter Command, Dowding played a major role before and during the Battle of Britain. His refusal to send ever-increasing numbers of fighters to France was one of the key decisions of the war.

Douglas Bader (2nd from right, seen here with pilots of 616 Squadron) was the main exponent of the Big Wing tactic of No. 12 Group during the Battle of Britain, which proved then, and ever since, to be a contentious area.

In the early years Hermann Göring (left) was able to build the Luftwaffe from nothing to the most effective air arm in Europe. However, his weak leadership and the political machinations of the Nazi hierarchy sowed the seeds for the Luftwaffe's ultimate failure.

Above: In the early war years the Bf 109 was the best fighter in most of the theatres in which it fought, but the Germans stuck with the aircraft too long and eventually ran out of both engine and airframe capability for further development. A Bf 109F of JG 27 is shown.

Right: The RAF initially had no response to Luftwaffe night raids, but the Beaufighter night fighter, fitted with airborne radar, soon became very effective.

Right: Pilots of 80 Squadron pose with a Spitfire at West Malling, July 1944. Fighter Command had been fighting an offensive war since 1941, with mixed success, but by summer 1944 the Luftwaffe had all but retreated to the defence of the Reich.

The RAF's training system was established early in the war and was able to produce the large number of aircrew needed for both expansion and replacement. With the addition of overseas training locations and specialist training units, this was a key aspect in eventual success.

Whitley crew members from No. 58 Squadron, Linton-on-Ouse 1940; the aircraft of No. 4 Group flew leaflet drops over Germany from the start of the war. These early experiences of the problems of navigation and finding targets at night were invaluable.

A Wellington crew of No. 149 Squadron arriving at their aircraft for a mission. The initial daylight attacks by Wellingtons revealed the vulnerability of the RAF's bombers to fighter attack; Bomber Command had to change to night operations.

Wellington crews at Marham for the August 1940 attack on Berlin that was partly responsible for Hitler changing the Luftwaffe's strategy in the Battle of Britain.

Above: The advent of four-engined bombers gave Bomber Command a strategic weapon never available to the Luftwaffe. The problem was finding targets and surviving the defences. This underside view of a Halifax shows how vulnerable it was from below – no guns.

Right: Many Luftwaffe night-fighter pilots, like Egmont Lippe-Weissenfeld, were able to make multiple victories in a single night by 'swimming with the stream' and using their *Schräge Musik* guns to good effect.

Above: The Junkers factory at Leipzig after the Bomber Command attack of 3/4 December 1943. Despite the seeming devastation, much of the heavy machinery at such targets remained undamaged and the Germans proved adept at restoring production.

Left: Tactics and leadership were vital in all aspects of the air war (on both sides); Gp Capt John Searby (centre), seen here at Wyton in August 1943, was one of the first Master Bombers.

The vigour with which Air Marshal Harris (centre) pushed the case for strategic bombing, and defended it in military and political circles, meant that Bomber Command survived and ultimately thrived. On Harris's left is AVM Saundby, successively Senior Air Staff Officer and later Deputy C-in-C of Bomber Command.

The RAF owed much of its tactical development and campaign success to the likes of leaders such as (left to right) Coningham, Broadhurst and Tedder. This was especially true for the Middle East campaigns and in North-West Europe.

Cartoon showing the last moments of Lancaster 9 Squadron, lost on 9/10 July 1943. Crew names are listed along with their fates; the cartoon was drawn by one of the escapers, Sgt Hughes.

Oil became a key strategic target for the Allies. This is a target photo for a Bomber Command daylight attack on the Bec d'Ambes depot in south-west France on 4 August 1944. The aircraft was from No. 514 Squadron and the photo shows that it dropped 7 × 1,000 lb and 4 × 500 lb bombs.

Hitler failed to appreciate the massive productive capacity of the United States; a B-24 production line at Fort Worth is shown. Bomber and fighter aircraft rolled off the production lines in enormous numbers, enabling massive expansion as well as replacement of losses.

Looking up and seeing a sky full of contrails must have had a major impact on the morale of the German people; it is also one reason Hitler preferred bombers to be shot down over Germany, so their destruction could be seen.

A B-17 Flying Fortress of the Eighth Air Force seen during an attack on the Focke-Wulf factory at Marienburg, 9 October 1943. Smoke is rising from the target so it seems to have been an accurate attack, but it was one with a heavy cost.

The B-17 Flying Fortresses and B-24 Liberators of the Eighth Air Force were the main contributors to the day bombing over Germany; a formation of B-24s of the 44th BG out of Flixton is shown.

Right: As well as seemingly endless numbers of aircraft, the USA also seemed able to supply almost endless numbers of young men willing and able to face the dangers of daylight operations over Germany. The flight crew and groundcrew of 'Thundermug', a B-17G of the 305th Bomb Group, pose in front of their aircraft, June 1944.

Right: Groundcrew maintaining a B-17. Working in all weathers and under difficult conditions the groundcrew personnel deserve far more recognition that they are usually given.

Below: A flak hit on a B-24 from which only two crew escaped. Whilst fighters remained the biggest threat, flak claimed numerous bombers and for many aircrew this was more terrifying as they had to plough through it to drop their bombs.

Left: The first of the American single-engined escort fighters was the P-47 Thunderbolt. Initially looked on with disdain by those pilots who had flown 'sleek' Spitfires, its rugged nature and effective armament soon won then over. Here, fighter ace Don Gabreski poses with his groundcrew.

Left: The P-51 Mustang is often credited with being the fighter than saved the daylight offensive, primarily due to its long range. Lt Stapp and Lt Manahan of the 305th FS, 353rd FG, demonstrate tactics for the camera.

Below: General Bill Kepner took over command of the Eighth AF fighter groups in September 1943 and brought in new tactics for fighter escort.

Right: Adolf Galland was not only a successful fighter pilot but also a notable fighter leader; he fared less well when trying to deal with Goering and the Nazi hierarchy. He was able to push for a growth in the Reich fighter force but in both equipment and pilots this was all too late.

Below: The Me 262 jet fighter was never the threat to the Allies that it could have been; delays in development and mistakes in tactical use meant that by the time it entered the battle Allied air dominance was so great that it could have little impact.

Oil had been a target priority from 1940, but at that time Bomber Command had no real capability of destroying such targets. By 1944, with the Combined Bomber Offensive in full effect, it was a different story, and the lack of oil supplies, especially aviation fuel, curtailed training and operational flying for the Luftwaffe.

The end of another German fighter. A Fw 190 is on the receiving end of fire from an American fighter. Luftwaffe pilot losses became so high that it was impossible to maintain unit strength, even with inexperienced pilots.

afternoon on 7 September 1940, some 400 bombers and 600 fighters were converging in waves on London. The defending fighters rose to meet them, but it was to be a day of mixed fortunes with some squadrons suffering heavy losses and others claiming high scores for little loss. All too often it depended on how well the ground controllers had predicted the situation and thus put the fighters in an advantageous position. The controllers were getting better and the aircraft supply situation was reasonable, which meant that the Spitfire squadrons were never truly short of aircraft, although the careers of some aircraft lasted only a few days – as did some pilots. Some squadrons were still having trouble with tactics.

Although not realised at the time, this was the opening shot in what was to become the destructive air campaign that would eventually flatten German cities and cripple their industries. It was also the point at which the Germans failed in Strategy 101 by moving away from the air superiority campaign before it was completed. RAF Fighter Command was on the ropes and in the last days of August losing more pilots than the Luftwaffe. There were a number of factors in the decision to move away from the RAF's airfields and go after London. First and foremost, Hitler was furious that Berlin had been bombed. After all, Göring had promised that no bombs would fall on Berlin. In the manner of all dictators Hitler went into a rage and threatened the destruction of London and other British cities. Secondly, the Luftwaffe and German intelligence were bad at numbers. With claims that the RAF had lost at least 800 aircraft from its initial fighter strength of just over 900, and with replacements estimated at only 200–300 a month, they predicted that the RAF had been almost destroyed. They were, of course, totally wrong. The RAF entered the deciding weeks of the battle in September with 750 fighters, more than at the start the battle. The squadrons themselves had a combination of inexperienced pilots with some excellent COs and flight commanders not hidebound by pre-war tactics and with some other successful pilots in the mix; in other words, they were far better placed than before, especially now their airfields were being left alone.

This is thus one of those turning points in 'how the RAF beat the Luftwaffe', a point that was reached by dogged determination across a number of aspects, and the strategic failure of the Luftwaffe to stick with the plan of air superiority.

Major Luftwaffe daylight attacks continued into late September. Losses suffered led thereafter to a reduction of the forces engaged on any single day to one Ju 88 *Gruppe*, and from the beginning of October to the use of fighter-bomber formations only (Bf 109s each carrying one 250 kg bomb). The individual bomber *Gruppe* as well as the fighter-bomber formations with a strength of up to 120 aircraft, were escorted in their outward and return flights by two or three fighter *Geschwadern*. When the weather situation did not permit attacks by regular formations in the prescribed form, use was made of cloud cover for nuisance raids by single aircraft. The month of October saw the continuation of the war of attrition against London and the final shifting of the main weight of attack from daylight to night raids. In September, these had been carried on simultaneously with daylight attacks.

The last of the massed daylight raids took place on 30 September and was given a very rough handling by a Fighter Command that was now much stronger than it had been at any point in the Battle. In that simple equation, one could assert that the RAF had now defeated the Luftwaffe, in that the latter was no longer able (or willing) to maintain the intensive daylight campaign over England. 'The struggle for mastery of the air, when discontinued by Germany, had not been fought through to a conclusion' (Bechtle). Sounds like the kid who is not having fun taking his ball home!

Morale Then and Later

On 20 August Churchill made his famous 'never in the field of human conflict' speech, in part inspired by what he had seen on his visit to Uxbridge a few days before. As with so many of his wartime speeches it was designed to boost morale amongst all who heard, civilian and military, and it certainly gave those 'Few' a morale boost. It also had a positive impact on American political and public opinion; the resilient 'mother country' had faced down the aggressor, with all the benefits that could bring, and it allowed the RAF to build the confidence that it was as good as, if not better than, the strutting enemy.

> Nobody ever thought we were going to lose this battle. Morale was always very high. It never crossed our minds that the Germans might defeat us and destroy the RAF. We lost odd chaps. Most of those chaps I had only known for three of four weeks. I joined the Squadron in July, and I had never met any of them before. They were fellow pilots; they weren't old buddies or friends.   (Bob Foster)

Bob Stanford Tuck was flying Spitfires with 92 Squadron with some success, having notched up 14 kills by September 1940 when he was promoted to squadron leader and sent to take over 257 Squadron at Debden, a Hurricane squadron. The squadron had lost eleven of its original pilots since May, and both its flight commanders had been killed on 11 September, the day before Tuck arrived. Needless to say, morale was rock-bottom. Tuck's first impression of the Hurricane was not good: 'After the

Spitfire she was like flying a brick – a great lumbering, farmyard stallion compared with a dainty and gentle thoroughbred. It nearly broke my heart, because things seemed tough enough without having to take on 109s in a heavy kite like this.' As a great leader he put such thoughts aside, and indeed soon came to appreciate the qualities of the Hurricane as a sturdy, stable and reliable gun platform able to take significant damage. Leading from the front, he took the squadron into the battle of 15 September and they emerged with a number of victories for no loss, a boost to their morale. Whilst inspiring by example he also drew a stern line with those he considered not up to the mark, such as those who turned for home without, in his view, valid cause, even drawing his revolver and threatening two such pilots.

Other leaders met similar problems:

> I soon discovered that 92 Squadron, my new command, had not only lost four Commanding Officers, three of them in the past month, but the total losses had been more than double those of 303 Squadron in the same period. Not unnaturally morale was at a pretty low ebb, which was reflected in the inevitable lack of discipline resulting from the fact that the squadron had been virtually leaderless. The upshot of all this was that I was appointed to take over a disorganised, undisciplined and demoralised collection of first-class material. Although they had suffered terrific casualties, they had also inflicted severe losses upon the enemy and, under the circumstances, they felt they knew far more about air fighting than any Squadron Leader who might occupy the chair of office for a day or two. The Station Commander, Group Captain Dick Grice, who really was a first-class commander, told me that the Air Officer Commanding had decided to move No. 92 to the north for a well-earned rest. I argued that if this was done, the squadron would be finished and I begged to be allowed to keep it at Biggin as that would give me the chance I needed to get it into shape — while the stigma of having 'had it' could not be attached to it.   (Kent, *One of the Few*)

Luftwaffe Morale?

When Erhard Milch, as Inspector-General of the Luftwaffe, visited bomber groups based in Holland he was faced by leaders who

> . . . made no secret of their indignation. The squadron leaders who had actually flown in these operations bluntly told the field marshal that it was impossible to produce the results required of them with

the aircraft, bomb-sights and armament at their disposal, that the British fighters were just as superior to the German bombers as German fighters were to British bombers and that night bombing could have no decisive effect, as we had neither the bomb-sights for night operations nor enough bombers.   (Baumbach)

On 7 September Göring publicly assumed command of the air battle and turned from daylight to night attack and from the fighter bases to the built-up area of London. Dowding had every right to be pleased with the performance of his fighter squadrons but he was also realistic enough to know that the battle had been finely balanced and that there were many lessons to be learnt.

The Royal Air Force far from being destroyed was triumphant. A strong flow of fresh pilots was provided. The aircraft factories, upon which not only our immediate need but our power to wage a long war depended, were mauled but not paralysed.

(Churchill, *Second World War*)

Typical stuff from Churchill, and without doubt his wartime communiqués to the British people and its armed forces were important in both strategic and morale terms, although as mentioned in the Leadership section, there were downsides to his overall approach.

The Reward for Success – Dismissal!

The two men who had led the RAF to victory in the Battle of Britain, Dowding and Park, were victims of RAF politics and intrigue as soon as the Battle was over. Dowding was given a special assignment in the USA prior to his retirement, whilst Park was sent to become AOC Flying Training Command. The last was admittedly an important post and Park was able to bring his knowledge and expertise to making changes to the way RAF aircrew were trained, which was the foundation of the squadrons – the better they were trained the more effective they would be.

Park later replied as follows to a note from AOC No. 13 Group:

It was a shock to be told that I was to be taken away from my Command after only seven months but it was a greater shock to hear the name of my successor, in view of the little support that No. 11 Group has had from No. 12 Group since way back in May. Your Group and No. 10 Group have always sent properly trained squadrons to relieve war-weary squadrons from the front line. Moreover, your Group has always cooperated in helping out with junior leaders and providing properly trained pilots required to replace wastage. On the other hand, a number of pilots provided by No. 12 Group were rejected by squadrons because they had not been trained after leaving their OTU.

Dowding and Park were replaced by the two men who had opposed them during the Battle; Sholto Douglas became head of Fighter Command and Leigh-Mallory took over No. 11 Group. It could be argued that the RAF was faced now with a different strategic situation, one in which the fight had to be increasingly taken to the enemy so they could not rebuild strength and return to the attack, so did this need fresh blood and new ideas?

Did the RAF Win?

The RAF won, or beat the Luftwaffe, in late summer 1940 by dint of the fact that the air assault on Britain moved to a night attack against cities, and the amphibious assault was postponed; the German requirement for air superiority to protect an invasion had not been met, which equals an RAF victory, but did the RAF actually 'win'? One could argue that it was a strategic victory in that the enemy ceased his planned campaign, but on the tactical front – the way that operations were flown, the loss rates, the combat effectiveness – the result was perhaps not so clear cut.

In his 1946 lecture, AVM Elmhirst stated: 'They [the Germans] also began to realise that our fighter pilots were a well-trained meat of high morale and good shots, brilliantly led and mounted, and brilliantly controlled from the ground to intercept raids.' Good jingoistic stuff and the core of the legend that has come down since 1940. Whilst elements are true, the detailed view of each of these aspects, and which we have briefly covered above, needs comment, as there are implications for later operations.

Some studies have suggested that less than 50 per cent of the RAF fighters airborne made contact with the enemy, and in part this was blamed on the rigidity and poor quality of the ground control. Squadrons were scrambled too late and so did not have time to make combat height or be in a position to engage, even if they had been vectored to the enemy. It took Hurricane squadrons longer than Spitfire squadrons to make combat height – and by that do we mean the combat height of the bombers or the fighters? Radar was great at picking up raids building up over France, but by the time they had become a mass of radar returns, the ability of controllers to differentiate the types (bomber of fighter), the heights and even the tracks of the raids became limited. Additional data from the Observer Corps was very useful, especially for height, but was late in the overall picture as by the time it came in the attackers were close. Other sources, including RAF aircraft sent out to observe and report, added value, but controllers still had to assimilate it and then put a plan into play – and all of this was new. It is amazing how well it actually worked, considering there had been little in the way of pre-war testing and training of the overall system. Some cynics have even said that the intercept rate was higher when squadrons were put in a general area and left to find the enemy.

The outdated squadron formation tactics meant that most pairs of eyes were focused on staying in formation rather than scanning the skies for the enemy. If you cannot see it then you cannot attack it – or avoid it. Many losses were down to this lack of eyeballs, and several failures to intercept could be attributed in the same way. The traditional view of the fighter pilot with his head on a swivel is true only when he does not have to focus on keeping formation; he can still glance but he cannot search. This was greatly improved by the adoption of more flexible tactical formations.

The 'well-trained meat of high morale and good shots' comment is also somewhat contentious; as we highlighted above, many pilots had not fired their guns prior to their first combats, although this was later addressed in the training system, as was the lack of tactical training. As to being good shots, most were anything but good shots – some were exceptional but most usually missed what they aimed at. This also brings in the question of even if they hit the target, was critical damaged caused? The short answer is that for the bombers, especially the rugged Ju 88, the lethality of the Browning machine-gun was just not there; again, as mentioned above, many pilots reported emptying their guns into (or near) the target, seeing hits, but with no result – damage maybe but not destruction. Some studies have suggested that if the RAF pilots had been better trained, especially in gunnery and tactics, and had different weapons (0.5 in. machine guns or 20 mm cannon) then the destruction wrought on the Luftwaffe would have been up to 500 per cent higher – and brought a convincing victory in a matter of weeks. The RAF certainly learnt this lesson, and weapons and training continued to improve – at least for Fighter Command, though the defenders of Malta were later to report the same issues with aircraft and weapon performance. The other part of Elmhirst's comment – high morale – held true for most of the battle and was without doubt one of the deciding factors whereby RAF pilots came out with the belief they were as good as, or even better than, the much vaunted Luftwaffe, and morale is a war-winning (or losing) element in military operations. This was certainly a factor for the rest of the war, and the legacy of the heroic 'Few' helped build the RAF's morale.

There has also been debate about pilot effectiveness. In a combat situation, it could be argued that the main measure of a pilot's effectiveness was his proven ability to cause fatal damage to the enemy – ideally shooting him down or at the very least causing critical damage and a withdrawal from the battle. There are other measures that could be considered, a pilot who prevents a colleague being shot down, the effects that the mere sight of a large number of fighters could bring, such as the enemy dropping bombs early, turning for home, or simply an impact on their morale. However, in essence it is about shooting down the other guy. One study has suggested that no more than about a third of RAF pilots in the battle claimed any role in the destruction of an enemy aircraft, and for many of those it was a 'half shared', that in actual fact could be shared by six or seven pilots for the same aircraft. So, it seems that far less than half of pilots had any direct combat effect, and the number with multiple kills was quite small – only around 17 pilots laid claim to 10+ enemy destroyed, the top-scorer being Sgt Josef František. One figure that has been given for these 17 was 241 destroyed, which was a high percentage of the total of around 1,200 Luftwaffe losses! Imagine if more pilots had scored double figures, or even high single figures, the Luftwaffe would have been decimated.

So, what about the 'brilliantly led and mounted'? Without trying to start an avalanche of debate on the merits of the Hurricane vs. the Spitfire and which type was more important/more effective in the battle, we do need to consider the merits and deployment of the two main fighters. Rugged gun platform with good turning circle and comfortable cockpit, including view, for pilot, versus the more constrained cockpit of the Spitfire and its better climb and overall speed performance. Assuming that the Spitfire had the edge, which in most key respects it did, then the question of where and how the two types were deployed comes into focus.

If the threat was just bombers and Bf 110s then the Hurricane was more than suitable – and for all group areas other than No. 11 Group, this was the situation the RAF faced – so why were so many Spitfire squadrons based in those other groups? Should the Spitfire squadrons have been concentrated in No. 11 Group, with perhaps some at the nearest airfields in No. 10 and No. 12 Group? If the RAF had an average of twenty Spitfire squadrons during July–October 1940, why did the number of Spitfire squadrons in No. 11 Group average six or seven, with twice that number of Hurricane squadrons, plus between two and five Blenheim squadrons? Would it have made a difference? The argument adds that the time to height of a Spitfire squadron was less, which would mean they could be better placed to intercept; some historians have even suggested that if the Spitfire squadrons had been based on coastal airfields they could have been sent out to meet the Germans whilst they were still forming up! Who made the decisions on which squadrons would go where and what was the basis for such decisions?

In terms of tactics and squadron leadership, it was not until after the battle that the RAF truly adopted, and even then with some exceptions amongst the 'old school'; of leaders, the 'Finger Four', which was essentially the same as the *Schwarm* used by the Luftwaffe. From this point on, with the RAF having a new breed of combat-experienced young leaders, not bound by the old ideas, the RAF never again fell behind its opponents in the field of fighter tactics. Indeed, tactical flexibility was one of the key elements in the RAF's eventual success.

Result

No matter how you slice and dice the Battle of Britain, the result was RAF 1 Luftwaffe 0 – they had lost, in that had not achieved their aim and had terminated the operation. This was their first defeat, which always plays hard with a team that up to that point was used to winning, seemingly without effort. Not only that, but it had cost the Luftwaffe a high percentage of its experienced combat leaders and pilots, who could not be readily replaced. Furthermore, in the Spitfire they had found an enemy fighter that was as good as and, in some respects, better than their own Bf 109s, whilst the Bf 110 and Ju 87 had been discredited and were, effectively, virtually redundant in the Western theatre of operations.

Chapter 4

Luftwaffe Night Raids and V-weapons

The German move to night bombing created challenges for the RAF; the radar network was able to pick up the raiders and sector control could guide fighters to the area . . . but what fighters? Despite the fact that bombing of the UK in World War One had primarily been a 'night game', which the RAF gradually won, there had been little effective development of night defence in the 1930s.

At the first meeting of the Night Interception Committee, 14 March 1940, Air Marshal Peirse had stated that: 'Defence against night attacks was one of the biggest problems we had to face. Even if the enemy began by raiding in large numbers by day, our good defences would force him to adopt night bombing.' Fighter Command had realised in the late 1930s that night interception would be required and in November 1938 Air Fighting Committee Report No. 57 addressed this issue:

> A few recent experiments carried out at night have indicated that it should be possible to navigate fighters by means of D/F intercept techniques to within about 4 miles of an enemy – providing sufficient information regarding track and height of the enemy is available. The accuracy of interception by D/F at night will be such that fighters will usually be unable to sight the target unless the latter is illuminated by some means or unless further detection aids are provided.

Trials looked at the interception methods that could be adopted, concluding that visual pick-ups, even with the assistance of searchlights, were not effective, but the option for an airborne radar (AI – Air Interception) was promising if the fighter could be guided by ground control to a position at which the AI operator could pick up the target. This work was late, but it was another of the important technical and tactical decisions that helped the RAF defeat the night aspect of the Luftwaffe campaign over Britain.

The Night Interception Unit (soon renamed Fighter Interception Unit) was formed at Tangmere in March 1940 with six AI Blenheims and a remit to make the technology work. When AI Mk IIIB was introduced in May

1940, with a maximum range of 9,000 ft and minimum range of 600 ft, along with greater reliability, a practical set had at last arrived. Early trials concluded, however:

> The effective field of AI vision was restricted to a fairly narrow cone directly in front of the aircraft and unless the fighter [pilot] found himself between 6,000 ft and 1,000 ft behind the enemy aircraft, and flying in the same direction at roughly the same height, he had very little chance of completing the interception.

On the night of 18 June, the Luftwaffe launched its first night raid against Britain. It was to prove an enlightening experience for attacker and defender alike. The attack was to be made by Heinkel He 111s of KG 4, based at Merville and Lille-Roubaix, and the primary targets were the airfields at Honington and Mildenhall. Oberleutnant Ulrich Jordan, the lead pilot in the attack force, had been reassured 'We have no night fighters ourselves and I am sure that the British have none either.' The result of a confused series of combats, with Spitfires and Blenheims involved, was the loss of six Luftwaffe bombers, but at a cost of three Blenheims and a Spitfire. The Luftwaffe was no longer in any doubt that the RAF could, and would, contest the night skies over Britain.

June also saw the Luftwaffe begin night raids over other parts of the British Isles: small-scale bombing or reconnaissance missions to coastal areas and, on occasion, as far as Bristol and Merseyside. The searchlight organisation now comprised some 4,000 searchlights of various types, but there were still gaps in the planned zones. Nevertheless, at this stage they were the critical night asset, operating with fighters, as demonstrated by the June action detailed above, and guns. However, by the end of June it was concluded that:

> The success enjoyed by the searchlights had been short-lived. By flying at greater heights and by employing tactics of evasion, enemy aircraft had managed to avoid illumination. The fitting of AI to the Blenheims, however, held promise that an alternative system of operating against unilluminated targets could be developed – but the conditions to be satisfied before such interceptions could take place were formidable. The fighter had to be placed within several hundred yards of the enemy and on the same course.

The FIU had noted that the lack of AI production was a problem, so the contract for the new version, AI Mk IV, was given to EMI. The company was to base its work on new principles, especially the suppression of close-range clutter, to achieve a minimum range of the order of 400 ft. Progress was rapid, and the FIU had the first sets back for trials in late June. They were greeted with great enthusiasm as, on first impressions, they appeared to be a huge improvement on what had gone before. The decision was also taken to fit them to Beaufighters, as Blenheim performance was not good enough, but with the slow delivery of the Beaufighter, three Defiant and three Hurricane squadrons were also assigned to night defence.

Even amongst the AI-equipped units, most action was still due to visual acquisition, often aided by searchlights or the gun barrage. On the night of 28/29 August Blenheim 'D' of No. 600 Squadron was scrambled:

> I was told to get off as soon as possible and to patrol base at Angels 17. For the next hour we received a good number of vectors and investigated innumerable searchlight concentrations. It was not long before I saw the exhaust flames of an aircraft close in front and above, so turned and went flat out after him, to find that we could hardly climb any higher, and all controls were sloppy. So, having staggered into a line astern position at approx. 400 yards, I let go a good burst. The enemy aircraft turned and dived, proving too fast for us to catch. A bit later I saw exhaust flames below us to starboard, so dived after them and was getting in really close when we were illuminated from behind. One searchlight coming in from the front, flicked over the aircraft in front before fastening on to us. It [was] sufficient to show that we were very close, so I opened fire before the searchlight blinded us entirely. Exhausted the remainder of my ammunition and again saw enemy aircraft dive away too fast for me to catch.

Up to late August no urban centre night raids had involved more than twenty aircraft. From that time onwards the raids comprised up to a hundred or more bombers. In August, Fighter Command operated defensive missions on twenty-six nights, flying 828 sorties but making only three claims. In a speech delivered on 9 September 1940, Adolf Hitler decreed: 'We are giving our reply night after night. If the British declare that they will attack our cities heavily then we will wipe out their cities.' Even allowing for the heavy political rhetoric, the message was clear: the Luftwaffe would be ordered to intensify its night offensive. Just a few nights earlier, on the 4th, the growing effectiveness of the RAF's night defences was ably demonstrated when Pilot Officer Herrick and Sergeant Pugh, in a Blenheim, shot down two enemy bombers, an He 111 and a Do 17: 'The pilot stated that the searchlights were most effective, and, of course, entirely responsible for enabling him to sight and fire at the enemy.' Merrick was awarded a DFC for this action; nine days later he claimed another He 111.

The first phase of the night Blitz on London lasted from 7/8 September to 13/14 November and Fighter Command was worried that the Germans would be

> ... able to bomb this country with sufficient accuracy for [their] purposes without even emerging from clouds. The most depressing fact which has emerged from the past weeks is that the Germans can fly and bomb with considerable accuracy in weather in which our fighters cannot leave the ground. Their navigation is doubtless due to the excellence of their radio aids.

The Luftwaffe night effort on 15/16 October, for example, was heavy, with approximately 400 sorties flown. Some crews flew two missions that night, and the standing order was for aircraft to stay over their targets for as long as possible and 'nuisance bomb' every few minutes. The RAF responded with forty-one sorties, but only two resulted in intercepts, one by an AI-equipped Blenheim of No. 23 Squadron which was unable to achieve a firing position, and the other a successful engagement. The raid caused heavy damage to London, some 900 fires, many of them classed as major, being reported. The poor showing of the defences caused serious questions to be asked within Fighter Command; there were still those who doubted the use of AI and considered that resources should be used elsewhere.

John Cunningham was destined to become one of the great night-fighter aces, but his early experiences with the AI aircraft caused serious doubts:

> We had vectors from Sector Control and were then instructed to 'flash your weapon' [use the AI radar]. The AI op was unable to pick up the target, then I saw the bombs go down. The magician was still kneeling on his prayer mat of blankets muttering to himself, the green glow from the CRT flickered on his face. A witch doctor, I thought, a witch doctor and black magic – and just about as useful.

It could be argued that up to this point the Luftwaffe was winning, since the RAF was unable to prevent the Luftwaffe from conducting bombing raids. The last months of 1940 saw the RAF introducing new capabilities, such as the Beaufighter with AI Mk IV, and the use of improved Ground Control Intercept (GCI) radar, as well as better training for night-fighter crew, including the Radio Operator (Air): 'It is of the greatest importance that the AI operator should be intelligent, keen, and of a patient and painstaking disposition. He is, after all, the brains of the aircraft up to the moment when the pilot actually sees the silhouette of the enemy aeroplane and opens fire.'

The first true GCI station, at Durrington, became operational in October and added a vital link in the chain of engaging enemy aircraft at night (and by day).

The British lead in radar development remained a key factor in the RAF's defensive success as the campaign developed:

> From the middle of November the massed night attacks were extended to the industrial cities and ports of the Midlands. The tactics of air war by night developed during the ensuing winter months. Concentration of attack in one place and at one time was not necessary because of the weak defences. The individual units proceeded to the targets along separate courses. To increase the strain on the morale of the population the duration of the attack was prolonged as much as possible. To facilitate locating of targets and the individual objectives within the target areas themselves, the major attacks were carried out by moonlight. London, offering a large target area, was attacked chiefly during moonless nights . . . The month of November saw 23 major GAF attacks on vital British centres. In each attack 100–600 tons of bombs were dropped on these targets. During the period of 1–15 November 1940, 1,800 bombers dropped 1,900 tons of H.E. and 17,500 incendiary bombs on London alone. Of the towns attacked, Coventry, a centre of the British aircraft industry, must be mentioned. During the night of 14/15 November, 454 aircraft raided this town, dropping 600 tons of H.E. and incendiary bombs. Coventry has become a by-word wherever operational air war is discussed as a result of the extensive damage caused by this raid.

The attack on Coventry on the night of 14/15 November was indeed particularly effective – and worrying to the RAF; although the RAF flew 110 night patrols there were no combats.

When Sholto Douglas took-over as C-in-C of Fighter Command in late November one of his first concerns was to address the problem of night defence. His report of 8 December also stated that: 'I am convinced that the main obstacle to frequent intercepts by night is the lack of accurate tracking inland from the coast, and most important of all, lack of accurate information with regard to the height of the enemy bomber.' He also saw the need for 20 AI-equipped squadrons with better airfield facilities and that 'Special training using the AI by day with crews wearing dark glasses should be carried out; and that crews selected for night fighting should be specially tested for vision.' All of this was gradually put in place and with the advent of the AI-equipped Beaufighter the RAF finally had an effective night fighter.

By early 1941 the RAF's GCI network for night operations was beginning to come together. With both ground controllers and aircrew needing to become familiar with equipment and procedures, the squadrons undertook intensive training by day and night. Six GCI sites were operational in January (Avebury, Sopley, Durrington, Willesborough, Walding Field and Orby), each associated with a sector control. The standard GCI technique was the 'curve of pursuit'. Using a map on which target and fighter tracks were plotted, the GCI controller positioned the fighter some 6–8 miles behind his target and on a same-altitude parallel track. He then transferred to his screen to calculate and monitor the actual curve of pursuit so that the fighter ended up astern at 2 miles, at which point the intercept could be taken over by the crew: 'It is very important that, when handed over to AI, the fighter should be directly behind the bomber, on the same course, at the same height and with an overtaking speed of not more than 30–40 miles per hour.' The last aspect was one of the hardest to achieve; too fast, and the pilot would inevitably overtake his target without getting into a firing position.

The German attack on Liverpool during the night of 12/13 March 1941 was typical of the offensive operations being undertaken at this period. Some 169 aircraft of Luftflotte 3 were scheduled to take part in this raid, although it appears that only 146 found the target, along with 170 aircraft from Luftflotte 2. Most of the German crews had little trouble identifying the port city and the first bombers were over the target at 2040. This was the first of nine distinct waves of attack that lasted for some six hours. Many German crews reported sighting fighters and it was, indeed, a busy night for Fighter Command, with 178 sorties flown but only four enemy aircraft claimed destroyed, plus a few more probable or damaged. The 96 Squadron war diary recorded the night's activities: '18 trips hunting for the enemy' and the result: 'no large numbers of enemy aircraft blazing on the ground, but just a drawing of enemy blood in "probables", and a squadron with tails well up and a few gunsights and gun muzzles that had spat forth fire at the enemy machines'.

Fighter Command Report No. 235 summarised the 'trend of air defence at night':

> The month of March [1941] saw the beginning of effective operations by the GCI system, and the use of 'Fighter Nights' over target areas. The success of fighters rose month by month; 24 enemy aircraft were destroyed in March, 52 in April, and 102 in May. During the period March, April, May 1941, about 40 per cent of fighter success was obtained with GCI/AI technique. Since then the enemy has made

only slight, dispersed raids, ideally suited to the GCI/AI technique, and the percentage has risen considerably, so that at the present time AI machines carry out practically all the night interceptions of these dispersed raids.

A report of 18 April 1941 really shows the advantage of AI-equipped aircraft over their single-seat colleagues. This report covered the period 2/3 March to 12/13 April, when the twin-engined aircraft (Beaufighter, Blenheim and Havoc) flew 492 sorties with a total claim of 98 contacts, 64 combats and 33 enemy aircraft destroyed. The single-engined aircraft (Defiant, Hurricane and Spitfire) flew 1,211 sorties resulting in 78 contacts, 54 combats and a claim for 24 aircraft destroyed. The report stated:

> Owing to the lack of certain returns it has not been possible to assess the relative efficiency of different methods of night fighter control, but it may be reasonably assumed that the best control at present in use is that which employs GCI in conjunction with the AI-equipped Beaufighter. Of the average results obtained by this combination, under conditions of bright moonlight and clear visibility during the months of March and April, it may be stated that of the attempts to intercept enemy aircraft, 15 per cent resulted in combats, and of these combats 70 per cent resulted in the destruction or probable destruction of the enemy aircraft.

May was to prove the busiest month of the year for Fighter Command's night defences, with almost 2,000 sorties flown and 96 enemy aircraft claimed as destroyed. Two-thirds of this effort (1,345 sorties) was by the single-engine squadrons. One of these, 255 Squadron, still at Kirton, had its busiest and most successful month:

> This moonlight period (till 17/5/41) was one of intense enemy 'blitzing' of target areas in NE and Central England and in conse-quence a considerable strain was thrown on the Squadron. Each night one Flight was at 'readiness' with the other 'available', and on some occasions during the peak moonlight period as many as 16 planes have been at 'readiness'. From the assumption of this dusk state on 2/5/41 till the end of night state on 17/5/41 (15 nights) a total of 132 operational patrols were flown.

The war diary quite rightly commented on the events of 9 May: 'This remarkable achievement – 6 enemy bombers destroyed, and one damaged inside half an hour with no loss to the Squadron's personnel or planes, evoked a deluge of congratulations.'

The night defences were not yet perfect, but the scale had certainly tipped. On 12 May, the day the great enemy night assault came to an end, the C-in-C Fighter Command told the Night Air Defence Committee that 'AI with GCI was the most profitable means of night interception, notwithstanding the successes obtained by Cats Eye fighters'. By the end of 1941, Fighter Command had flown 11,980 night-defence sorties, with 4,967 being by AI-equipped aircraft. The fighters had claimed 258 enemy aircraft out of the estimated 25,334 aircraft that had flown over the UK in this period, with a further 131 falling to anti-aircraft guns and 44 to 'other' causes.

The most significant technological development in 1941 was the adoption of centimetric AI sets. Although the theory of employment of such wavelengths had been proposed as early as 1936, it was not until the development of the Randall–Boot cavity magnetron valve that it became a practical proposition. Improvements were made at the General Electric Company laboratories and the first trials were flown in March 1941, although it was some time before the AI Mk VII/Beaufighter combination was fully operational in numbers, and the shortage meant that the 'Fighter Nights' single-seat contribution remained important. The RAF continued to improve its night capability and the Luftwaffe, whilst continuing night attacks and with occasional success, suffered heavy losses disproportionate to the effort being made, albeit it tied up significant military assets for the British. It is safe to declare that by the end of 1941 the RAF had defeated the Luftwaffe in the night skies over Britain. The Luftwaffe had certainly not abandoned its night war over Britain, but the increasing effectiveness of the defences meant that it was less effective – and more hazardous.

A major German campaign was launched in April 1942, the so-called Baedeker raids against British cultural centres, the first attack being on Exeter on 23/24 April. By this time 255 Squadron was operating from High Ercall and had completed its re-equipment with AI-equipped Beaufighter VIs; on the night of 25 April the first success with the new aircraft was made:

> F/O Wyrill (R/O Sgt Williams) on a non-operational patrol, at 2300 hours was taken over by Honiley and passed to Comberton. After a series of vectors, a blip was obtained in the vicinity of Hereford at 12,000 ft, E/A being slightly below. After a burst of 2 seconds from dead astern, the E/A took violent evasive action, and visual was lost in the mist. Visual was regained and after a second burst of 4 seconds, E/A was seen to burst into flames and to dive vertically. There had been no return fire, A few seconds later, an open parachute was

seen descending, and E/A was seen to hit the ground and explode. This success brought much encouragement to all members of the Squadron, as well as to the Station, and congratulatory messages came from Group, Sector and various sections of the Station.

(255 Squadron)

The victim was a Ju 88.

In the period 2/3 April–26/27 August, 40 raids were made, with an average of 50–70 bombers, although the two raids on Bath involved 164 bombers (25/26 April) and 83 bombers (26/27 April). This was out of an average German bomber force in the West of 430 aircraft, of which 50 per cent or so were normally available.

'In September and October 1942 operations were confined to nuisance raids by day and night and mining operations, the aim being to shield the squadrons from loss as far as possible. But even this did not result in any noticeable reduction in the losses' (Bechtle lecture, February 1944). By late 1942 German bombing attacks on Britain had almost ceased.

> During these two months [October and November], only 199 enemy aircraft were plotted within 40 miles of the coast, excluding the Shetlands area. A further 59 aircraft were plotted in a more distant area outside the normal range of our night defences. The only serious raid during the period was against Canterbury on the night of 31 October/1 November. It was made by two waves of enemy bombers estimated at a total of 35 sorties, and of these, four were destroyed by AI night fighters. Smaller raids were made on the East Midlands on the nights of 21/22 October and 24/25 October, consisting of eight and twelve enemy sorties respectively. In addition, there were two small attacks on Tyneside on the nights of 11/12 October and 16/17 October by eight and seven aircraft respectively.

In response to the German activity, Fighter Command flew 124 sorties, all but four being by AI aircraft, resulting in eight combats and six enemy aircraft shot down (the other two combats ended in claims for a probable and a damaged). The Fighter Command summary for 1942 stated: 'For Fighter Command, the year was thus largely one of consolidation and unremitting patrol work. If there were no spectacular achievements, Fighter Command's success must be measured not by the number of aircraft shot down but by the relatively few occasions on which British towns and industries were troubled by night air attack.'

The German night bombing of Britain continued to be low key into 1943, as it had been in the later months of the previous year. As the year opened,

Luftflotte 3 had a mere 67 serviceable long-range bombers, primarily the Do 217s of KG 2 and the Ju 88s of KG 6, although it was anticipated that this strength would increase over the next month or so. The German High Command was calling for a major assault by Angriffsführer England during the winter months at the start of 1943.

The low scale of German raids had led to a reassessment by Fighter Command of its night defences, and the deployment of assets to other tasks. This had come about as a combined result of the reduced threat and the crisis in the Bomber Command offensive that was being caused by the increasingly effective German night-fighter force. The only large-scale raid against England in January 1943 took place on the 17th/18th in response to a Bomber Command attack on Berlin the previous night. Some 118 German bombers approached in two waves, London being their target, but very few bombs fell in the target area. Fighter Command flew 119 defensive sorties and claimed the destruction of four Ju 88s and one Do 217, other aircraft falling to the anti-aircraft guns in what was another poor night for the Luftwaffe. The bombers' usual tactics consisted of low-level, high-speed nuisance raids, against which the existing types of AI proved ineffective. However, the introduction of a limited number of Mk VIIIA sets, initially with FIU and 219 Squadron, changed things. The first victory with the new kit occurred on 20/21 January, when an FIU Beaufighter shot down' a Do 217. This success was followed up in the next few weeks to confirm the capabilities of the new radar.

Most of the night raids over the next few months caused little damage and, according to RAF sources, the raiders suffered an average 12 per cent loss rate. After a quiet period in which bomber units conducted training, new equipment was introduced, the Do 217 and Ju 88 were replaced and the Luftwaffe returned:

> From April 1943 massed air attacks, chiefly against targets close to the coast. Despite these innovations there was only a slight decrease in losses. Counter-measures were introduced against the very harassing effects of long-range British night fighters in collaboration with the light flak allocated to GAF stations. These measures are now being adopted throughout the GAF (switching off some flare path lights, staggering light flak guns along the line of approach of landing aircraft).   (Bechtle)

The two features of enemy night attacks later in 1943 were attacks by intruder aircraft on airfields in the Midlands and East Anglia in retaliation for the increasingly powerful combined bomber offensive and, secondly, renewed attacks on London by fighter bombers in the autumn, accompanied by the dropping of '*Düppel*' (German equivalent to the Allies' Window anti-radar counter-measure). From July to December 1943, the enemy flew some 818 long-range bomber, 165 fighter-bomber, and seven reconnaissance sorties overland – a total of 990. The RAF claimed destruction of 66.5 and the guns another 20.5. Once again, the majority of interceptions were made under GCI control. To put these figures into perspective, a typical Bomber Command raid of late 1943 was that to Berlin on 22/23 November, in which 764 bombers took part; the city was heavily hit, and the RAF lost 26 aircraft.

Following the late 1943 heavy attacks on Berlin, Hitler was determined that reprisal attacks should be made against London. The night of 21/22 January 1944 brought Operation Steinbock, the Luftwaffe's largest raid for some time. The attack comprised 447 sorties in two main attacking waves, primarily of Ju 88s and Do 217s. The bombers used *Düppel* in an attempt to blot out the GCI network, but in the event many of the attackers did not even cross the English coast. Nevertheless, it was still the busiest night that the RAF defenders had seen for a while, and various squadrons were active at some time. Among those scoring victories was Flight Lieutenant J. Hall of No. 96 Squadron, who claimed a Do 217 and a Ju 88. Another attacker that failed to make it home was a Heinkel He 177 of KG 40, the first of the type to be shot down over the UK.

There were some successes for the Luftwaffe during this 'Baby Blitz' of early 1944, but overall the loss rates, in part due to increased use of the new AI Mk X, made such raids too costly and ineffective. Whilst night activity, including intruders continued into 1945 there is really nothing significant to add to this study.

The RAF had won the night war over the UK, but the UK had to undergo one more offensive campaign.

Defeating the V-weapons

The German development of missile weapons was to provide the Allies with another challenge, and as some of these were operated by the Luftwaffe, the defeat of the weapons is in the scope of this study, and some mention must be made. Speer: 'The jet plane was not the only effective new weapon that could have been slated for mass production in 1944. We possessed a remote-controlled flying bomb, a rocket plane that was even faster than the jet plane.'

Civil Defence Operational Review No. 7 of 14 November 1944 stated:

> The serious attacks, which began 13/14 June 1944, lasted about twelve weeks. Altogether, more than 8,000 flying bombs were

launched during this period, and of these more than 5,000 came overland. The flying bombs that fell on London represent those that escaped our defences. London remained the primary target. The scale of launchings varied greatly between nearly 1,000 and little over 100 per week. In all, a total of 3,916 flying bombs had been destroyed by the end of August; of these, 1,942 were credited to fighters, 1,730 to AA and 244 to balloons. This represents an overall rate of destruction of 48.5 per cent of the total launched, but this makes no allowance for the appreciable number of flying bombs which fell in the sea from unknown causes before they could be attacked. The effects of the attacks by flying bombs were primarily the damage to a considerable amount of property. By the end of August, in London alone more than 1.1 million houses had been damaged; it is interesting to recall that in the nine months of bombing, September 1940 / May 1941 inclusive, the number of houses damaged in London was 1.15 million. Civilian casualties are estimated at 5,205 fatal and 15,611 serious. The effect on the essential war effort mainly comprised loss of man-hours estimated to have reduced output by as much as 20–25 per cent.

This summary is interesting for a number of reasons: firstly the damage data show the extensive damage caused even though the number of flying bombs making it to London was limited; secondly, it is clear how quickly the defensive and offensive (bombing the sites) reaction was able to minimise the danger. With the number of flying bombs destroyed by fighters and by the reduction of the attack capacity caused by Allied bombing, one could argue that Allied air power defeated the Luftwaffe V-weapon campaign! But what if the weapons had been available in greater numbers, and earlier, what would have happened if hundreds of V-1s had targeted the invasion build-up areas? Allied air power most certainly played a role in delaying the development of the weapon, so let's start there.

Peenemünde

The Allies had been acquiring evidence that this was the site of advanced weapon research, especially missile technology, and by late June 1943 the War Cabinet had scheduled Peenemünde as a high priority target for Bomber Command. Air Marshal Harris requested a delay until the longer nights of late summer would make his aircraft less vulnerable and on the night of 17/18 August a force of 596 bombers converged on the target. The initial markers were slightly off the aiming points but the Master Bomber, Gp Capt John Searby performing this role on its operational debut, was able to call on the backer-up aircraft to re-mark the target and to pass bombing instructions to the Main Force. It was a clear moonlit night and the target was well and truly plastered, although the moonlight was also perfect for the night fighters; fortunately, they were late arriving and only caught the last wave. Bomber losses of forty were considered acceptable for the level of destruction on such a vital target.

The German Flak Regiment 155 (W) was formed on 16 August 1943 with the intention to start V-1 operations on 15 December 1943. The original scheme called for 64 main firing sites and 32 reserve sites in a belt from St Omer to Cherbourg. Each site was to have storage accommodation for 20 bombs, assembled and ready to be fired, with a maintenance building holding another two or three bombs. The scheme also called for eight heavily reinforced supply centres each capable of holding about 250 flying bombs, plus a few heavily reinforced firing sites, each with a stock similar to the supply sites, and with two firing channels.

Problems with construction rates of the weapons, the number of modifications required to make them operational, and the manning and training of the firing batteries contributed to delays in the planned operational date. And in December 1943 the Allies at last woke up to the threat; a combination of human intelligence, often from French workers, and air reconnaissance, had enabled planners to pinpoint many of the sites, and led to:

> ... the commencement of determined Allied air attacks on 20 December 1943. These attacks were carried out on a scale and with a persistence which made it quite clear that the locations of the Regiment's sites had been accurately plotted, and that the enemy fully realised the potential threat inherent in the preparations which were going on.   (ADIK report 411/1945)

The offensive against the V-weapon sites was carried out under the codenames of Crossbow and Noball. Bomber Command expended many sorties against launch sites and storage facilities. This campaign also involved the USAAF's Eighth and Ninth Air Forces as well as the RAF's 2nd Tactical Air Force and Air Defence of Great Britain.

By spring 1944, Flakgruppe Creil, as Flak Regiment 155 was also now known, was established at its sites in France. 'New sites of a simplified nature were surveyed and prepared, and because of their simplicity lent themselves more easily to camouflage. At the same time a new chain of supply was laid down for the transport of bombs from the dumps within Germany.' The regiment was ordered to begin its offensive on the night of 12/13 June. The target was to be London from all sites with two salvoes to be fired, one at 2340 on 12 June and one at 0040 on 13 June. However, at zero hour many sites reported they were unserviceable, and so the salvo idea was abandoned and instead harassing fire was ordered. The first daily report showed that of the fifty-five sites that were ready, 'Only ten rounds of harassing fire were launched, and four bombs were observed to crash.'

The V-weapon Blitz

At 0418 in the morning on 13 June 1944, the peace at Swanscombe, near Gravesend, Kent, was shattered by a fierce explosion. The first of Hitler's new 'terror' weapons had landed on English soil. Within an hour, three more of these V-1 flying bombs had come to earth, one crashing into a railway bridge at Grove Road, Bethnal Green, in London, and causing six deaths and a substantial amount of damage. In the 24-hour period from 2230 on 15 June to 16 June 1944, British records show 151 reported launches, with 144 V-1s crossing the English coast. Of those, 73 reached the London area. The defences notched up only a modest score, seven V-1s falling to the fighters, 14 to the guns and one shared, whilst a further 11 were shot down by the guns of the Inner Artillery Zone. The V-1, spanning a little over 17 ft 6 in., was a very small target, and it flew fast (300–400 mph) and low. The official RAF account summarised the speed problem: 'as for the fighters, the short time in which interception had to be made, demanded that they should be quickly and accurately directed on to the course of the bomb'.

The Hawker Tempests of No. 150 Wing at Newchurch had been at readiness for defensive patrol since dawn on 15 June. Early the following day the wing leader, Wing Commander Roland Beamont, and his No. 2 were airborne on such a patrol when they sighted a V-1. Giving chase, the fighters were eventually able to carry out an attack, and Beamont scored his first flying bomb 'kill', the missile crashing near Faversham. By the third week in June the defences had started to settle down with guns and balloons in place and with eight single-seat fighter squadrons and four Mosquito squadrons deployed on patrols. It was also planned to increase the gun belts to include 376 heavy and 540 light guns and for an increase in balloons from 480 to 1,000.

The Luftwaffe launch rate rapidly increased; the 1,000th flying bomb was launched on 21 June and the 2,000th only eight days later. Colonel Wachtel, commanding 155 Regiment, made the most of this early success and pressed for a major increase in strength, suggesting additional regiments and the creation of a brigade, as well as over 60 new launch sites. He also noted that the Allied defences, and the attacks on launch sites, would rapidly increase. 'The Regiment did not deceive itself as to the steadily mounting success of Allied defences, and to the fact that the speed and altitude of the bomb were such that both fighter and AA defences were getting better results than had been anticipated.'

The bombing campaign against V-weapon sites was intense and involved the RAF and the USAAF. Reconnaissance and intelligence, including human intelligence from the local population and agents, were vital in locating and determining the threat. But, having found the sites, the challenge was to destroy them, or at least disrupt their operations. This included attacks on production and storage facilities. Wachtel's report on 1 July summarised the effects of bombing to that date and noted that: 'Two sites have been completely destroyed, 22 have suffered heavy, 8 medium and 10 slight damage.' In the following 15 days, reports recorded that 2 more sites were destroyed, 16 suffered damage, 7 medium damage and 14 slight damage in air raids. Considering the total number of sites, this was considered acceptable and proved that camouflage was working. 'It was in the field of supply that the effects of air attack were the most apparent. Transport broke down to an extent which made it impossible for the regiment ever to function to full capacity. One of the results of the failure of the supply system was that the time interval between shots averaged 60–90 minutes, against a firing sequence of 26 minutes.'

On 7 August 1944 the Regiment war diary recorded: 'the first official recognition of the fact that not only was the new weapon not going to prove decisive, but that many of the sites from which it was at present being launched would have to be evacuated'. Work on many new sites was stopped and new sites at the extreme range of the weapon but away from any likely Allied advance were chosen. By now, though, there were so many Allied aircraft operating out of Normandy that any movement or construction in northern France attracted fighter-bomber and bomber attention.

By mid-August the Air defence of Great Britain (ADGB) effort was at its height, with 15 day-fighter and 10 night-fighter squadrons tasked with the Diver campaign, as the British counter-measures programme was known. This was a large commitment of resources, but it had developed into a reasonably effective force. The first phase of the flying bomb campaign ended on 1 September 1944, with the Allied capture of those V-1 launching sites within range of London.

The V-1 campaign also involved the RAF's first jet fighters, the Gloster Meteors of 616 Squadron, which scored a number of successes. Flt Lt Graves landed off his 3 August sortie cursing a Mustang pilot who had got in his way just as he was setting up to finish off a 'bomb'. Success eventually came the next day with 616 destroying two of these weapons.

Mid-afternoon and 'Dixie' Dean was airborne patrolling under the control of Biggin Hill:

> At 1616 he spotted a bomb at 1,000 feet near Tonbridge and was cleared to give chase. Diving down from 4,500 feet and reaching 450 mph he soon caught up with his quarry and positioned to attack it from astern . . . at which point his cannon failed. Determined that it shouldn't get away he flew alongside and positioned his wingtip under the wing of the 'bomb' and then pulled up sharply; this sent the weapon out of control and it crashed about 4 miles south of Tonbridge.

Another historic event had thus been notched up – the first jet air-to-air victory. The Meteor, though, never came face to face with its Luftwaffe counterpart, the Me 262.

In the whole campaign the Germans launched some 9,252 flying bombs, of which just under 5,900 crossed the English coast and 2,563 of those reached the London area. Around 4,000 flying bombs were destroyed by the defences, the Fighter Command summary claiming that 1,847 were destroyed by its fighters.

The conclusion can only be that the RAF, and its counterparts in the defence scheme, had the measure of the V-1s and would have taken an increasing toll of the weapons, so we can declare victory over the flying bombs.

No Answer to Ballistic Missiles

Although operated by the Army and not the Luftwaffe, brief mention of how Allied air was involved in the anti-rocket campaign seems appropriate. The first V-2 to reach England landed in west London on 8 September 1944, killing three people. In all sixteen V-2s were recorded as landing on London, and a further eighteen outside London in the first three weeks. During October–December 1944:

> The total number of rocket incidents was 357. Of these 20 fell in the Norfolk area, of the remaining 337, 162 fell in the London region. The most serious incident occurred on the morning of 25 November, when a rocket fell at New Cross, demolished the local Woolworth store, killed 260 people, and seriously injured 108.

Attacks continued into 1945, with 663 rocket incidents in the January–March period; the final attack was on 27 March 1945, the rocket landing in Orpington.

This weapon was impossible to stop once it had been launched and the only effective counter was to destroy the production, storage and launch facilities. The Allies expended a huge effort on this type of site for all the

V-weapons; ADGB/Fighter Command's part comprised 4,300 sorties (and 1,000 tons of bombs) hunting for the sites; with a rocket that was about to be launched being the prime (but rare) target. These Big Ben missions were flown by Allied fighters and fighter-bombers.

If the German rocket force had been ready earlier then it could well have had a strategic impact; the Allies never really defeated these weapons, but they reduced the risk until the time the threat was removed by the liberation of the launch areas.

Chapter 5

Bomber Command's Night Offensive

With the declaration of war, Bomber Command might have expected to be let loose for its destruction of key targets in Germany. It was not to be. With the decision taken that attacks on land targets were, for the present, banned, 'fleeting targets at sea' were the focus of attention. On the evening of 3 September 1940, a force of nine Wellingtons from Mildenhall and eighteen Hampdens, nine each from Scampton and Waddington, went in search of German warships but found nothing. Overnight ten Whitleys from Linton-on-Ouse dropped propaganda leaflets in Area 1(a) – the Ruhr – with 5.4 million leaflets being dispensed. The following day, however, Bomber Command suffered its first operational casualties with the loss of two Wellingtons and five Blenheims (four from 107 Squadron) during attacks on shipping. The order for this raid stated: 'The greatest care is to be taken not to injure the civilian population. The intention is to destroy the German fleet. There is no alternative target.'

This remained the pattern of activity for the next few weeks, the Whitleys flying by night over Germany on leaflet-dropping and the other types trying to find and bomb German warships. A Bomber Command report for 29 September 1939 summarised one such attack:

> Eleven Hampdens from Hemswell carried out a reconnaissance of the Heligoland Bight area with instructions to search for enemy surface craft and if found to attack. The target was attacked and seven 500 lb bombs were dropped by the first three aircraft. No results were observed except that large splashes were seen in the water near the destroyers. Heavy anti-aircraft fire was experienced, and one aircraft was hit and one of the crew wounded. The other flight of five aircraft failed to return.

After the first few weeks of operations, Bomber Command had achieved no real result and had started to take losses, as well as realising that its aircraft and the capabilities of its crews were facing challenges. The real lessons had yet to come, however. The bombers were still a 'force in waiting' and theories of strategic bombing remained largely untried. There were mixed opinions as to the wisdom of daylight attacks but no conclusive evidence either way. This changed in early December with two Wellington attacks that proved that daylight raids were too costly. On 14 December 1939 twelve Wellingtons from 99 Squadron were sent to patrol the Elbe Estuary and the Frisian Islands to attack shipping.

> At 1425 hours a force of one battleship, one cruiser, three destroyers and one submarine were sighted, but owing to low cloud no attack could be made. Fighter attacks were made by 20 enemy aircraft, Bf 109s and Bf 110s, two of which were definitely destroyed and two more were probably shot down. Heavy anti-aircraft fire was encountered when the enemy aircraft were clear of our formation. One Wellington was shot down, two collided and fell in flames, two are missing and one, on arriving at Newmarket, collapsed and three of the crew were killed.

On 18 December No. 3 Group sent twenty-four Wellingtons from three squadrons to patrol the Schillig Roads and Wilhelmshaven to report on any enemy naval forces.

> In Wilhelmshaven a battleship, two cruisers and four destroyers were seen in the harbour and alongside. They were not therefore attacked. There was heavy anti-aircraft fire and some 25 Me 109s and Me 40s [sic] attacked – at least 12 of which were shot down. Twelve of our aircraft failed to return; of these two are known to have descended into the North Sea on the way home.

Ignoring the ridiculously optimistic report of shooting down twelve fighters and of claims of some bombing success when there actually was none, the loss rate at last brought bomber leaders to the realisation that daylight bombing was a non-starter; there was no discussion of fighter escort, as there were no suitable fighters that could reach even the closest targets.

Air Chief Marshal Edgar Ludlow-Hewitt had been AOC Bomber Command since 1937; he was considered one of the best strategic thinkers in the RAF and he had early on recognised that his force was ill-equipped for its proposed task in the Western Air Plans. He could not shake the overall faith others had in the 'bomber will always get through' but he was one of the driving forces behind two key forward-looking plans: the development of the four-engined long-range heavy bomber and, even more significantly, the establishment of a robust and scaleable training system. He recognised that a future war would again be a war of mass, and that masses of trained aircrew would be needed. He improved the allocation of resources, firstly by assigning operational squadrons as Group Pool Training squadrons and then with the creation of bomber Operational Training Units (OTU). If this had not been established as early as it was then Bomber Command would not have been capable of the rapid expansion that it would need. Ludlow-Hewitt was replaced as AOC in March 1940, but he took over the role of Inspector-General of the RAF (for the rest of the war), a post in which he was able to influence several key decisions. Ludlow-Hewitt is one of the ignored RAF commanders, but he deserves more credit as one of the group of leaders who helped the RAF win the air war.

The net effect of daylight losses saw Bomber Command's strategic effort convert to night operations. This had two effects: it started the growth of German night-defence capability, albeit slowly as the RAF threat was minimal at this time; and demonstrated a lack of accuracy in bombing operations, although this was not to become clear until 1941, of which, more later. Bomber Command had already been flying night sorties over enemy territory, the Whitleys of No. 4 Group spreading 'Nickels' (propaganda leaflets) far and wide. These sorties operated with impunity as there was no German defensive capability, the only, but not insignificant, threats being the weather, navigation and aircraft reliability. The Luftwaffe had won this round, RAF daylight strategic bombing was over.

In January 1940 the Wellingtons and Hampdens joined the leaflet-dropping campaign, not because it was considered to be effective but as a way of giving crews valuable experience in night operations. This routine continued into spring 1940 and the only aggressive actions were those of No. 2 Group which maintained its low-level attacks, with shipping still being the favoured target. On 16 March 1940 Air Marshal Charles Portal had taken over as C-in-C Bomber Command, the appointment being seen by many as political – Portal was thought to be less likely to make waves. He did not remain at the helm for long, being replaced in October by ACM Richard Peirse, whilst Portal moved up the tree as Chief of the Air Staff, a role in which he proved adept at juggling politicians and other service chiefs. However, within days of taking over Bomber Command he oversaw some significant developments. He authorised the first attack on a land target in Germany; the seaplane base at Hornum being chosen for this reprisal for a German attack on Scapa Flow. A force of thirty Whitleys and twenty Hampdens dropped a mix of incendiaries, 250 lb and 500 lb bombs; although results were poor it had been a significant operation for the Command. On 13 April 1940 a new bombing directive was issued to the RAF, stating that, in the event of general air action being called for, Bomber Command was to implement WA 8 (Western Air Plan No. 8), the night attack on Germany, with priorities given as:

- Oil installations.
- Electricity plants, coking plants and gas ovens.
- Self-illuminating objects vulnerable to air attack.
- Main German ports in the Baltic.

A full-scale bombing offensive against German industry meant that the defences of the Reich would have to be modified to meet the threat.

On 14 May the Luftwaffe launched a major air assault on the Dutch city of Rotterdam, the first overt bombing of a city by either side in the western theatre of operations. To many in the British War Cabinet this was looked upon as the final straw; an all-out bombing offensive could now be implemented. The following day, Churchill authorised the bombing of targets east of the Rhine. To use an overused but appropriate phrase, the gloves were off and Bomber Command was given clearance to employ its supposedly 'war winning' plan of attacks on German industry. That same night, 15 May, ninety-nine RAF bombers attacked oil and rail targets in the Ruhr and the strategic bombing offensive was under way. The aiming points were industrial sites at places such as Sterkrade and Castrop-Rauxel and eighty-one of the bombers reported attacking their designated targets, although in the light of later evidence of navigation errors and the problems of finding targets, especially in the perennially hazy Ruhr, this seems unlikely. One Wellington (115 Squadron) crashed in France, becoming the first RAF casualty of the strategic bombing offensive, Flt Lt Pringle and his four crew being killed.

The small scale of Bomber Command 'attacks' (with leaflets) during the period up to spring 1940 did little to encourage the Germans to create an effective night-defence system. The Luftwaffe concept for Reich defence was primarily to rely on anti-aircraft guns and searchlights, and whilst the threat was low this seemed adequate. It was, however, yet another strategic failure by the Luftwaffe, although in line with its overall concept of air power as an offensive and not a defensive weapon. As we have seen, Bomber Command losses were insignificant during this period, and it is likely that most were due to other causes (bad weather, especially icing, running out of fuel, and so on), rather than good shooting by the German flak gunners. The initial impetus to improve the defences was not so much a fear of the material damage, but rather the loss of face to the Nazi regime, especially with the likes of Hermann Göring making such bold statements as 'No enemy aircraft will fly over the Reich territory.' Spring 1940 had seen the introduction of the Bf 110 to the night fighter role following trials by I./ZG 1. An aircraft that was proving a failure in its much-vaunted daylight *Zerstörer* (destroyer) role was about to become a significant element in the night defence of the Reich; although many favoured the adoption of the Ju 88 with better performance, this aircraft was not available (yet), whereas the Bf 110 was in need of a new role.

Throughout the war, flak was a major problem for the RAF's bombers, and as it was operated by the Luftwaffe it could reasonably be included in this study. However, as the night war developed it became much more of an aircraft vs. aircraft combat zone, and it is that aspect that we will focus on, and which will be used to determine who won.

The British strategic offensive had been continued throughout the anti-invasion period, and it was intensified following the 24 August 1940 German attack on London, with Churchill ordering a raid on Berlin in retaliation. Churchill was an advocate of the bombing offensive, and in early July had told Beaverbrook: 'The only one sure path to victory is an absolutely devastating, exterminating attack by very heavy bombers from this country upon the Nazi homeland. We must be able to overwhelm them by this means without which I do not see a way through.' This support would be relied on many times, especially by Arthur Harris, amidst attempts to remove bombers for other tasks and change the focus of resources. Churchill without doubt was a difficult political master, at times as difficult as Hitler, but he was firm on air power and especially the need to strike hard at Germany.

The 'Big City', as Bomber Command crews came to know Berlin was the objective of over eighty bombers in that first retaliatory raid. Poor weather caused problems, especially in the target area, but some bombs did fall on the Reich capital; Berlin was attacked twice more before the end of August and Göring's boast that 'no enemy plane will ever fly over the Reich' was well and truly laid to rest. Although it would be another two years before the RAF's bombers were capable of inflicting significant damage, the air war had entered a new phase. On the night of 23/24 September the Command made a maximum effort attack on a single target for the first time; the target was Berlin and 129 bombers took part. Three aircraft were lost, and results were poor, crews being unable to identify their targets because of a thick haze, made worse by the glare of searchlights. It was, however, a new tactic.

The basic Luftwaffe fighter interception technique was still that of the 'cat's eye', the so-called 'Helle Nachtjagd' (illuminated night fighting), whereby the roving fighter pilot relied on the searchlights to reveal his prey and then on the eyes of his crew to close in for the kill. The system initially had three zones in the neighbourhood of the Zuider Zee and Rhine estuary, thus covering the direct route to and from the Ruhr. The area covered was 56 miles long by 12 miles deep. The roving night fighters were not permitted to stray over flak zones, as it was still thought that flak had the best chance of bringing down bombers over the targets. The night-fighter squadrons were at first moved from base to base to cover the most likely operational areas. This so-called 'Kammhuber Line' (after Josef Kammhuber, then in charge of night-fighting) was established clear of the flak-defended areas, Germany's major cities being left in the care of the flak units.

New night fighter crews were given a standard briefing from the 'old hands':

> The only possibility then is the trapping of the enemy in the search-light beams. For this purpose, in front of the Ruhr we have created a barrage of night-fighter sectors which are covered by two waves. Each of these sectors is provided with searchlight batteries to catch the enemy bombers in their beams when the weather is fine. When one of them is caught in the searchlights we attack at once. We must be careful not to overshoot the mark. The bombers fly at 220 mph and we dive on them at between 280 and 310 mph. Moreover, the Britisher is a sportsman but very tough. He sells his skin dearly, and as soon as he sees a night fighter, he blazes away with everything he's got . . . You must always think, with each bomber, death and destruction fly over our cities. Protect your country, your women and children from death out of the skies. Put all your efforts into the defence of your country.　(Wilhelm Johnen, *Duel Under the Stars*)

The advent of ground radar – the Würzburg A type had been introduced in the autumn of 1940 – had improved matters, as a system basically similar to that perfected by the RAF was introduced. An experimental radar station was in operation at Nunspeet, Holland, by early September, working primarily with II./NJG 1. The initial application of radar was in conjunction with the searchlights in the *Helle Nachtjagd* system, whereby one Würzburg was used to control the night fighter and another controlled a searchlight cone for illuminating the bombers. This system included a plotting room able to control one night fighter for each zone. Although the system achieved a modicum of success, the Germans found, as had the RAF, that such techniques were severely limited by bad weather and cloud, and the capacity of the control organisation. Radar had proved its effectiveness, though, so Kammhuber pressed for more equipment. The availability of radars and the introduction of new types, such as the Giant Würzburg, allowed a refinement of the system to take advantage of GCI.

From September 1940 onwards the Luftwaffe records of the Quartermaster-General's Department of the Air Ministry give the weekly establishment and availability of night fighters. Hitherto they had been included as part of the overall fighter total. The first statistics, for 14 September, showed an establishment of 116 aircraft but an availability of only 55. Although the totals rise through the year, peaking at an establishment of 186 in late November, the serviceability does not improve, remaining at about 60 per cent. The German night-fighter serviceability rate remained low, down to 40 per cent at times, throughout the war.

By March 1941 three new British heavy bombers had entered service, the Short Stirling, Avro Manchester and Handley Page Halifax, virtually doubling bomb loads and greatly increasing the RAF's offensive capability. Attention was also paid to self-defence, and the four-gun rear turret was a standard feature, along with nose and mid-upper turrets, although the 0.303 in. machine gun remained the standard weapon. The Stirling flew its first mission on the night of 10/11 February 1941, with 7 Squadron contributing three aircraft to the 43-bomber force. Each aircraft carried an 8,000 lb load (16 x 500 lb bombs).

The report said simply: 'The Squadron carried out its maiden operational trip, three aircraft successfully bombed the target area at Rotterdam, all returned safely.'

A few weeks later, on 10 March, it was the turn of the Halifax, with 35 Squadron, led by Wg Cdr Collings, sending six aircraft to Le Havre. This was a significant point in the strategic air war: the RAF had the first of its true long-range heavies in operation, whilst the Luftwaffe still refused to recognise the need for this type of aircraft, and even when it did, with the He 177, the insistence was that it must be able to operate as a dive-bomber. In the air–land war the Luftwaffe concept provided the Army with an admirable set of aircraft for the Blitzkrieg but by making bombing essentially subservient to the Army, the Luftwaffe failed to recognise or develop the strategic bombing capability that the Allies eventually used to destroy German industry and cities. If the Germans had conquered Britain and then had only a one-front war in Russia, their air–land doctrine and the aircraft that supported it would have been recorded by history as a brilliant and innovative stroke. However, on the other side, with early lack of success and high loss rates, Bomber Command's war could have been over before it really started. The fact that the RAF leadership (Portal) and British political leadership (Churchill) kept faith in the bomber weapon, and that the earlier decisions to build four-engined bombers and create a training system to produce crews had now started to bear fruit, gave the Command a breathing space, but it still had to prove itself.

An extension of the bombing directive to include smaller towns had no immediate effect and the bombers were back to their usual haunts of Berlin, Cologne, Essen and Frankfurt for much of August 1941. Other industrial centres were also hit, and intelligence reports occasionally provided feedback on results; for example, the 8/9 September attack on Kassel was believed to have caused severe damage to a factory making railway rolling stock.

After a reduction In the bombing effort against German cities, the focus of attacks having related to the maritime war, Bomber Command resumed its strategic offensive with a directive to disrupt the transport system and destroy the 'morale of the civilian population and of the industrial workers in particular'. The weight of attack steadily increased, and the defence system received greater impetus to achieve success. German air resources were already being stretched, with three active fronts in North Africa, Russia and over Germany. Cologne, Hamburg, Mannheim, Essen, Hanover, Frankfurt, Nuremberg, Berlin and other German cities were on Bomber Command's list that autumn, operations taking place on most nights. The scale of effort gradually increased, almost 400 aircraft being involved on the night of 7/8 November 1941; 169 went to Berlin, and 21 were lost. This loss rate of 12.4 per cent was far higher than Bomber Command could sustain, it being generally accepted that a sustainable loss rate was less than 5 per cent. Berlin, however, was a particularly hard target. Not only were the flak defences of the city strong, but the bombers had a long flight over enemy territory, increasing the chances of interception by night fighters.

There was also the question of how to find and hit targets; the Butt Report of August 1941 had revealed shocking statistics concerning bombing accuracy. The report had based its findings on analysis of bombing photos taken by the bombers as they completed their bomb run. The key finding was: 'Of those aircraft recorded as attacking their target, only one in three got within 5 miles.' For the effort being expended and the casualties being suffered, the direct results, the actual bombing of targets, were totally in-adequate. Several changes resulted, some of which were already in the pipeline. Those who remained convinced by the bomber weapon said you needed far more bombers that were able to concentrate a devastating load of bombs on their target area, and you needed a better way of finding the target. The 'target area' soon became area bombing and included the concept of de-housing the industrial workers as part of the overall disruption of German industry.

The search for electronic aids to assist navigation and permit 'blind bombing' was of critical importance to Bomber Command. The earliest successful device, and then only partly so, was TR1335, otherwise known as 'Gee'. In July 1941 the Wellingtons of 115 Squadron were fitted with Gee sets in order to conduct operational trials. On the night of 11/12 August a force of twenty-nine Wellingtons, including two Gee aircraft, attacked Mönchengladbach. This trial and others on the next two nights appeared to be successful, the navigators having no trouble obtaining Gee fixes for most of the route. It was then decided to halt the experiment until sufficient sets were available to equip the majority of the bomber force, a figure of 300 bombers being set as a minimum. As was stated at the Chiefs of Staff Conference on 18 August: 'It made the theoretically desirable policy of concentration in time and space practicable.' It was some months before the requisite number of aircraft had been equipped and Gee was once more used operationally. It was an immediate success with the crews, not so much as a blind-bombing aid – it never achieved the accuracy for such a role – but as a general navigation aid to help the bomber get to the target area so that the crew could visually acquire the target itself. However, another essential part played by Gee was in helping the bomber find its way back to base. Statistics showed that after the introduction of this equipment the number of aircraft landing away from base dropped. It also saved many a crew from the fate of flying on past England and ending up in the Atlantic as their petrol ran out.

Ron Tettenborn, an observer with 9 Squadron, was amongst the first to use Gee on operations:

> First impressions were of staggering accuracy, on practice use in UK, – you could say to the pilot 'we should hit the SW corner of the airfield in . . . minutes', and did, to the astonishment of the crew! On the Continent it was obviously not so accurate as over the UK but was said to be within about a mile at Ruhr range; on a good night, with height, you could use it about as far east as Heligoland, with accuracy of 4–5 miles. It was most comforting on the way home but tended to leave the lazy navigator in trouble if it failed!

It was also essential for Bomber Command to reduce its losses. It thus became important to disrupt or destroy the enemy night defences, and it was this desire that led to the expansion of the RAF's night-intruder campaign, with the dual intention of attacking enemy night-bomber airfields as well as night fighters. Although there was still only one unit, 23 Squadron, fully engaged on night-intruder operations (this unit flew 488 of the 559 intruder sorties recorded for the 142 operational nights of 1941), the concept had certainly become well established by the spring of 1942. By the end of the summer a significant number of squadrons, mainly Hurricanes, had become involved in this type of work.

Throughout the second half of 1941 Kammhuber continued to refine the basic system in the west, extending the coverage of his 'boxes' and providing purpose-built operations rooms (known as 'Kammhuber cinemas'). However, even with such refinements the system remained limited by its ability to handle only one target (and fighter) per box. It was also found that the boxes were not deep enough: the British bombers crossed the danger zone too quickly. As the RAF's bomber operations continued to grow in scale, the defence system was rapidly swamped. Nevertheless, RAF planners were growing concerned. During 1941 Bomber Command operated on 240 nights, dropping 31,700 tons of bombs; it had been a frustrating year in which proof had been provided that only a small percentage of bombs were falling anywhere near their targets. This, added to the rising losses, led many to question the future of the bombing offensive. At this point the Luftwaffe was beating the RAF but when defending against a bombing offensive you only win if you stop the bombing, and that the Luftwaffe was never able to do.

Whilst 1941 was a year in which the RAF was making great strides forward in airborne radar for its night fighters with the introduction of centimetric radar, in the later months of the year Göring made a decision that would put the Germans some way behind the Allies in the development of AI equipment. He rejected proposals to develop centimetric-wave sets, contending that the reflection factor would make them unusable.

Air Chief Marshal Sir Norman Bottomley summarised the official view of events so far in a post-war conference:

> The Luftwaffe very quickly reacted to our night bombing offensive. As early as September 1940 they had developed a night-fighter force of 120 aircraft out of their day fighter units. By the end of 1941 the effectiveness of the enemy night-fighter system resulted in such heavy losses to our bombers that it was decided to restrict bomber operations over Germany until the spring of 1942. By June 1942, the number of night fighters had risen to 250, by July 1943 it was 550 and by the spring of 1944 over 800. The night-fighter force remained efficient to the very end of the war. In the face of these defences, losses were considerable. The rate of night-bomber losses was highest in 1942, with a loss rate of 4.1 per cent. A casualty rate of 4 per cent meant that on average there was a turn-over of aircrews in squadrons in about four months due to casualties.

1942: The First Real Test of Strength and Will

The Germans were now being forced to devote much attention, manpower and resources to the problem of the defence of the Reich. By January 1942 the total number of flak guns had almost doubled, and the night-fighter system, with its associated radars and control networks, had been greatly expanded, thus draining resources of men and material from other combat uses. In this study I am not looking at the overall strategic value (for and against) of each of the air war scenarios, but rather the 'win/lose' of each of those scenarios. Nevertheless, the allocation of resources, the political imperatives that drove resource allocation, were of course influenced by the wider strategic situations.

This year was to see major changes for both sides in the air war over Germany. For Bomber Command it was a make or break year, as results had been generally poor to date and there was pressure to move resources to other critical war areas, such as the maritime war. The Command did not have the ability to find its targets and to deliver a telling weight of attack, and loss rates continued to cause concern. Unless this could be remedied, the entire campaign seemed pointless to some. This was not strictly true of course as there was the diversion of German resources and, a point often overlooked, the morale boost to Britain and the Allies from the fact that Germany was under attack: the Allies were hitting back. Several things changed in 1942 in Bomber Command's favour, and some of those reflect the 'how the RAF won' aspect. One of the most significant was the appointment of a new commander.

In February 1942 Arthur Harris was given the task of guiding Bomber Command; he was determined that the Command should be run his way and that its offensive power should not be bled away to other areas. It was a policy that brought many heated arguments, but it was undoubtedly a policy that, in general terms, was correct, and he was fortunate in having the support of Churchill. There were naturally errors and mistakes, areas in which a little more flexibility might have produced a better result – but much of this can only be said with the benefit of hindsight. The cost of the campaign was high, earning him the name 'Butch' or 'Butcher' Harris from the crews, although in most cases this was not meant in quite such a blunt way as it sounds. To the press he was usually 'Bomber' Harris. Without the guiding hand of its commander, it is most unlikely that Bomber Command would have become such a potent offensive force; a lesser leader would have given way to some of the pressures that tried to pull the Command in different directions. There has been much argument since the war as to the way that Bomber Command was used, and Harris has received a great deal of vituperation, being accused of running a 'vindictive campaign' against the German cities.

Bomber Command mounted its largest operation yet, with 235 aircraft attacking the Renault factory at Boulogne-Billancourt near Paris on 3/4 March 1942. The major significance of this for the present study is the level of concentration (by time) of the bombers over the target: previous attacks had averaged 80 aircraft per hour, but on this night the bombers achieved 120 per hour, the tactic being aimed at both increasing the weight of the attack and reducing the attackers' exposure to the defences. Many 'experts' had feared that too great a concentration would bring about an unacceptable level of collisions, but this did not prove to be the case and concentrating bombers into a very short time span over a target became a standard Bomber Command tactic.

Concentration of effort also meant picking on one target: Essen was attacked on 8/9, 9/10, 10/11, 25/26 and 26/27 March (the 10/11 raid being significant as the first Lancaster attack on a target in Germany). Although these attacks were Gee-guided, they failed to achieve any level of concentration or accuracy on the target. The night defences continued to take a toll, the final raid losing almost 10 per cent of the 115 aircraft taking part, most falling to night fighters along the inbound and outbound routes.

After the series of attacks on Ruhr targets, during which the night fighters had become an increasing threat, many bomber crews reporting sightings and combats, 28/29 March saw Bomber Command launch its most effective raid of the war to date. The target was Lübeck, and 234 aircraft, mainly Wellingtons, were tasked in three waves, the first of which comprised experienced crews using the Gee navigation aid to make the first bombs accurate, thus enabling subsequent waves to bomb the fires. Conditions were perfect, and extensive damage was caused, while losses among the bombers were under 5 per cent (twelve aircraft), the majority falling to night fighters.

However, overall success was still elusive and Harris determined that only a decisive blow by a very large force of bombers would prove the value of his Command and ensure the political backing he needed; whilst Churchill was in general supportive, he still needed to be shown that his support produced results. Thus were born the 'Thousand Bomber Raids'. Harris was in no doubt that: 'The bombing strength of the RAF is increasing rapidly, and if the best use is made of it, the effect on German war production and effort will be very heavy over a period of 12 to 18 months, and such as to have a real effect on the war position.'

The first Thousand Bomber Raid was intended to demonstrate the full power of a co-ordinated bombing plan. The target was the city of Cologne, and on the night of 30/31 May 1942 a force of 1,047 bombers, including 338 four-engine 'heavies', left their bases in Britain. Just under 900 were recorded as bombing the target. Losses were 41 aircraft, roughly half of which fell to night fighters between the coast and the target (inbound and outbound), with flak claiming 16 and fighters 4 over the target area. Although this was the highest number of losses so far suffered in a single night, it was also by far the largest raid, and the loss rate was considered acceptable in view of the predicted level of damage inflicted upon the target. The Thousand Bomber strategy was repeated against Essen (1/2 June) and Bremen (25/26 June), the last also being significant for the first intruder operations by Boston and Mosquito aircraft. Although the three raids had not perhaps been the clear-cut demonstration of potential that Harris had intended, they certainly impressed many, including Churchill, and eased some of the pressure on the Command. This was just as well, as the Thousand Bomber force had to be broken up to allow the large numbers of OTU aircraft used to return to their vital training role. The demonstration had, however, also impressed the Nazi leaders, and greater efforts were demanded from the defence forces, with Hitler also demanding reprisal attacks.

The use of greater numbers of aircraft gave Bomber Command additional problems in getting aircraft safely to, and over, the target. It also prompted the tactical experts to look at new ideas. Two innovations had been employed during the Thousand Bomber raids: the use of a bomber stream and attempts to condense the overall time over the target, to saturate the defences in time and space. A tight stream of bombers, constrained within a particular geographic area but using height separation, would penetrate the fewest number of defensive boxes, thus reducing the chances of interception and exploiting the major limitation of the GCI boxes. The same basic argument applied to concentration over the target, as this would saturate directed flak (but not, of course, barrage flak). As various German targets were attacked through the summer, bomber losses began to mount once more as the defenders amended their tactics to suit the changing situation. In terms of finding and hitting targets the introduction of the Pathfinder Force became a key element in successful bomber operations; however, whilst it ensured the bombers were more effective, other than the extent that targets that had direct relevance to air-defence capability were hit (aviation and oil, for example), its role sits outside this present study.

According to the post-war debrief of General Frydag:

> By the end of 1941 the German government, in view of the possible threat of air attack, albeit not taken very seriously in official circles, had decided upon a policy whereby the armaments industry as a whole should be obliged to undertake further expansion only at sites geographically separated from existing industrial concentrations and it was the smaller towns with populations ranging from 5,000 to 20,000 inhabitants which were chiefly selected for this purpose.

However, it was not until 1943 that any significant attempt at such dispersal was made; this could have been a strategic error but, as we will see later, shortage of defending aircraft was never the problem.

There was a reorganisation and expansion for the Luftwaffe's night-fighter force. May saw the creation of a new command structure intended to make XII Fliergerkorps less unwieldy. Despite these cosmetic changes, which did have some impact, there were still major problems. Aircraft and equipment still had a low priority, partly because Kammhuber had managed to upset a large number of senior officers. Nevertheless, the overall effectiveness of the system had increased, and by August 1942 there had been a sharp increase in the delivery of Lichtenstein B/C radar sets, thus giving the crews more tactical flexibility.

By summer 1942 the new heavy bombers had been operating for some time, and all had been found lacking in various important respects. A report of 2 June 1942 compared the Manchester and Stirling loss rates for the period September 1941 to March 1942: Manchester 626 sorties for loss (Failed to Return or Category E damage) of 27 aircraft (4.4%); Stirling 639 sorties for loss of 17 aircraft (2.7%). It appeared that the Manchester was far more vulnerable to flak than either of the other types; the explanation given was that 'the Manchester has two main petrol tanks and two small ones, whereas the Stirling has fourteen', the implication being that critical levels of damage were thus sustained more easily by the Manchester.

A report of 30 July also had harsh things to say about the Halifax, the loss rate of which had risen to an average of 5.3 per cent from its 1,467 sorties in the year to June 1942. This time the conclusion reached was that the losses were mainly due to night fighters, perhaps because unsatisfactory exhaust shrouds on the engines made the aircraft easier for the night fighters to pick up. The Halifax 'problem' was the subject of many reports throughout 1942 and into early 1943; one conclusion reached in October was that it was 'essential that pilots posted to Halifax squadrons should be detailed to complete at least three, preferably five, sorties as 2nd pilot or against lightly defended targets before being employed on main operations'. The importance of such reports was that improvements in equipment, tactics and training could be made.

The Halifax remained under the spotlight. A few more months of statistics and the Halifax was under review again, with particular reference to the experience levels of pilots in No. 4 Group as a factor in loss rates:

> There is no reasonable doubt that pilots on their first two operations have a casualty rate well above the average and that those who had survived 20 sorties had a rate well below the average. This must be aircraft-related as the Lancaster does not suffer the same problem. The record on lightly defended targets is good; the problem comes on highly defended targets. New pilots are a bit nervous of the

aircraft, the aircraft having gained a bad name for instability in manoeuvres. It thus may happen that a new pilot is reluctant when he meets defences to manoeuvre his machine sufficiently in combat or that in a sudden emergency, he puts his machine into an attitude in which he has had no previous experience of controlling it.

The solution proposed by the report was for more general handling training to be carried out at the OTUs and fighter affiliation when on the squadron. Other reports had highlighted the benefits of fighter affiliation sorties, suggesting that the loss rates of squadrons were significantly influenced by the amount of such exercises undertaken. The crews quite enjoyed the chance to take their aircraft out over the sea to meet up with a Spitfire for a spot of mutual training; the gunners calling the evasions so that the pilot could throw his aircraft into a stomach-churning manoeuvre. The point here for our study is once again to stress the importance of such analysis, which was fed through both to the squadrons and the training units, and where appropriate to the technical folks to make changes in equipment.

August 1942 saw the first American bombing raid and whilst what was to become the double blow of day and night in the combined bombing offensive was still some time away, the downfall of Germany had started. From now on the defenders would be battered continuously, and fighter resources would be harder to come by.

Disruption and destruction of the German night-fighter effort was thus of great importance. The scale of RAF intruder operations rose to a peak in the summer of 1942, 336 sorties in June being the highest monthly total. The emphasis on German night-fighter airfields that became evident in the last few days of July was maintained over the coming months. By October virtually all intruder effort was against such targets, with Leeuwarden, Deelen, Twente and Venlo being favourite haunts.

The RAF history summarised general intruder operations for the second half of 1942:

> The number of operations carried out has steadily diminished. This was owing to the small scale of enemy activity and to the weather. To give pilots experience, however, the long-range aircraft were sent deep into central France to operate against enemy night training centres. Compared with the successes earlier in the year, the results were disappointing. Between August and December, we claimed the destruction of only two enemy aircraft, although we claimed to have damaged 54. The AOC-in-C has decided that during periods of enemy inactivity the intruder force should carry out offensive

patrols over enemy territory by day as well as night. Should the enemy recommence large-scale attacks on the United Kingdom, the force would revert to its original role.

Victory in the skies over Britain had enabled more effort to support the night war over Occupied Europe.

The effects of this campaign were summarised in the RAF account:

> The effects of intruder activity on the German Air Force are not precisely known but prisoner of war reports at the time showed that such activity caused the diversion of returning bombers either to waiting areas or alternate airfields, the adoption of special landing procedures and the use of illuminated decoys and dummy airfields. Enemy crews were therefore forced to operate with restricted facilities and at a higher than normal nervous tension Again it is impossible to measure the effect of such tension, but it seems likely that it impaired the efficiency of the enemy bomber force in some degree at least. It is probable, for example, that as a result of intruders, the enemy accident rate was increased.

The increased use of radar and other items of equipment had turned the air war into an electronic battlefield, a situation that was recognised by October, when the Senior Air Staff Officer (SASO), Bomber Command, chaired a meeting to discuss the adoption of radio counter-measures (RCM). The general conclusion reached was that the organisation of the German night defence system offered four possible targets for attack by radio counter-measures. These were:

- The early warning system, the radar components of which were mostly Freya sets, situated around the coastline of Germany and Occupied Europe, supplemented by further Freyas inland. All of these operated on frequencies of 120–130 mc/s.
- The close-control system at GCI stations, which was based on the use of two Würzburgs, one for plotting the fighter and one for the bomber. The frequency was around 570 mc/s.
- The channel of communications between ground controllers and night fighters. Instructions were passed by R/T in the 3–6 mc/s band.
- Enemy AI radars operating on 490 mc/s.

It was recommended that an effective airborne jammer be developed to counter the Würzburg, and that an airborne 'Mandrel' jamming barrage should be established. In the interim, a temporary expedient known as 'Shiver' was introduced to provide some disturbance of the Würzburgs. The

Mandrel jammer was primarily aimed at the early-warning radars and had been in service since late 1942. However, it was the more widespread use of the equipment, and the tactic of creating a Mandrel screen (with aircraft flying a race-track pattern) that eventually produced results as an element within the overall RCM campaign. Various marks of Mandrel equipment entered service to counter different radar bands. Certain of the specialist squadrons were later given Shiver to supplement the Mandrel equipment, the Shiver system being intended to jam the GCI (Würzburg) sets and flak fire-control radars. Steps were also taken to disrupt the fighter control frequencies, the earliest system being that of transmitting engine noise, using microphones placed in engine nacelles, to blot out the controllers' voices. This counter-measure, 'Tinsel', was first used in December. The complexity and constant need to improve and respond to enemy counter-measures meant that the research, development and evaluation of new equipment and tactics was constant; the RAF and its research establishments, as well as industry, proved more adept at this than the Germans. This was another of the factors in why the RAF did not lose the night war.

A very significant meeting of the Chiefs of Staff Committee took place in November 1942, which included 'an estimate of the effects of an Anglo-American bomber offensive against Germany'. This meeting took a wide-ranging view of the whole question of air bombardment in the strategic sense and had as its starting premise that: 'A heavy bomber force rising from 4,000 to 6,000 heavy bombers in 1944 could shatter the industrial and economic structure of Germany to a point where an Anglo-American force of reasonable strength could enter the Continent from the West.' The important aspects of concentration of effort and dedication of resources to the primary aim were therefore included as key elements of the plan. Using the assumed increase in the size of the Anglo-American bomber force, the paper estimated that by the end of 1943 some 50,000 tons of bombs would be dropped every month, rising to 90,000 tons in late 1944 when the total of 6,000 heavy bombers would be available. It is interesting to note that the total German tonnage dropped in the 12 months from June 1940 was only 55,000 tons.

1943: Destructive Power – but Crisis of Confidence?

It is noteworthy that, on 1 January 1943, some 37 per cent of all Bomber Command pilots were from the Commonwealth (Canada, Australia, New Zealand), including an entire Canadian Group; plus, of course, all the Commonwealth aircrew other than pilots. Add to this the volunteer aircrew from other nations and it becomes apparent what a truly cosmopolitan organisation Bomber Command was – and the availability of this source of manpower was the only reason that the RAF, and Bomber Command in particular, was able to replace its losses whilst at the same time grow overall strength. This access to a large supply of manpower was another of the factors in how the RAF was able to defeat the Luftwaffe, as was the ability to train aircrew, including British aircrew, in the safety of overseas locations. It was not quite the same with the groundcrew, although as 'national' squadrons were formed within RAF Bomber Command these did contain some national groundcrew.

Whilst 1942 had been a critical year for Bomber Command's survival, 1943 was to be the first year in which it began to deliver the long promised destructive power – and with previously unheard-of accuracy. A Bomber Command analysis put forward the hopes for 1943:

> Prior to the winter victories of the Soviet armies, Bomber Command was contributing an essential element to the failure of the enemy's campaign in Russia by drawing off the German fighter force, reducing the productivity of German industry by bombing, and hampering it further by locking up very large manpower resources in flak and civil defence measures. Now the Germans are in retreat and everywhere on the defensive . . . in these circumstances the bomber offensive if concentrated on Germany will, in the immediate future, be not merely important, but decisive in crushing the German power to wage war.

The January 1943 Casablanca Conference confirmed much of Anglo-American strategy for the remainder of the war. It restated the 'Germany First' strategy and the planned massive increase in American air power in Europe which was to lead to the inevitable destruction of the Luftwaffe. Various proposals had been prepared at staff level, including Portal's paper outlining the proposition that a heavy bomber force of 6,000 aircraft could end the war, and were the basis for the discussions. The outcome was a broad statement of the intent behind the Combined Bomber Offensive for 1943: 'Your primary object will be the progressive destruction and dislocation of the German military, industrial and economic system, and the undermining of the morale of the German people to a point where their capacity for armed resistance is fatally weakened.' The directive issued by the Combined Chiefs of Staff on 21 January went on to detail five main target systems for attack, none of which were new and all of which had, at one time or another, been scheduled for attack by Bomber Command: submarine construction yards, aircraft industry, transport, oil plants and 'others in the war industry'. This kind of broad instruction suited Harris admirably as it meant that he was not tied down to using his resources against what he termed 'unprofitable and unsuitable' targets. This single-minded approach by Harris time and again ensured that, with some exceptions, his bomber force remained focused.

At the end of January, the latest in a series of technical additions went into operation, a raid on 30/31 January, to Hamburg, being the operational debut for the H2S radar system. This was to prove of enormous value not only in target finding but also in general navigation, although in the early months, until operators became experienced, there remained problems of identification unless it was a coastal or river target, where radar returns were easier to interpret.

> In 1943, RAF Bomber Command forced the GAF to form its first functional command. Air Fleet Reich was charged with the air defence of Germany. Our night attacks were taking too big a toll. The United States Air Force had commenced its attacks in daylight, but it was not until September 1943 that the GAF realised what these attacks were going to mean for them. There were demands for an ever-increasing number of day and night fighters. (Elmhirst lecture)

The Luftwaffe night-fighter force underwent expansion, re-equipment and reorganisation during 1943 in response to the increasing weight and accuracy of attacks being delivered by Bomber Command. New units were created, but wastage of crews and aircraft remained high, partly through the insistence of some commanders that the night fighters should also take part in repelling the American daylight raids. They were no match for the agile American fighters, and irreplaceable experienced crews were lost for little good reason. One such loss was that of Hauptmann Ludwig Becker of NJG 1 on 26 February: he had achieved 44 night victories and would likely have become one of the very high-scoring night pilots.

The German position was not as simple as many post-war studies suggest. There was always a great deal of in-fighting within the various elements of the Nazi military machine. Göring held a significant planning conference on 22 February 1943. Among the many comments that came from this conference, the following are relevant to this aspect of the air war. Discussing Kammhuber's insistence on production of the Ta 154 night fighter, Göring said:

> If it were left to him, only night fighters would be built and nothing else. He is emphatically egotistical about it. He says to himself, 'If no one else can use this aircraft then my allocation will be secure.' That is a point of view that should not carry any weight with us. If the aircraft is not superior to the Ju 188 then it will not be built.

Jeschonnek said:

> I would like to add something about this night fighter [the Ju 188]. It has been laid down that sufficient aircraft are to be produced to provide us with 18 complete night-fighter *Gruppen*; but at the moment we can only put between 24 and 28 aircraft into operational *Gruppen*. Our ultimate objective is to have 24 *Gruppen* at full strength by 1 July 1944. There won't be sufficient quantities in 1943 to attain our targets.

And Milch added: 'The Ju 188 will definitely be one of our best night fighters for a long time to come.'

On 18 March 1943, Göring once more addressed his commanders at Karinhall:

> I now have to produce the means whereby at least some kind of counter-stroke may be delivered in view of the constantly increasing number of British bombers. Do not deceive yourselves, gentlemen, the British will carry out attacks with an ever-increasing number of these slow four-engined 'crates' which some of you hold in such contempt. He will deal with each and, every city; he can navigate to Munich or Berlin with the same precision. Nothing bothers him. The night fighters are successful on some occasions and unsuccessful on others. The flak can only play a defensive role or have a deterrent effect. The equipment with which they have to navigate and hit the target even in bad weather is ideal, while our instruments are always going wrong so that the night fighters are always coming to grief and cannot do much about it.

No doubt many in Bomber Command would have been heartened to have heard these comments. By 1943, though, Göring had lost virtually all his influence with Hitler, primarily because the Luftwaffe was failing to protect Germany from the Allied bombing campaign and was not making effective reprisal attacks. This meant the Luftwaffe had no political power to protect its interests in the increasingly paranoid conferences presided over by Hitler.

Battle of the Ruhr

Harris saw a raid of 5/6 March 1943 as a turning point. Led by an Oboe-equipped Pathfinder force, 442 bombers attacked the industrial city of Essen and this elusive target received heavy damage for the loss of only fourteen aircraft: 'Years of endeavour, of experiment, and of training in new methods have at last provided the weapons and the force capable of destroying the heart of the enemy's armament industry.' This raid was the opening move in the new offensive aimed at flattening the Ruhr and its vital industries. The Casablanca Directive was a clear call to the advocates of strategic bombing to prove their case; in March 1943 Bomber Command launched a sustained attack on Germany. The first part was the 'Battle of the Ruhr', from March to July, aimed at destroying the vital war industries of the region.

In the period until mid-May, about 60 per cent of Bomber Command Main Force effort was tasked against targets in the Ruhr, Duisburg being the most frequently visited. Other large raids went to Essen, Bochum, Mannheim, Dortmund, Nuremberg, Munich, Stuttgart, Berlin, Frankfurt, Stettin and, farther afield, the Skoda Works at Pilsen. On 13/14 April, Mosquitoes began night harassing raids, the idea being to keep the sirens going throughout Germany, a foretaste of the much larger-scale and more effective raids by the Light Night Striking Force.

Air Gunnery

One of the routine series of operational analyses undertaken concerned the use of the bombers' guns for self-defence. The whole question of a 'policy' for air gunners had been examined on previous occasions, with no firm conclusions, and it was still very much a matter of crew tactics. Some gunners never fired their guns in anger during an entire tour of operations, some never even saw a night fighter. In some crews it was policy NOT to open fire unless the fighter came into the attack; a quick glimpse of a fighter in the darkness did not always mean that he had seen you – to open fire would certainly give the aircraft away. Amongst others, and this was somewhat more in line with the general guidance given, the policy was to fire at anything that moved as this showed that the bomber crew were awake and ready – maybe the fighter would go away and pick on somebody else. Statistics showed that the rear turret was most frequently in action, for example, in the period November 1942–February 1943 of 139 instances of heavy-bomber gunners engaging targets, no fewer than 123 had been by the rear gunners. The average number of bullets fired was 235, the maximum 1,000, and this from a total available of 6,000 rounds for a Lancaster rear turret (4,800 for a Stirling, 3,000 for a Halifax). The scientists contended that a limit of 3,000 rounds be imposed, thus giving an appreciable weight saving, and associated improvement in performance. At other times it was argued that the removal of the front and mid-upper turrets, with the associated weight saving and improved aerodynamics, would give the aircraft an improved performance that would far outweigh the loss of firepower.

Arguments had also been raging for some time concerning the 0.303 in. guns with which the RAF bombers were equipped, and heavier calibre turrets such as the Rose turret with 0.5 in. guns were trialled. The standard guns were certainly reliable, and they pushed out a high rate of fire, but the effective range was very limited. The 'wise' fighter pilot could stand off from the gunners and take shots with his highly destructive cannon. The AOC-in-C of No. 5 Group, Ralph Cochrane, amongst others, argued that the air gunners should fire more often, letting loose at the faintest shadow, the additional 'own goals' which might result from this would, he suggested, be far outweighed by the gains. Others, including Don Bennett, head of the Pathfinders, argued strongly against this idea. In the event it was individual crew choice as to which technique they thought gave them the best chance of survival.

The Bomber Command Quarterly Review often included references to night-fighter tactics and engagements that had taken place. The issue for April–June 1943 included a feature on 'Encounters with Night Fighters', which stated in part:

> The enemy High Command has gradually built up a truly formidable defensive front against Allied air attacks, and it is only because our own tactics and equipment have developed at least as fast that we can continue to operate successfully and on a larger scale than before. In spite of the deepening of the controlled-fighter zone, which now extends in a solid belt from the Ruhr to the Dutch and Belgian coasts, our losses during the past quarter show no appreciable increase as compared with last year. Reports from air crews indicate that night fighters frequently give up the attack without firing a shot if they see that the bomber has discovered them. It is very seldom that a crew that carries out the correct defensive procedures comes off worst. During the April–June period some 50 night fighters were driven off in a seriously damaged condition, while 55 are considered to have been completely destroyed.

A typical engagement was recorded in the Quarterly Review:

> Wellington 'T' of No. 431 Squadron, returning from the raid on Stuttgart on the night of 14/15 April, observed a square of four white lights on the ground some 60 miles north-west of the target. These lights changed to a single line of white lights when the Wellington had passed, as if indicating its track. Presently the wireless operator, who was in the astrodome, reported a Bf 110 at about 400 yards' range on the starboard quarter. As the bomber turned in towards

the attack the rear-gunner fired a short burst. The enemy broke away immediately without firing and, passing underneath, came in again on the port quarter, opening fire at 300 yards. Meanwhile our aircraft was corkscrewing, but the rear gunner was able to reply with an accurate short burst, hitting the Messerschmitt in the nose. This was followed by a longer burst which caused the fighter to explode with a brilliant flash. Meanwhile a second Bf 110 attacked from astern and underneath, fired a short burst which missed, broke away to starboard. As the intercom was u/s, the rear gunner signalled these attacks to the pilot by means of the call light. The enemy came in again on the starboard quarter but broke off without firing at 200 yards, when the rear gunner gave him a short burst. The Wellington was now flying at a very low level as the pilot had dived repeatedly to avoid attacks from below. But the Messerschmitt attacked once more, on the port quarter, firing a long burst that passed over our aircraft. At 200 yards' range the rear gunner fired and observed some hits on the Hun's starboard engine. As he passed overhead flames were seen coming from the nacelle of this engine. There was slight damage to the Wellington's port wing.

Bomber Command Morale in the Dark Days

However, for now, Bomber Command was approaching crisis point. The ongoing loss rate had averaged 4–5 per cent, a non-sustainable figure, and morale had begun to suffer as crews calculated that their chances of survival were not good. Throughout the war there were instances of aircrew who had lost their nerve and had to be withdrawn from flying. This was usually officially referred to as LMF (Lack of Morale Fibre) but was often a much more complex problem: 'Fear was a subject that was never talked about except perhaps in a jocular manner after a few beers, yet it was present to a varying extent in each one of us. Normally the feeling was just bottled up.'

In May 1941 there was an attempt to 'codify' the procedure to be taken in respect of these 'W' (Waverer) cases of individuals: 'whose conduct may cause them to forfeit the confidence of their Commanding Officer in their determination and reliability in the face of danger'. There were seen to be two categories of individual, those who maintained a show of carrying out their duties, and those who simply refused to. It was no light matter to declare that you were not able to go on another operation; the first feeling was that the crew was being let down, this thought alone was enough to make many think again and once more hide their individual fear. If the feeling was too strong, or the 'powers that be' became aware of it, then the situation was still kept at an informal level within the squadron, with the flight commander and squadron commander trying to persuade, in some cases cajole, the individual into carrying on. Once it became obvious that nothing would change the decision then it was judged imperative to remove the individual from the squadron and his usual circle of contacts – to prevent 'contamination'. The medical officer would become involved and make his report as the matter was referred to group and the individual posted as soon as possible. From mid-1941 loss of the flying brevet had become automatic.

All this may seem harsh but in truth it wasn't. Every effort was made to try and persuade the man to return to flying, with no stigma attached. Only when this was of no avail did the system take harder action, with the intention of protecting the rest of the squadron and preventing a general collapse (although such an event seems unlikely to have resulted even in the darkest days of winter 1943/44.) Considering the many thousands of young men who flew on these hazardous missions, in full knowledge of their limited chances of survival, the problem was very small scale. Certainly, all were afraid at times, but it is remarkable that so many had the will to go on – and on.

Indeed, despite the heavy losses, morale at the squadrons remained high. In many ways the life of a Bomber Command aircrew member was a strange one; unlike the soldier in the field, he went to war from the peace, security and relative comfort of a well-established airfield to face danger and hardship for a few hours, then to return to England, perhaps a trip down to the squadron's pub or a night at a local dance (with all that such an event entailed!), but with the knowledge that the skies of Germany would soon call again; next time would his aircraft be the one that 'Failed to Return', would it be his personal effects that were quickly and quietly removed from the room, a new face then to appear in his place. So many faces didn't re-appear, they were gone – so what, pass another beer and sing another song. It was an attitude of mind that few other than operational aircrew could understand; it made them appear hard and indifferent, yet it was the only defence against mental collapse. It would always happen to the other fellow, and if it didn't – well, enjoy it while you can. Squadron life, and squadron songs, were an essential part of the picture, they bound everyone together with a sense of purpose and belonging.

This 100 Squadron song was typical of the many 'created' by Bomber Command units:

SONG – THE 100 SQUADRON BOYS
(Air – 'McNamara's Band')

We are 100 Squadron – we're the boys who know the score,
If anyone denies it, we will spread him on the floor,
At bombing and beer and billiards and all the Cleethorpes' Hops,
We have got the gen – we're the leading men – we certainly are the tops.

    CHORUS:
While the bombs go bang
And the flak bursts clang
And the searchlights blaze away,
We weave all over the starlit sky
And wish we'd gone by day.
Pattison, Pattison save us now
We can't abide the noise.
A credit to Butch Harris, the 100 Squadron boys.

Oh, we love to nip in smartly to a little buzz bomb site,
And smartly nip off home again and get to bed at night.
We're saving our night vision up for other earthly joys.
And now we're safely in the Mess, meet the 100 Squadron boys.

My name is William Irving, and I'm from the Middle East
And what you think about me here, I don't care in the least
I'm in command of 'A' Flight though you may not think it so,
There is not a pub in Lincolnshire or a WAAF that I don't know.

My name is Harry Hamilton, I'm an unpretentious Scot,
And although in a way I have little to say I sometimes think a lot
 If you ask my crew if I have any faults, they'll tell you in accents sweet
You can see the ants as I stooge over France at altitude ZERO FEET.

My name is Traff and I joined the RAF – well pretty near the start,
My trade is navigation, but I'm a bit of a wolf at heart.
I've a popsy here and a popsy there and I don't care if they're wed
So long as their husbands don't come home and find me still in bed.

Bomber Command Training

The concept of tightly knit crews was a foundation of morale and worked remarkably well within Bomber Command; airmen were loyal to, supportive of, and afraid to show up, their crew. Crews were formed at OTUs:

> Then they go to the OTU where they are formed into a crew and begin to learn teamwork. The duties of all members of the crew are carefully defined as far as the principal tasks are concerned, but the captain of each aircraft is responsible for arranging the duties of his crew and for seeing that they carry them out punctually and efficiently.

A new pilot would start the trawl to find the rest of a crew, the decision being left to the individuals as far as possible rather than the 'system' just putting names together. It worked remarkably well. This was outlined in an Aircrew Training Bulletin: 'The aircrew meet for the first time at the OTU and during the first two weeks of the ground course are given certain discretion in sorting themselves out into complete crews (with the exception of the Flight Engineer who does not arrive until later.)'

John Long went through the crewing up 'process' at Moreton-in-the-Marsh (No. 21 OTU):

> On arrival we were directed to one of the hangars where the completely undirected process of crewing up took place. Pilots, Navigators, Wireless Operators, Bomb Aimers and Gunners all milled around, making their categories and names known to each other as the random selection went on. Having crewed-up, through the rest of the training we became a 'unit'. We were learning not only how to operate our war machine but also about each other.

The introduction of specialist schools, such as the Lancaster Finishing Schools (LFS) also helped. Bomb aimer Don Clay on the LFS:

> The ground work consisted mainly of getting to know our various stations and equipment as well as escape procedures for baling out and dinghy drill. One of our final sorties at the LFS was fighter affiliation and by the end of the exercise our 'lad' left us in no doubt that, given the correct 'gen' by the gunners, no Jerry fighters would ever mark us down as a kill. With our last exercise at LFS we were sent home on leave for a week and told to report back before being posted to an operational squadron.

June 1944 was the high point for the training machine in terms of aircraft numbers, with a strength of 2,018 aircraft at 44 units, comprising 22 OTUs,

15 HCUs (Heavy Conversion Units), three LFSs and four 'miscellaneous training units' such as the Pathfinder Navigation Training Unit (PFNTU). These aircraft were housed at 59 airfields and employed thousands of air and ground personnel: an incredible organisation and a key element in the overall success of Bomber Command.

New Directive: Pointblank

As the height of the Ruhr offensive yet another directive landed on Harris's desk. The Allied Conference held in Washington during May 1943 took a further look at the progress of, and future plans for, the Combined Bomber Offensive. One of the plans under consideration was that presented by the American bomber commander, General Eaker. The so-called 'Eaker Plan' had been outlined in April with its central argument being that it is 'better to cause a high degree of destruction in a few really essential industries than to cause a small degree of destruction in many industries'. The target systems outlined in the Casablanca Directive were turned into seventy-six precise targets, the destruction of which was to be seen as an essential pre-requisite to the Allied invasion of the Continent. Eaker stressed that this could only work if there was an adequate bomber force and so suggested that the two bomber arms should work together to this general plan. The Washington Conference was in general agreement with this proposal but disagreed with some of the target systems and allowed for greater flexibility of action by increasing the number of targets (at the request of the Air Staff). Having American air power in the war over Europe was to prove essential, but it came with a degree of political and doctrinal baggage that many of the experienced RAF leaders found 'challenging'.

A new directive reached Bomber Command on 3 June 1943; code-named Pointblank; It recognised that the German fighter threat, especially by day, was still far too great: 'If the growth of the German fighter strength is not arrested quickly it may become literally impossible to carry out the destruction planned and thus to create the conditions necessary for ultimate decisive action by our combined forces on the Continent.' The overall strategic plan called for the US VIII Bomber Command to attack the stated targets by day and for RAF Bomber Command to hit the *same* area by night, truly a combined offensive. In the event, this very rarely happened. However, this was the true start of the devastating day–night war against Germany that saw the destruction of the Luftwaffe. Whilst in this study I treat the night offensive and the day offensive as separate entities, they were very much linked, especially in the pressures on the Luftwaffe in terms of aircraft, crews, training, fuel and all the other aspects essential for war fighting.

The directive had various target types listed, and it was frequently adjusted; however, for some time it made German fighter strength the first priority, and stated four specific areas for attack:

- The destruction of airframe, engine and component factories, and the ball-bearing industry on which the strength of the German fighter force depends.
- The general disorganisation of those industrial areas associated with the above industries.
- The destruction of those aircraft repair depots and storage parks within range, and on which the enemy fighter force is largely dependent.
- The destruction of enemy fighters in the air and on the ground.

The Bomber Command Operational Research Section (ORS) continued its investigations into a wide range of tactical questions. One of the regular series of reports was that which concerned the German defences, their composition and strength, and the relevance of various tactical methods. The work of the ORS has often been ignored by historians, and it was known to very few of the crews during the war itself, but it played an essential part in the creation of new ideas and tactics: 'a fruitful alliance between the air force and the scientists which enabled Bomber Command to evade the German air force and, with increasing accuracy, to find and hit its targets'. The scientists were certainly kept busy. Bombers were given warning and protective systems as part of the increasingly complex contest between the bombers and the Luftwaffe. The 'Monica' tail-warning system was introduced into service in mid-June, intended to give bomber crews warning of the presence of aircraft closing in from behind. A small transmitter installed in the tail of the bomber had a range of 1,000 yards to 4 miles and should, in theory, have given the rear gunner advance notice of a fighter sneaking up from behind. The warning was an audio one; the nearer the contact, the more rapid the 'pips. However, this proved to be a nuisance, as in the bomber stream the equipment picked up almost constant contacts from other bombers. One attempted solution to this was the Mk IIIA, with a visual indication (lights), though the problem of too many contacts remained.

New kit continued to appear, such as the Boozer warning device. According to one air gunner:

> This gadget consisted of an external aerial fitted to the tail of the aircraft and a small panel of three lights above the pilot's instrument panel. There were two red lights and one white light. The red lights

were for ground activity and the white light for enemy fighters. If a Luftwaffe 'sod' had your aircraft on his interceptor monitor, then this light would flash a brilliant white. As soon as this appeared, evasive action of one sort or another without further ado. It worked for me twice – and I'm still here!

Luftwaffe Attempts to Get More Fighters Involved

At a conference on 6 July 1943, Major Hans-Joachim ('Hajo') Herrmann presented his view that: 'The subject in question is the employment of single-engined aircraft on night-fighter operations. I consider the prospects of successful operations by this type of aircraft to be particularly good as it is highly manoeuvrable.' They had a notable early success during an attack on Cologne:

> We had twelve aircraft in the air and the only arrangement we made was that we would co-operate with local flak. After the first contact with the enemy I was surprised that the flak did not cease firing at enemy aircraft picked up by searchlights. Our pilots pressed home their attacks splendidly! The aircraft could be clearly identified first as silhouettes, then by the exhaust; with the small single-seater aircraft it was possible to bank quickly and keep on the enemy's tail without difficulty. We flew five Fw 190s and seven Me 109-G4 and G6. At first, we flew in echelon formation up to an altitude of 10,000 m, so that we could come down on the enemy very quickly. We made contact and fired on enemy aircraft sixteen times and made contact without firing seventeen times.

This *Wilde Sau* ('Wild Boar') tactic became a major element of the night-fighter force for the next year or so.

The RAF was also maintaining the pressure on German night-fighter airfields, both with bombing sorties and with intruder missions. Fighter Command aircraft were tasked to undertake more intruder operations. Under the code-name Flower, the Mosquitoes of 605 Squadron flew the first such operations on 11/12 June. This was to prove very much a growth industry, and before long major efforts were being put into this tactic. Air Defence of Great Britain (ADGB) issued the basic 'Rules of Engagement' in mid-June: 'Aircraft, excepting four-engined bombers, burning navigation lights over the continent are to be attacked on sight. An aircraft without navigation lights might be attacked if it was acting in a hostile manner – e.g. taking-off or landing at an enemy airfield, or if it had definitely been recognised as hostile by visual means.'

Harris had asked for 100 intruder/bomber support sorties on each night that a major raid was mounted. Such a requirement stretched resources to the limit, so it was decided to use a number of single-engine fighter squadrons for 'night rhubarbs' (Nos. 1, 3, 198 and 609 being chosen) during moonlight periods.

Of more immediate benefit to the bombers was the decision that 'Window' (strips of foil dropped from aircraft to give misleading radar returns) could now be used. With Bomber Command losses averaging 4–5 per cent in early 1943, and with suggestions that this could be reduced by a third if Window was used, Harris insisted on its deployment. The attack on Hamburg on the night of 24/25 July 1943 was to be the operational trial for Window, and proved an immediate success, throwing the German defences into confusion. This device was simplicity itself and yet proved to be one of the most significant developments introduced during this critical period. Only twelve bombers were lost (1.5 per cent). The introduction of Window not only saved aircraft from being shot down by fighters, but it also improved the flak-damage statistics. The level had been running at around 15 per cent, but post-Window this fell to 5 per cent, with consequent savings in repair time and higher availability of aircraft, as well as the morale-boosting effect of fewer aircraft being hit.

Night-fighter ace Wilhelm Johnen recalled the problems caused by this simple device:

> It was obvious that no one knew exactly where the enemy was or what his objective would be. An early recognition of the direction was essential so that the night fighters could be introduced as early as possible into the [bomber] stream. But the radio reports kept contradicting themselves. Now the enemy was over Amsterdam and then suddenly west of Brussels, and a moment later they were reported far out to sea in map square 25. The uncertainty of the ground stations was communicated to the crews . . . All the pilots were reporting pictures on their screens. I was no exception. At 15,000 ft my sparker announced the first enemy machine on his Li [Lichtenstein]. Facius proceeded to report three or four pictures on his screen. I hoped that I would have enough ammunition to deal with them all! Then Facius suddenly shouted: 'Tommy flying towards us at a great speed . . . 2,000 metres . . . 1,500 . . . 1,000 . . . 500.' This was soon repeated a score of times. Then the ground station suddenly called: 'Hamburg, Hamburg, a thousand enemy bombers over Hamburg. Calling all night fighters, calling all night fighters, full speed for Hamburg.'

The Hamburg raid was the subject of a report by the ORS:

> The very low casualties incurred in the first two attacks were largely due to the temporary disorganisation of the German fighter defences by a new counter-measure which precluded the vectoring of controlled night fighters. The final attack was ruined by unexpected deterioration of weather conditions over the target. Eighty-seven aircraft is a high price in itself, but in comparison with the loss sustained by Germany in the almost complete annihilation of her second city, it can only be regarded as minute. The 'Hafen' with its imposing array of shipbuilding yards, docks, warehouses and administrative buildings was the basis of Hamburg's contribution to German economic life. All parts of the city and dock were shattered – all four main shipbuilding yards were hit, five floating docks were sunk or badly damaged, 150 industrial plants were destroyed or badly damaged, plus massive distortion of communications and power.

Albert Speer:

> Our Western enemies launched five major attacks on a single big city, Hamburg, within a week, from July 25 to August 2. Rash as this operation was, it had catastrophic consequences for us. The first attacks put the water supply pipes out of action, so that in the subsequent bombings the fire department had no way of fighting the fires. Huge conflagrations created cyclone-like firestorms; the asphalt of the streets began to blaze; people were suffocated in their cellars or burned to death in the streets. The devastation of this series of air raids could be compared only with the effects of a major earthquake. Hamburg had suffered the fate Göring and Hitler had conceived for London in 1940. Hamburg had put the fear of God in me. At the meeting of Central Planning on 29 July I pointed out: 'If the air raids continue on the present scale, within three months we shall be relieved of a number of questions we are at present discussing. We shall simply be coasting downhill, smoothly and relatively swiftly. We might just as well hold the final meeting of Central Planning, in that case.' Three days later I informed Hitler that armaments production was collapsing and threw in the further warning that a series of attacks of this sort, extended to six more major cities, would bring Germany's armaments production to a total halt. 'You'll straighten all that out again,' he merely said. The next day I informed Milch's colleagues of similar fears (Conference with chief

of Air Force Procurement, 3 August 1943): 'We are approaching the point of total collapse . . . in our supply industry. Soon we will have airplanes, tanks, or trucks lacking certain key parts.'

Harris and his men would have had a boost to their morale if they had seen this assessment.

The RAF had brought in a new tactic and had concentrated its efforts on a single target, and the bomber theorists had always said it would come down to weight of attack (assuming you hit what you aimed at). Hamburg confirmed this, and yet with no follow-up attacks, the city recovered. The resilience of the German population was proving a match for Bomber Command. As the tactical advantage switched to Bomber Command, the Luftwaffe also made changes. The organisation of the night defence system was reviewed, and Kammhuber was replaced as General der Nachtjagd by Generalmajor Josef Schmid. It was considered that both Kammhuber and his 'line of defensive boxes' lacked the flexibility to deal with the ever-changing and growing bomber threat.

On the night of 17/18 August Bomber Command sent 596 bombers on Operation Hydra, the attack on the German research installation at Peenemünde. It was a moonlit night, but the plan included all the spoofing, deception and decoy tactics that the Command had been developing in recent months, including the use of a Master Bomber, the role being performed by Gp Capt John Searby of 83 Squadron. The first two waves of bombers benefited from the plan, suffering only 11 losses, but the final wave of 166 aircraft was caught by the night fighters that were racing to the area, and lost 29 aircraft. It is estimated that diversionary missions caused some 200 night fighters to move towards the wrong target, including a number that fell into what has been called a Serrate (another electronic aid) trap set up in the Friedland area by Beaufighters. Total German night-fighter losses amounted to 12 aircraft, 9 having been shot down by bombers or fighters. However, the most significant event was the probable first operational use by the Luftwaffe of a new weapon, '*Schräge Musik*' (meaning oblique or jazz music) upward-firing guns. Most pilots using *Schräge Musik* preferred to fire at the inner part of the target's wings in the hope of destroying fuel tanks and starting fires that would destroy the bomber. Unless the first burst was badly aimed there was little hope of escape for the bomber. As the RAF bombers had no underside guns, there was little defence once a fighter had sneaked into a firing position.

At a conference in late August, Field Marshal Milch explained the problems, stressing that the day and night air attacks against German armament production had to be stopped or the war would be lost:

Everything must be staked on the 110. Only the 110 in sufficient numbers can give us the necessary relief at night . . Germany itself is the front line and the mass of fighters must go for home defence. You can set up five times as many AA batteries; it will make no difference to the figure of 1–2 per cent [kills]. But if we put twice as many fighters in the air, the number of successes will be at least twice as high. If we put four times as many fighters, the number of successes will be four times as high. [Such] success rates would make the enemy stop his bombing day and night.

Other senior commanders, such as Jeschonnek, did not see a problem: 'Every four-engined bomber the Western Allies build makes me happy, for we will bring them down just as we brought down the two-engined ones, and the destruction of a four-engined bomber constitutes a much greater loss to the enemy.' Many Allied leaders would have agreed.

It now became a test of strength; could the bombers be destroyed in high enough numbers to stop the offensive? Certainly, business as usual for Bomber Command was becoming harder and harder; the rising toll of casualties was having a serious effect on the front-line strength and experience level of the Command – Bennett for one was complaining that the experience level of the crews being sent to the PFF had dropped in recent months. The adaptability of the German military throughout the later years of the war deserves much praise. No sooner did the RAF come up with a new tactic to swamp or confuse the defenders than they devised a counter, or at least a method by which they could still operate effectively. With streams of British bombers heading for a single point of the Reich, they realised that much could be achieved if the ground control broadcast a running commentary of where the enemy were and where they were going. It was then up to the fighters to make contacts, by radar or visual means. Typical of such commentaries was that for the night of 23/24 August:

2133	Bombers approaching Amsterdam
2155	Bombers flying east; orbit searchlight beacons
2217	Bombers approaching Bremen
2238	Berlin is possible target
2304	All fighters proceed to Berlin
2332	Bombers over Berlin

In this way the controller could keep his options open, not committing his forces too early and ensuring that he had the maximum forces to counter the main attack. The fighters could move from beacon to beacon, keeping pace with the stream until the time to attack. As soon as a fighter found the bomber stream, often with the aid of the commentary from 'observer aircraft' that, having found the stream, joined it and passed position updates, it was down to individual combat techniques. It was also common for fighters to drop flares or markers around the stream to attract the attention of their colleagues.

The see-saw nature of the night battle continued with the Luftwaffe introducing new equipment such as Naxos and Flensburg. The most significant of these was the FuG 350 Naxos Z, designed to pick up the transmissions from the bomber's H2S radar. As H2S was still in short supply, most sets were fitted to the Pathfinder aircraft, prime targets for the fighters. Flensburg was designed to home in on Monica, and so a device designed to protect the bomber against the fighter now became lethal. October 1943 also saw the Luftwaffe introduce a new AI radar, the SN2, which at first was immune to the RAF's jammers. The maximum range was just over 3 miles at approximately 18,000 ft, but the minimum range was as much as 1,000 ft. The latter proved problematical, as crews could lose their targets in the critical final stages.

The continuing high attrition rate of night fighters was causing its own problems, as the following memo to the Personnel Office of the Air Ministry, dated 17 October, illustrates:

> In recent nights, heavy casualties have occurred among the commanders of *Gruppen* and *Staffeln*. If these losses continue, suitable *Gruppe* commanders would not be able to be found from the ranks of the night-fighter formations. It is requested that about ten commanders of bomber units with operational and night-flying experience be transferred immediately.

A post-war RAF report using Luftwaffe data stated:

> During the period 1 August 1943 to 1 February 1944, General Schmid estimated that losses, direct and indirect, of men and material in the single-engine night-fighter units amounted to 45 per cent, the equivalent of at least two full-strength day-fighter *Geschwadern*, at a time when every day fighter counted.

The unit formed by Hajo Herrmann had been praised for its earlier success, but this appeared to be more propaganda than reality. Herrmann himself, according to the report,

> . . . conducted his operations without the slightest regard for losses. Weather conditions and aircraft endurance were scarcely taken into consideration at all, 'if fuel runs out and there is no possibility of

landing, bale out', was the watchword, and soon the majority of
pilots had more parachute jumps on their records than victories.

(ADIK Report 416/1945, 'History of German Night Fighting')

Throughout 1943 the RAF had also been introducing new RCM devices
aimed at reducing the effectiveness of the German night defence. Among
those entering service during 1943 were 'Ground Grocer' (April) to jam
AI, and three systems designed to jam or confuse R/T control frequencies:
'Ground Cigar' (July), 'Airborne Cigar' (ABC, October) and 'Corona'
(October).

The last of these went into use on 22/23 October; Bomber Command's
major attack that night was against Kassel, and as soon as the German night
fighters were airborne, they started receiving conflicting R/T instructions,
thanks to German-speaking operators at the ground station in England.
According to the war diary of I Jagdkorps: 'Thus was the first enemy use of
spoof R/T orders to our night fighters, but they were easily identified because
of pronunciation.' Radio counter-measures within Bomber Command were
reorganised on 23 November with the creation of No. 100 (Special Duties)
Group, under the command of AVM Addison, whose duties were to:

- Give direct support to night bombing or other operations by
  attacks on enemy night-fighter aircraft in the air or by attacks on
  ground installations.
- Employ airborne and ground RCM equipment to deceive or jam
  enemy radio navigation aids, enemy radar systems and certain
  wireless signals.
- Examine all intelligence on the offensive and defensive radar,
  radio and signalling systems of the enemy, with a view to future
  action within the scope of the above.
- Provide immediate information, additional to normal
  intelligence, as to the movements and employment of enemy
  fighter aircraft to enable the tactics of the bomber force to be
  modified to meet any changes.

Flying Officer M. Kelsey and Pilot Officer E. Smith of No. 141 Squadron
were airborne in Beaufighter VIV8744 on one offensive patrol in late
December. Their combat report is typical of such missions; they had made
a number of Serrate contacts and then:

On the way back to the Düren area, a Serrate contact was obtained
50 starboard and 5 below and 10 miles to the north. A/C turned at
300 ASI towards E/A who was flying south very fast, and decreased
height gently to get below the E/A. When 5 miles away E/A turned due

east, turned with it to reduce the distance and shortly afterwards AI contact was obtained at 14,000 ft range. When immediately behind and slightly below, visual was obtained on E/A which was a Ju 88 burning green and white resins. Pilot was of the impression that the E/A was drawing away so opened fire at 1,000 ft range, with cannon and MG, causing E/A to slow down. Pilot continued his burst for 7 seconds closing to 300 ft. Strikes were seen all over E/A who turned steeply to port and dived straight down with flames streaming from both engines and the fuselage, to explode on the ground where a glow could be seen through the clouds.

However, the 'teeth' for the offensive task were provided by Mosquito squadrons transferred from other groups, the first being No. 141 Squadron, which re-equipped and moved to West Raynham in early December. By mid-December the group had four such squadrons plus two special flights.

Fighter Command was also still very active in supporting the night offensive and flew 3,278 night offensive sorties in 1943, losing 60 aircraft and making claims for 72 enemy destroyed, although it must be remembered that for many sorties destruction of enemy aircraft was not the primary aim. The busiest, and most successful, month was August with 551 sorties claiming 12 aircraft. This month included the first Mahmoud sortie (22/23 August); this type of mission was defined as: 'operations by night fighters against enemy night fighters outside the radius of Bomber Command operations or on nights when Bomber Command was not operating'. By the end of the year 119 Mahmoud sorties had been flown.

Battle of Berlin

Harris had already decided that his next major campaign would be against the 'Big City' and the Battle of Berlin duly opened on the night of 23/24 August when 727 bombers, almost half of which were Lancasters, took part in a Master Bomber attack. The results were disappointing with scattered bombing, the markers having fallen on the southern part of the city. The defenders took a heavy toll with 56 aircraft (7.9 per cent loss rate) being lost, the highest number in a single raid so far; it was a particularly bad night for the Stirlings with 16 of the 124 aircraft involved being lost.

The summer 1943 Berlin offensive was a failure from the RAF point of view: the loss rate was far in excess of the sustainable 4 per cent. Based on pure statistics like this, the defenders appeared to be winning the battle in the night skies over Germany. What the British did not know was that the defenders were having their own problems, not least of which was the high accident rate among the night-fighter units, all of which combined to reduce the availability of aircraft and crews.

In October 1943 Bomber Command ORS issued a series of notes on tactics, dealing with the basic organisation and operation of the German defensive system. In part, these stated:

The German Air Force uses GCI. This starts when coastal Freyas of the Aircraft Reporting Service warn Sector HQs of approaching aircraft. Fighters get airborne to orbit forward beacons of the box to which they are allocated, with maybe a reserve fighter at an inner beacon. The GCI follows the fighter on a Giant Würzburg, when a raider enters the box it is tracked by a second Giant Würzburg and the fighter homed by R/T. The fighter takes over when it has visual or AI contact with the enemy. Post-combat the night fighter returns to orbit the beacon . . . The aim of the night bomber is to gain immunity from attack through concealment. Make the GCI's task harder by weaving, including use of height – this is best at short range, say 1–2 miles, just before AI contact – then put in an orbit to throw off the fighter. However, this will only be possible when the radio-location aids are available. Until then it is best to go straight and level, using the concentration corridors.

Over the target fly straight and level unless picked up by search-lights, keep above 15,000 ft to avoid the worst of the flak. Best to get out of gun-defended zones as soon as possible. It cannot be too strongly emphasised that when massed searchlights fasten on to an aircraft, which happens swiftly, and is followed almost immediately by the noise and buffet of continuous near shell bursts, no human being can consider calmly the best way to turn. Escaping the searchlight cone is more a matter of mental discipline than tactics.

Air combat. The endeavour of the bomber is to finish the combat without being seriously damaged, and this can only be achieved by manoeuvring so that the fighter's fire goes wide and making up for the lighter armament of the turret by firing accurately at the fighter. During the corkscrew the pilot should call the next manoeuvre so that the gunners can allow for it . . . 'going down, port' . . . 'going up, starboard' . . . the striking power of a .303 is adequate to damage the frontal portion of a night fighter, which has a large frontal area scarcely protected by armour.

The Battle of Berlin took place in a number of phases and lasted to February 1944, by which time the Command had mounted 9,099 sorties against the 'Big City', dropping 29,804 tons of bombs; overall losses were 501 aircraft. The second attack of the introductory phase took place on the last night of August 1943 and once again the bombers failed to do much damage and suffered high casualties with the loss of 47 of the 622 aircraft, with the Stirlings once more having the highest percentage losses (17 of 106 aircraft).

The initial raid in the first real phase of the Battle of Berlin took place on 18/19 November when 440 Lancasters attacked Hitler's capital, with a second force attacking Ludwigshafen to split the night-fighter response. A combination of poor weather and poor PFF marking led to a scattered raid, although this time losses were light. Four nights later the weather forecast was near perfect and the Command mounted a maximum effort against Berlin, 765 aircraft taking part. The outbound route was near direct, which meant an increased bomb load. However, the weather was worse than forecast but this was an advantage as it proved more of a problem for the defenders than the attackers and marking was accurate with Berlin being hit hard. The Stirlings suffered a high loss rate again (10 per cent) and Harris reluctantly ordered their withdrawal from this target. Indeed, this was very much a Lancaster Battle as the Halifaxes too had to be withdrawn as their loss rates had increased, although they later returned.

Speer:

> Instead of paralysing vital segments of industry, the Royal Air Force began an air offensive against Berlin. I was having a conference in my private office on 22 November 1943, when the air-raid alarm sounded. It was about 7:30 p.m. A large fleet of bombers was reported heading toward Berlin. When the bombers reached Potsdam, I called off the meeting to drive to a nearby flak tower, intending to watch the attack from its platform, as was my wont. But I scarcely reached the top of the tower when I had to take shelter inside it; in spite of the tower's stout concrete walls, heavy hits nearby were shaking it. Injured anti-aircraft gunners crowded down the stairs behind me; the air pressure from the exploding bombs had hurled them into the walls. When the rain of bombs ceased, I ventured out on the platform again. My nearby Ministry was one gigantic conflagration. On 26 November 1943, four days after the destruction of my Ministry, another major air raid on Berlin started huge fires in our most important tank factory, Allkett.

With fog forecast for the areas in which German night fighter airfields were concentrated Harris ordered another attack on Berlin on 16/17 December. For 97 Squadron it was a particularly bad night with seven aircraft lost. Arthur Tindall was a WOP/AG on the raid:

I can still recall the Met Officer saying that the weather would close in by the early hours of the following morning and he anticipated the raid being cancelled. In the event it wasn't, with disastrous results. Our squadron lost seven aircraft that night. We were airborne for 7 hours 45 minutes compared with usual Berlin raids of 6–6½ hours. The following morning our ground crew said we had less than 50 gallons of petrol. In other words, we were very lucky to have made it.

The final raid in December 1943 was a maximum effort with the Halifax units joining in to send 712 bombers and with a longer outbound route, combined with poor weather, the German controllers failed to bring many fighters into contact with the bomber stream and only twenty bombers were lost. It was a relief to the planners that the loss rate had dropped but they could take little comfort from the course of the Battle of Berlin to date.

It was more of the same throughout January. When the briefing curtains were drawn back on 20 January crews groaned as they saw the tape leading once more to Berlin, although the direct route had been changed in favour of a more indirect approach. This was another maximum effort with 769 bombers, 264 of which were Halifaxes, but it followed the same pattern as previous raids with fighters getting in amongst the bombers and with a cloud-covered Berlin proving hard to hit. It was not a promising return for the Halifax, with 22 of the 264 aircraft being lost. It was 102 Squadron's 'turn' to suffer and the Pocklington-based unit lost 5 of its 16 Halifaxes over enemy territory plus another two that crashed in England (it lost a further 4 aircraft the following night).

There were only two more attacks on the city during the Battle of Berlin. The first of these came after a respite due to the phase of the moon making bomber operations unwise; on 15/16 February nearly 900 bombers, the largest force yet to attack Berlin, left England for the northern route. With a near direct route home planned, bomb loads were high and the total dropped this night was a record 2,642 tons. The German fighters were out in force and combats began over southern Denmark. Most of the 43 bombers that failed to return fell to fighters. Despite cloud cover the city was hit hard and in general this was a successful raid. The raid of 24/25 March was a maximum effort with 811 bombers taking part; 72 (8.9 per cent) of these aircraft failed to return – the highest single loss to date. It is estimated that 50 of the losses were caused by flak.

The Battle of Berlin was over; Harris's prediction of 500 bomber losses was correct – and that was only RAF losses – but his hope that Berlin would be destroyed from end to end was not fulfilled, although almost 30,000 tons of bombs had been dropped. Nevertheless, the effect on the extensive industrial, economic and administrative activities of the Reich capital was significant both in direct (destruction) and indirect terms (evacuation or personnel, resources spent on repairs, and so on).

Late 1943 Allied discussions, notably at the Quebec Conference, focused on the needs of the invasion of north-west Europe, and how German land and air strength could be reduced, through destruction of assets or the diversion of assets to other areas. One aspect of the planned build-up of Allied strategic bombers in Italy was an intention to attack the German aircraft industry in areas that could be more easily reached by Italy-based bombers; indeed, it was thought that 65 per cent of fighter production was in such areas and if this was threatened it was estimated that one-third of day- and night-fighter assets would be re-deployed to meet the threat. This was not the only area of concern about dispersion of assets for the Germans; the likely withdrawal of Italy from the Axis would entail risks not only in Italy but also the Balkans, along with Greece and strategic locations such as Crete, which were important in the overall Mediterranean theatre. Allied intelligence sources had already reported a doubling of enemy air strength in Greece and Crete, and the creation of a new Luftwaffe command for south-east Europe.

The situation at the turn of the year was such that many in Bomber Command were expressing concern at the continued high loss rates, attributed primarily to the Luftwaffe night-fighter force, although flak was by no means an insignificant element. By January 1944 the total of Luftwaffe flak units covering Germany and the Western Front had increased to 7,941 heavy guns and 12,684 light/medium guns (along with 6,880 searchlights). This total did not include Army and Navy flak units. Conversely, the night-fighter force had shrunk, albeit marginally, with a strength of just under 600 aircraft and a daily availability of about 400. Despite the German successes, the picture for the defenders was thus by no means simple. Losses were running at around 3 per cent, deliveries of equipment were slow, serviceability was poor, and the electronic war was proving increasingly difficult and, furthermore, Bomber Command was continuing to destroy German cities. The contribution made by the flak arm was considered vital, and frequent co-ordination meetings were held; 'The prime objective must always be to bring that arm into action which would prove most effective at any given time.'

At a divisional commanders' conference on 25 January 1944, Schmid stated that:

> The number of aircraft being shot down by day and night is still
> too low and better results should be possible, given full exploitation

of all resources. *Zahme Sau* had proved itself to be the best night-fighter operational technique and such aircraft should be fed into the enemy stream carefully and at an early stage.

The following day an order was issued to disband one *Staffel* within each night-fighter *Gruppe*. This was followed by a series of conferences at the highest levels of the Luftwaffe command, culminating in a major reorganisation of the Reich air defences into three areas of responsibility:

1. Jagddivision   Hanover–Magdeburg
2. Jagddivision   Oldenburg–Bremen–Rothenburg
3. Jagddivision   German–Dutch frontier

Experienced crews were being lost, new crews were given inadequate training, and tired crews were not allowed enough rest; the strain on the squadrons was becoming extreme. Considering the difficulties, they were achieving major successes: it was not beyond reason that, given adequate resources, they could drive Bomber Command from the night skies. Indeed, the year started well for the Luftwaffe. The Battle of Berlin had been costly for the RAF and the Nuremberg raid of 30/31 March 1944 was nothing short of a disaster for the attackers. That night, 795 bombers (including 572 Lancasters) took off for the primary target, while other, much smaller formations prepared to attack decoy targets or undertake intruder missions. As this large raid began to build over England, the German reporting system was already passing the first of its situation reports, and the night-fighter units were brought to maximum alert. The bomber stream formed up and moved across the Channel, and the first of the night fighters were waiting as they approached the Ruhr.

Les Bartlett was bomb aimer in a No. 50 Squadron Lancaster:

> As we drew level with the south of the Ruhr valley, things began to happen. Enemy night fighters were all around us and, in no time at all, combats were taking place and aircraft were going down in flames on all sides. So serious was the situation that I remember looking at the other poor blighters and thinking to myself that it must be our turn next, just a question of time. A Lancaster appeared on our port beam converging, so we dropped 100 ft or so to let him cross. He was only about 200 yards or so on our starboard beam when a string of cannon shells hit him and down, he went.

The night-fighter force flew 246 sorties and claimed 101 RAF bombers destroyed, plus a further 6 probables, for the loss of 5 of its own aircraft. Royal Air Force records show losses of 95 aircraft.

The German controllers had not been fooled by any of the deception techniques and had ordered aircraft to orbit beacons Ida (Aachen), and Otto (Frankfurt), ready to be fed towards the stream. It was a clear night with almost perfect conditions for the defenders. The bombers made no effort to hide their approach and flew, unknowingly, straight towards the waiting fighters.

The German controllers continued to give an accurate commentary on the stream's course and height, but as soon as the first combats took place this was almost superfluous, as the night sky was lit by burning aircraft and the ground track was marked by burning wrecks.

Taking off from Mainz-Finthen at 2345, Hauptmann Martin Becker of 1./NJG 6 made contact with the stream at about 0010. Ten minutes later he began a devastating attack on the Halifax bombers he was tracking, shooting down six within the space of thirty minutes. He returned to base determined to rejoin the fight, and on his second sortie of the night shot down a seventh victim.

He was not the only one to make multiple claims. Hauptmann Martin Drewes claimed three and Lt Schulte four. All had used *Schräge Musik* guns to deadly effect.

From March 1944 onwards a significant amount of Bomber Command's effort was assigned to the pre-invasion bombing plan. According to the Bomber Command ORS of 3 May 1944:

> A substantial proportion of the bomber force is now equipped with either Monica III or Fishpond. A survey of the operational record has shown that both had some success in reducing losses and the number of attacks by night fighters. In the period October 1943 to February 1944 this is estimated as a 15 per cent reduction.

Many Bomber Command crews would not have agreed, as they considered the equipment a liability. Later in the year it would be withdrawn from operational use (except by No. 100 Group), proof having been obtained that the German night fighters were equipped to home in on its signals. In mid-May the German night-fighter organisation was dealt a blow by Göring, who, having become concerned at the wastage rates among fighter pilots, stated:

> To exercise economy in unit commanders, three *Gruppen* of single-engine night fighters are to be dissolved and both aircraft and pilots transferred to the remaining six single-engine night-fighter *Gruppen*. At the same time two *Geschwadern* of single-engine night fighters are to be dissolved.

Although this had no effect on the more important twin-engine night-fighter units, who were by far the deadliest as far as Bomber Command was concerned, it did reduce the overall effectiveness of the system by reducing the defences in the target area. What was to have greater effect from this point onwards was the increased employment of night fighters in the day-fighter role, in an unsuccessful attempt to inflict crippling losses on the American bomber formations.

A German staff memo dated 2 July 1944 stated:

> The Führer, wishing to protect the homeland and secure the front, issued the order that fighters are to have absolute top priority and heavy combat aircraft are to be cancelled. The stock of fighters, destroyers and night fighters is to be increased to 10,000. This number is to include 5,000 new machines including 500 night fighters.

By midsummer the night-fighter force comprised some 15 per cent of total Luftwaffe front-line strength. Overall fighter strength was roughly equally split between day- and night-fighter elements, although the former did not suffer the same serviceability problems. The night skies were an arena for a deadly game of cat and mouse. If the night fighters managed to find the bomber stream, carnage would result and burning bombers would litter the countryside. If, on the other hand, the RAF could send the defenders to the wrong target or cause major disruption to their airfields and control facilities, then losses could be kept down.

By early 1944 the German defenders had seen most of Bomber Command's tactics. Experienced controllers were able to work through the electronic counter-measures and marshal their resources until the real target for the main force had become clear. Such was the case on the night of 18/19 July, when Bomber Command flew 927 sorties to a variety of targets. On most raids the losses were low, but this was not the case for the attacks against the marshalling yards at Aulnoye and Revigny. The total force employed against these two targets was 253 Lancasters and ten Mosquitoes, the intention being to destroy rail communications to the Normandy area as part of the interdiction campaign supporting the invasion. The Aulnoye raid went reasonably well, only two Lancasters being lost. However, the No. 5 Group attack against Revigny was caught by night fighters and lost twenty-four aircraft, almost 22 per cent of the Lancaster force involved. No. 619 Squadron from Dunholme Lodge, Lincolnshire, had a particularly bad night, losing five of its thirteen aircraft.

The concerted attacks on the German communications network were part of the Transport Plan, which was one of the two key strategic target sets, along with oil, that the planners had determined to be of specific value. Harris tended to interpret this as part of his regular attacks on cities, although with the pre-invasion bombing strategy, this became more focused and intense with specific targets, like the rail network, leading to the Normandy area.

> An appreciation in general terms, prepared by the Reichsverkehrs-ministerium [Transport Ministry] on 4 December 1944, remarked that whereas prior to the beginning of that year rail installations has suffered damage only adventitiously as a result of 'terror' attacks upon the large cities and towns, the Allies appeared from March 1944 onwards to have chosen German communications as their principal air objective with results disastrous to that system. In retrospect the Germans realised that the opening 'gambits' were part of a carefully conceived plan which was still to unfold itself.
>
> (ADIK Report 400/1945 'Effects of Allied Air Attacks on the German Transport and Communications System June 1944 to March 1945')

The overall Transport Plan is covered, in brief, in the chapter on the daylight bomber offensive; although Bomber Command's involvement was significant, daylight bombing played a greater role in this campaign.

In a comprehensive document dated 5 November 1944, 8th Abteilung summarised the 'problems of German air defence'. Sections of this document addressed the night fighter question:

> As regards night fighters, the position is rather more favourable at present. Substantial reinforcements have been received from disbanded bomber and transport units, and striking power has, therefore, greatly increased. Our total strength of approximately 1,800 aircraft enables about 200 fighters to take the air during each enemy attack. Night-fighter crews have been trained on an almost peace-time scale, and successes have been considerable. A plan must be devised for the concentration of our forces in western Germany. In this connection, the following suggestion may be borne in mind. Since the present fuel shortage only permits of the employment of night fighters for a few days each month, our forces should carry out operations at full strength on certain days and times as based on previous experience. Although a certain percentage of such sorties will be fruitless, it can be assumed that 50 per cent will succeed in contacting the enemy. This is the only way in which immediate protection can be given to the heavily bombed areas of western Germany.

In a port-war debrief General Schmid suggested that:

> Neglect of night-fighter training and the poor quality of the pilots produced was an important contributory factor in the rapid dwindling of German striking power from the latter part of 1944 onwards. Kammhuber's night-fighting organisation provided for two training units, NJG 100 and NJG 101, which were fundamentally well organised but lacked the necessary supervision to make them a success. Main stress was laid on the flying of single-engined fighters and training for *Himmelbett* [Kammhuber box] operations, whilst long distance flying, bad-weather landings and navigation were almost completely neglected. Moreover, since training instructors consisted in the main of rejects from the operational units, replacements were seldom trained up to the standard required for front-line operations and training often had to be completed at the operational units.   (AIDK report)

This failure to put in place an effective training organisation was a major oversight by the Luftwaffe and contributed to its ultimate failure; Bomber Command loss rates had been high, how much higher might they have been if more night-fighter crews had been effective? The RAF, on the other hand, had early recognised the importance of the training machine and had continued to develop it in terms of content, and assigned experienced personnel as instructors so that real operational lessons could be passed on. It was by no means perfect, but the fact that the value of this was recognised and acted on by the RAF was a key factor in its ultimate victory.

One of the major German problems later in 1944 was the reduction in effectiveness of the Air Reporting Service, in large part due to the loss of territory in northern Europe – in other words, the loss of forward radar coverage that had previously provided accurate information enabling the night fighters to begin their attacks even before the bombers had crossed the coast. While the numbers of fighters continued to increase, all other aspects were in decline. Fuel shortages limited crew training and even forced operational restrictions on the front-line units, and on many nights Bomber Command went virtually unhindered because certain night-fighter units were not permitted to fly. Furthermore, as far as the situation in the west was concerned, the transfer of units to the Eastern Front to counter Russian bombing attacks depleted operational strength yet more. In view of these and other factors, it is remarkable that the night-fighter force remained as effective as it did.

Allen Clifford recalled an attack on Homberg on 8 November 1944:

If ever there was a low point in anybody's life this was it, to be woken at 0400 hours knowing that you were going to war. I crawled out of a warm bed into a frozen Nissen hut at Methwold, gathered up towel and soap and shivered miserably in the wintry gap between the hut and the ablutions blocks to splash water over my face – but no time to shave. The breakfast of bacon and egg, and a mug of hot sweet tea preceded briefing. The red tape, which slithered disconcertingly across the map like a long tail of blood, led from Norfolk to a suburb of the huge German inland river port and industrial city of Duisburg. 'It's bloody Homberg again' we all thought.

This 8 November attack consisted of 136 Lancasters from No. 3 Group; only one aircraft was lost, a Lancaster of 218 Squadron.

The offensive against rail and oil continued into early 1945. Bomber Command was now ranging across Germany attacking a variety of targets, some in support of land operations as Allied forces closed in from west and east, and others in a more strategic sense. Although the bombers continued to suffer from both fighters, more rarely, and flak, loss rates had continued to decrease. The Command's final operational bombing mission took place on 2/3 May after a break without operations of almost a week. Mosquitoes attacked in the Kiel area; only one Mosquito, from 169 Squadron, was lost. The only heavies airborne were eighty-nine aircraft from No. 100 Group flying RCM support and tragically two of these were lost, probably in a mid-air collision. These three aircraft, from which only three of the Halifax crewmen survived, were the last operational losses suffered by Bomber Command. Thus ended nearly six years of war for Bomber Command.

The Command had been hammered at times, but it had never given up. The determination of its crews, supported by the efforts of the groundcrew and support personnel had forged an ineffective weapon into a highly destructive and, when it chose to be, accurate weapon. They had never been defeated by the Luftwaffe and in the end they emerged victorious.

Chapter 6

Daylight Offensive:
Destroying the Luftwaffe

Histories of the daylight bombing offensive usually focus on the USAAF's contribution, which in scale and effect is, of course, quite reasonable as they were the major proponents of the offensive from late 1942 to the end of the war. Bomber Command had been engaged in daylight operations from 1939 onwards, especially with the work of No. 2 Group. The Luftwaffe failed to make No. 2 Group or Bomber Command cease daylight operations, despite causing heavy losses; but the bombers failed in that their contribution, valid as it was and very hard won, had no major strategic outcome.

It could be argued that the Luftwaffe had won the daylight battle against the RAF's bomber offensive in 1939 and 1940, although the scale had been so small and the RAF's efforts based on false premises, that the Luftwaffe took away the wrong lessons. They also failed to learn the lesson that the RAF taught them in the Battle of Britain, that to defend successfully against concentrated daylight bomber operations a strong single-seat fighter force supported by radar and a control system was needed. The move of Bomber Command to a night war, covered in the previous chapter, meant that there was no strategic day bombing until the arrival of the Americans. And, as we shall see, fundamental flaws in the Luftwaffe command and equipment were already in place.

On 17 April 1942 the RAF flew a daring daylight raid right across Germany, when Lancasters of 44 and 97 squadrons attacked the MAN diesel works at Augsburg, as part of the anti-submarine strategy of attacking sources of supply, in this case U-boat engines. It was a low-level attack, it reached and bombed its target, but with some loss, including four Lancasters shot down by fighters near Paris. They were unlucky, for once a bomber was beyond the coastal defence zones there was no day-fighter defence in Germany. On 16 May Göring noted this, but did nothing about it, in part because of the conflicting priorities with the Germans now fighting on multiple fronts (Russia, Middle East, the skies over Europe, the Atlantic) and partly because the Luftwaffe view was that it was a one-off, too costly and unlikely to be repeated. Within a year that situation had changed, but the ability of the Luftwaffe to correct the fundamental failings was limited.

The Americans Arrive

From late 1942 the Allied offensive over Europe was an Anglo-American one; in terms of this study of 'how the RAF beat the Luftwaffe' this was the transition point to 'how Allied air power destroyed the Luftwaffe'. In a post-war interrogation, Göring spoke to General Spaatz, who asked him when did he realise that the Luftwaffe was losing control of the air, to which Göring replied: 'When the American long-range fighters were able to escort the bombers as far as Hanover, and it was not long until they got to Berlin. We then knew we must develop the jet planes. Our plan for the early development of the jet was unsuccessful only because of your bombing attacks.'

Having said that the Luftwaffe failed to learn the lesson of the need for a day-fighter defence, they were lucky in that the Americans had also failed to learn lessons from the RAF. At first the American bomber leaders still believed that the unescorted bomber would always get through, and that even if fighters did appear they would be countered by the concentrated fire of the bombers' guns from their formations. The 'Flying Fortress' would simply destroy the fighters and then drop its bombs in a 'pickle barrel'. Both contentions were way off, and the Eighth Air Force ignored the lessons of the RAF day raids and the Luftwaffe in the Battle of Britain.

General H. H. Arnold, head of the USAAF throughout the war:

> Some fighters may be superior to the bomber and capable of shooting it down, but it is none the less a fact that the bomber is the essential nucleus of an Air Force. The fighter is a defensive type of aircraft strategically, but the bomber is distinctively offensive in character. Battles and wars are won by a vigorous offensive and seldom, if ever, by the defensive.

Of all the wartime operations undertaken by the USAAF in Europe, the bombing offensive against Germany was the most intensive. It was also the most expensive in terms of aircraft and aircrew losses. It was an offensive from two sides – the UK and Italy. It was also a Combined Bomber Offensive (CBO) with the RAF's Bomber Command. The CBO was primarily flown from 'aircraft carrier England'.

The Eighth Air Force's bombing campaign against Germany was opened by six medium bombers of the 15th Bombardment Squadron on 4 July 1942, using American-built aircraft (Bostons) borrowed from the RAF. It was a modest start for what would develop into the most powerful air fleet ever assembled. Whilst the Eighth Air Force was to be the major American offensive weapon against Germany, it was joined in the task by the Ninth,

Twelfth and Fifteenth Air Forces. It was planned that the Eighth would have 60 combat groups by April 1943, comprising 3,500 aircraft, a massive total for which airfields would have to be constructed, or transferred from RAF use. When the German leadership first realised that they would face an American bomber onslaught they were dismissive of American equipment, productive capacity and fighting quality – and were wrong on all counts. At a time when the Luftwaffe was continuing to debate the value of a four-engine bomber, the RAF and the USAAF were turning them out in increasing numbers.

Before America entered the war, Hans Jeschonnek, Luftwaffe Chief of Staff, had received reports from General Bötticher, the German military attaché in Washington, concerning bomber production. In May 1942, after Hitler had dismissed concerns, he wrote:

> Bötticher, we are lost. For years I have, on the basis of your reports, forwarded demands to Goring and Hitler, but for years my requests for the expansion of the Luftwaffe have not been answered. We no longer have the air defence I requested, and which is needed for our German soil. Conflicting demands have been made by Hitler. We now no longer have any time . . . to provide ourselves with the weapons to fight the dreadful threat which you have predicted and reported to us. Then we will be covered from the air with an enemy screen which will paralyse our power to resist. They will be able to play with us!

The main voices crying out in 1942 for such a defence force were Galland and Milch, and both were ignored. In summer 1942 the average monthly production of single-seat fighters was 300 (the annual total for 1942 ended up as 2,647 Bf 109s and 1,850 Fw 190s) but that was to feed all theatres, and in 1942 the major efforts were in Russia and the Middle East, with the remainder assigned to North-West Europe and the area of RAF operations. Whilst some were calling for increased fighter production, Jeschonnek had commented that he 'would not know what to do with 360 fighters a month', this being the figure that Milch had requested. However, within a short while he himself was pushing for 900 fighters a month!

During summer 1942 the first USAAF B-17 groups arrived in the UK, with the 97th BG taking up residence at Polebrook in June. Fighters were also part of the original plan for the Eighth's operational composition, and pending the arrival of suitable US types, the first units were equipped with Spitfires. First into action was the 31st FG, six of its Spitfires joining an RAF sweep over northern France. It was not the best of starts, as Lt Col Clark was shot down and taken prisoner.

The first scheduled mission for the 97th's B-17s was to be on 10 August, although this was promptly cancelled because of bad weather. A second mission a few days later was also cancelled and it was not until 17 August that the B-17s made their first foray into enemy territory, the target being the rail yards at Rouen-Sotteville. It was policy at this stage to attack targets in Occupied Europe that were within range of the escort fighters provided by the RAF. One group of six bombers acted as a decoy raid, not crossing the coast, whilst the actual bomber force of eleven B-17s succeeded in dropping about 50 per cent of its bombs within the target area. The bombers were subjected to moderate flak, two aircraft being very slightly damaged, but only one enemy fighter got anywhere near the bombers, with no result. It was a small but promising (and misleading) introduction for the Eighth's commanders. The warnings being given by senior RAF commanders that daylight operations were near suicidal had yet to register with the air commanders. The first lesson to be absorbed was that European weather was changeable and often very bad, unlike the conditions in training areas such as Florida, and this alone presented major problems for formation flying and bombing accuracy. Nevertheless, what the crews lacked in experience they made up for in enthusiasm.

Two more B-17 groups, the 301st BG and the 92nd BG, arrived in August. The 301st flew its first mission (along with the 97th, now flying B-17Fs) on 5 September 1942, the target being Rouen. All 37 bombers returned with no problems. An attack on the same target the next day cost the first two B-17 combat losses, one from the 97th and one from the 92nd, the latter unit flying its first operation. By early autumn, six more bomber groups were either on route to or destined for the Eighth Air Force. A milestone was reached on 9 October when the Eighth put up over 100 heavy bombers for the first time, the target being a steel works at Lille. Bombing was poor and three B-17s and one B-24 failed to return; the gunners, however, put in claims for 56 destroyed, 26 probable and 20 damaged! This very high claim rate by bomber gunners was to be a feature of most missions and it was hard for intelligence officers to derive true figures.

At the end of 1942 nothing seemed to have changed, the Americans had failed to make any real impact, and the defenders had been doing well enough. On the German side some saw the writing on the wall, and if they had known of the American plans to increase strength to thousands of bombers, they might have been more concerned. Another chance to create the conditions for victory, or at least to stave off defeat, had been missed. However, to put this in context means looking at the war situation for the Germans. They had not expected to be fighting on multiple fronts by late 1942; their economy, their military doctrine and their force mix, were not structured for the scenario in which they now found themselves. During 1942 the Luftwaffe had trained 1,666 fighter pilots, not that dissimilar to the number for the early part of the war, and yet with losses and with expansion of the fighter force this was inadequate, and training is a pipeline – if you get behind it is very hard to catch up. In October 1942 the number of fighter pilot schools had been increased from five to ten, but that itself meant a drain on qualified pilots (as instructors) and other resources. In 1942 some units had been complaining about the quality of the pilots they were receiving and had to provide additional training to make them fit for combat flying. By late 1942 the German pilot situation had already deteriorated. Whereas in the early part of the war the total number of training flying hours for a pilot was similar for the RAF and Luftwaffe (on average 200 and 250 respectively), by 1943 this had tilted the other way, with Luftwaffe hours falling to around 150.

1943: Building up Strength – and Taking Heavy Losses

The Allied planners had decided that with increasing numbers of USAAF aircraft becoming operational, a combined bomber offensive was possible, the essentials of which were hammered out at the January 1943 Casablanca Conference, as described above.

On 27 January 1943 the USAAF made its first trip to Germany; 64 bombers intending to go to Vegesack were forced by bad weather to head for the secondary target, the docks at Wilhelmshaven, and 58 aircraft made successful bombing runs. Only one B-17 was lost as both flak and fighter defences proved ineffective, although over 40 bombers were damaged. Whilst the Spitfires and P-38s did their best as fighter escort, their limitations in range and endurance meant that the bombers were often on their own. The USAAF's main effort remained over France, and there were increasing combats with fighters; on 16 February the target was St Nazaire and the Luftwaffe claimed 6 B-17s destroyed (a further 2 were lost in a mid-air collision) and 30 bombers damaged (28 B-17s and two B-24s), out of 65 bombers that took part. The bomber gunners claimed to have destroyed 20 enemy fighters and damaged a further 12, although as was often the case the actual figures were much lower; multiple gunners firing at the same fighter would make a claim that they believed was correct. The figures were similar against a German target on 26 February: 65 bombers attacked Wilhelmshaven, losing 7 and having others damaged, and claiming 21 enemy fighters.

The surprising aspect to these early 1943 operations is that neither side seemed to be picking up on the lessons. The lack of effective fighter escort to Germany was because of a lack of a suitable fighter, although the mindset was still one that did not believe such as fighter was needed. Escort for the shorter-range missions was provided by Spitfires, which should have been more than capable of dealing with the current Luftwaffe fighter types. The Luftwaffe was still not focused on developing the next generation of fighters, an error that was to cost it dearly in the coming two years, but it was also failing to appreciate the potential of the American daylight campaign: these 50 or 60 bombers would soon become 500 or 600. Whilst the Bf 110 had rightly lost favour as a day fighter when faced with single-seat fighters, here was an opportunity for it actually to fulfil its planned role of bomber destroyer, so why did the Luftwaffe not use more 110s as part of the Reich day defence? This would have been effective, until the advent of the American long-range fighters.

On 4 April 1943, VIII Bomber Command attacked the Renault factory in Paris, a precision attack by 85 bombers that was escorted by no fewer than 18 Spitfire squadrons. This was the extreme range for the Spitfires and the mission planning tried to ensure coverage to and from the target; nevertheless, four bombers were shot down by Fw 190s of JG 26 before the escort could save them, as they were poorly positioned to intercept, and the Germans knew the fuel limitations – just like the Battle of Britain in reverse, at some point the fighter escort had to give up and go home. There was also, as with all fighter pilots, the innate desire to be free to roam and engage, to keep height to dive on the enemy, and a whole range of other tactical norms that were simply no longer totally valid. The Luftwaffe had to become more adept at making up for limited numbers by playing on the tactical weakness of the enemy.

The Eighth Air Force was looking to its 'own' fighter, the P-47 to help resolve the situation. The P-47 Thunderbolt, the 'Jug', was certainly a well-armed (eight 0.5 in. guns) and sturdy beast, but it did not look like a fighter when compared with the likes of the elegant Spitfire, and many RAF pilots did not rate its chances. With its initial internal fuel load its range was actually not much better than a Spitfire's. What was to make the difference was the conviction of the 56th Fighter Group that the P-47 was the right aircraft in the right place. The P-47 units had been working-up in early 1943 and made their first contact with the Luftwaffe on 15 April when a fighter sweep was flown by fifty-seven aircraft from the 4th, 56th and 78th Fighter Groups to the Ostend–St Omer area. They met the Fw 190s of JG 1 and claimed three for the loss of three of their own; however, German records suggest that no fighters were lost but some were damaged. Göring held a conference the following day with Galland and pilots from JG 1. They agreed that when the P-47s appeared with the bombers, the Fw 190 was at a disadvantage at high level and that the Bf 109G was better at taking on the high-flying escorts, leaving the bombers to the 190s. The concept was to have a 'light fighter group' of 109s in each of the fighter *Gruppen*, stationed in the forward areas to engage and separate the fighters from the bombers. As the RAF had found in 1940, the concept was a good one, but the application was difficult as it depended on warning time, positioning, numbers and other factors.

On the other side, in trials against a captured Fw 190, the Thunderbolt did not perform well – its low-altitude performance being particularly poor – and new fighter tactics had to be developed to make best use of the aircraft. It was through the determination of commanders like Hubert Zemke that the aircraft became effective – aggressive tactics and good use of the aircraft's assets made his 56th FG one of the most effective fighter units in the European theatre. After several sweep operations to let pilots gain experience, the first P-47 escort mission was flown on 4 May with 117 Thunderbolts from three groups escorting 79 bombers to Antwerp.

Whilst the P-47 was making some small impact, it was the next fighter that was to make the main difference, the P-51 Mustang. In early 1943 the AFDU tested the Spitfire IX against the Mustang X, an interesting comparison with what was to become the leading American fighter in Europe. Both aircraft were fitted with Merlin 60 series engines and the results were somewhat mixed with each aircraft having some performance advantages over the other.

The Manoeuvrability section stated:

> The aircraft were compared at varying heights for their powers of manoeuvrability and it was found throughout that the Mustang, as was expected, did not have so good a turning circle as the Spitfire. By the time they were at 30,000 feet the Mustang's controls were found to be rather mushy, while the Spitfire's were still very crisp and even in turns during which 15 degrees of flap were used on the Mustang, the Spitfire had no difficulty in out-turning it. In rate of roll, however, it found that while the Spitfire is superior in rolling quickly from one turn to another at speeds up to 300 mph, there is very little to choose between the two at 350 mph IAS and at 400 mph the Mustang is definitely superior, its controls remaining far lighter at high speeds than those of the Spitfire. When the Spitfire was flown with wings clipped, the rate of roll improved at 400 mph so as to be almost identical with the Mustang. The manoeuvrability of the Mustang, however, is severely limited by the lack of directional stability which necessitates very heavy forces on the rudder to keep the aircraft steady. (AFDU Report No. 64, February 1943)

The conclusions included 'The Mustang carries 150 gallons as compared with the Spitfire's 85 gallons. The latter can be increased by 30 gallons in a jettison tank.' This would later be particularly pertinent and encapsulates the major difference between what were undoubtedly two great fighters: the P-51 Mustang would be able to fight over Berlin from bases in the UK whereas the Spitfire was barely able to reach Paris. The 'legs' of the American fighter would be a decisive element in the Allied air effort over Europe and the destruction of the Luftwaffe.

Meanwhile, in April 1943 overall strategy was changed to give priority to attacks on the German aircraft industry. One of the first day missions by the Americans in support of this directive was on 17 April, the target being the Focke-Wulf factory at Bremen. Over 100 B-17s reached the target and dropped 265 tons of bombs in an effective attack that saw the factory lose 50 per cent of its capacity and the destruction of 30 Fw 190s in the factory area. But it was costly to the Americans. Sixteen B-17s failed to return; most fell to fighters and most were in the first bomber box: the 401st BS of the 91st BG lost six aircraft. Heavy losses amongst one squadron became quite common, if they were unlucky enough to be in a box that was broken up. In this case a further 39 bombers were damaged. The bomber gunners claimed 63 fighters destroyed and 15 probably destroyed, figures that were far in excess of reality, but helped maintain morale amongst the bomber force, who considered they were not only hitting their targets but also contributing to the aerial destruction of the Luftwaffe. Many of the B-17 losses had been to flak, and the American staggered box formations, whilst providing a degree of protection against fighters, made the bombers more vulnerable to ground fire, especially on the target run.

At the same time, VIII Bomber Command was undergoing a major expansion: four new Fortress bomber groups arrived in April 1943, making eight in action in total. Furthermore, seven extra B-17 Groups were assigned to the Command and were due to arrive by mid-summer. The other arrival was the first of the B-26 units, the 322nd BG (soon to be joined by two further groups with this type). This boosting of strength and the high numbers of German fighters claimed, helped to maintain morale amongst even those squadrons where losses had been particularly heavy.

Whilst bomber strength built up, and losses were replaced, the American fighters flew the same type of Rodeo sweeps as Fighter Command. The sweeps were intended to draw the Luftwaffe into combat where the Allied fighters could then destroy them; it was no more successful for the Americans than it had been for the British or the Germans, with the Luftwaffe ignoring fighter sweeps and only reacting when bombers appeared.

Then, on 4 May, the P-47s flew their first effective bomber escort, when 79 bombers attacked Antwerp for no loss. On 14 May, VIII Bomber Command was able to despatch over 200 bombers; American air power was growing on a weekly basis. The improving spring and then summer weather and more aircraft meant the command was also able to adopt new tactics, such as multi-targeting, and to fly on consecutive days. Clear weather also meant more accurate bombing and it seemed as if the bomber leaders were going to fulfil their promises. May, however, saw an increase in Luftwaffe day-fighter strength, as units were switched from other theatres to bolster the defence of the Reich; in part this was also a political move. A few hundred RAF bombers at night were invisible to the German population and most seriously affected only those whom they bombed. But hundreds of bombers flying over Germany in daylight were a sign to the German people that they were not being protected. This was also a reason why Hitler and his entourage preferred the visible destruction of bombers over Germany.

Plans for the Combined Bomber Offensive were set out more fully in the June 1943 'Pointblank' directive for attacks on factories producing fighter aircraft, components and ball-bearings. This was directly connected to the strategy of establishing air superiority over the Luftwaffe, and with effect from June 1943 the CBO was under way as an integrated day–night campaign, although not without its challenges, politics and detractors. Pointblank had five priority target sets, two of which related to German aircraft production and fighter strength, whilst the others were connected to U-boats, ball-bearing production, and oil refineries. RAF Bomber Command was meant to co-operate in this strategy, and Harris interpreted this as attacking towns related to the German fighter industry. From June to December 1943 some 25 per cent of the total American bomber effort was directed against Pointblank targets, the percentage rising to 50 per cent for the first four months of 1944.

In a series of raids on 21 May 1943 , the Americans lost twelve bombers, one of which was downed by a new weapon, the BR 21 air-to-air rocket, the first such success, scored by Hauptmann Eduard Tratt. The Luftwaffe was continuing to review its tactics and its weapons in face of the American bomber threat. The bomber loss rate was running at an average of 7 per cent on unescorted raids but less than 2 per cent on escorted raids, so it was clear that more escorts had to be provided, as 7 per cent was not sustainable. However, the American fighter pilots were not doing as well as expected in terms of engagements and kill ratios; of the P-47 groups, the 4th was still unhappy at having traded its Spitfires for Jugs, a mindset that impacted its performance, although the 56th was far more positive. This was largely because Zemke had focused on developing skills and practices that would take advantage of the P-47's performance, such as dive and rate of roll, which led to a general tactic or 'dive, fire, recover'. The effectiveness of this tactic was noted by their opponents, with Oberleutnant Hans Hartig, an Fw 190 pilot with JG2 6, later commenting:

> If attacked, we should draw the P-47s to a lower altitude (below 10,000 ft) by diving, then turn about suddenly. The P-47s will over-shoot; if they try to turn, they will lose speed and are vulnerable. The P-47 should zoom-climb and dive again. If we get into a turning combat, a P-47 can often get us on the first turn. If the Fw 190 climbs slightly in the turn it will gain on the P-47.

That was all very well, but the fighters had to be in the right place, and the P-47 did not have the required radius of action; a plan was in place for drop tanks but they were not the highest priority in the supply chain. The American bomber commanders still had to learn that unescorted daylight operations to Germany were untenable. The concept of the 'flying fortress' able to look after itself had proved invalid, and only a fighter escort could make the difference, especially as part of the idea behind the campaign was the destruction of the Luftwaffe, its aircraft and pilots.

As the Luftwaffe Reich defence continued to grow, with JG 3 now having a fourth *Gruppe*, and a part of JG 11 being declared operational, tough lessons for the American bomber force were not long in coming.

On 11 June 1943 the largest raid yet was mounted, with 248 B-17s attacking the U-boat yards at Wilhelmshaven; eight bombers were lost, mainly to fighters, and the raid was assessed as poor. Two days later whilst 140 P-47s were on fruitless fighter sweeps, the unescorted bombers over Germany suffered losses, Keil and Bremen being the targets. On the Kiel raid, 22 of the 72 B-17s from the 4th Bombardment Wing failed to return, whilst four of the 1st Bombardment Wing's attack on Bremen were also lost. The Kiel losses were particularly shocking and amongst the hundreds of American airmen who did not return to the UK that day was Brigadier General Nathan Forrest, the designated commander of the new 401st Bombardment Wing. One reason for the high losses was a new, and clearly ineffective, formation tactic that only served to make the Luftwaffe head-on attacks even more damaging.

In his *Luftwaffe Data Book* Alfred Price summarised the value and challenges of the head-on attack:

> The first major change in tactics was to deliver the attacks from head-on, where the bombers' defensive armament was less powerful and their armour protection less effective. The bombers cruised at

speeds around 175 mph and the fighters ran in at about 300 mph, so their closing speed was nearly 500 mph. That allowed time for only a brief half-second burst before the fighter pilot had to break away to avoid colliding with his prey. To bring down a heavy bomber with such a brief firing pass called for exceptionally good shooting. A few skilful pilots built up large victory scores using this method, but the average German fighter pilot achieved little. On the other hand, during a Staffel attack there was a good chance of damaging one or two bombers and forcing them to leave the relative safety of the formation. Aircraft flying alone could then be finished off at leisure.

This was a major issue for the bombers until an effective fighter escort was available; to fall out of the formation was to attract immediate and usually fatal attention from the Luftwaffe.

The fact that the German pilots were coming up with new tactics to avoid the danger of the bomber box's overlapping fire was a tribute to the formation discipline of the crews and the determination of the air gunners. Whilst the RAF had for some time devoted much effort and expertise into tactical evaluation, development and training, the USAAF was still relying on old ideas that had been established back in the States, and many RAF commentators make reference to the seeming unwillingness of the Americans to learn from the RAF. Whilst the courage and tenacity of the bomber leaders was never in doubt, their tactical awareness and leadership at this stage of the war were questionable.

The Luftwaffe, however, was close to its peak of effectiveness in terms of leadership, with the likes of Günther Specht taking command of II./JG 11. As Caldwell and Muller say in their excellent *Luftwaffe over Germany*:

> [Specht] strove for perfection and wrote detailed, analytical mission reports for the benefit of his pilots and his superiors. Within a few months II./JG 11 had gained a reputation as (arguably) the best unit in the day [fighter force], and Specht became known as one of the most reliable formation leaders in the Jagdwaffe.

The Allies were lucky that personalities and politics continued to dominate at the highest levels in Germany, and proposals for a restructuring and realignment of Luftwaffe air defence, promoted by the likes of Kammhuber, Galland and Milch, were often ignored or toned down by Göring and Hitler. Likewise, there was no significant movement of fighters away from the combat fronts and back to air defence, although in reality Reich air defence, day and night, was perhaps the most critical of all the combat fronts.

However, at long last questions were asked by the Americans about the need for an escort fighter, although asking the question and fixing the problem were not the same thing.

The Luftwaffe had so far faced the American daylight threat and had been victorious, as Milch noted in his summer tour of fighter units: 'The morale of the German fighter personnel is excellent, and under the circumstances imposed by their numerical weakness their performance deserves to be emphasised.' He also stated that the daytime fighter situation could be considered secure 'on the condition that adequately strong reinforcements are moved in'. What the German leadership still failed to grasp, and react to, was the capacity of the Americans to produce combat aircraft and crews and get them operational in the UK. Plans were already in place for thousands of bombers, as well as better and longer-range fighters. This capability, along with a dogged determination to slug it out and be victorious, were key factors in the ultimate destruction of the Luftwaffe.

After its losses in early June, VIII Bomber Command had focused on nearer targets, and so losses reduced. The fighters also had more 'trade' as the Luftwaffe could not ignore the bomber threat; on 26 June the P-47s had one of their biggest fights to date whilst covering the withdrawing B-17s, claiming four for the loss of four. When the weather cleared in late July, General Eaker launched a concerted series of attacks that became known as 'Blitz Week'; this was for many planners the first opportunity to test their theories. The basic idea was to fly seven major operations in seven days in order to stretch and stress the Luftwaffe. By this time Eaker was able to despatch over 300 bombers on major raids. The first targets of this new series, on 24 July, were in Norway, and 324 bombers participated – attacks were accurate and only one aircraft was lost. Attacking targets in Germany the next day, the bombers lost 19 of their number. The second day saw three missions to targets in Germany; the attack on Hamburg had the heaviest loss, 15 out of the 123 bombers, with a further 67 damaged. The most significant day was the 28th, as on this day the P-47s of the 4th FG operated over Germany with the first use of jettisonable fuel tanks. The only combats took place over Holland, with the P-47s claiming ten German fighters for the loss of one; however, 22 bombers fail to return, others crashed in the UK, and over 100 were damaged.

After two weeks in which the bomber groups recovered their combat strength, the offensive was renewed against targets in the Ruhr. An attack on oil targets on 12 August cost 23 of the 133 bombers, the highest losses to date. The P-47s were out in force flying penetration and withdrawal sorties, claiming four fighters for no loss, but not providing the level of cover needed by the bombers. Tactical lessons still needed to be taken on board.

However, the most significant raid in this phase was that on 17 August with two formations of bombers attacking targets connected with the German aircraft industry. The 4th Bombardment Wing had a 'shuttle mission' to bomb the distant Regensburg factory and then fly on to bases in North Africa, whilst the 1st BW was to attack Schweinfurt and return to England. The 4th BW despatched 147 aircraft, some acting as airborne 'spares'; however, one of the P-47 escort groups failed to arrive at the rendezvous and the rear group of bombers was unprotected – and soon under fighter attack. The P-47s with the front formation had to turn for home and both bomber formations faced increasing German attacks. In a running battle that lasted over an hour, the wing lost 24 aircraft; ten of these being from the 100th BG (which had flown its first mission on 25 June and was soon known as the 'Bloody Hundredth'). Nevertheless, bombing accuracy seemed good and the raid was assessed as a success. Meanwhile, the Schweinfurt aircraft had taken off – 230 B-17s in four formations. These too were subjected to very heavy attack, losing 36 of their aircraft. A total of 60 bombers (and crew) had thus been lost from a force of fewer than 500 aircraft; three groups had each lost ten aircraft or more. This was an unsustainable casualty rate, and a major blow to morale. The P-47s had claimed 19 Luftwaffe fighters, with 16 of those being claimed by the 56th FG, soon to become popularly known as 'Zemke's Wolfpack'.

According to the post-war USAAF Strategic Bombing Survey:

> The German anti-friction bearing industry was heavily concentrated. When the attack began, approximately half the output came from plants in the vicinity of Schweinfurt. An adequate supply of bearings was correctly assumed to be indispensable for German war production. In a series of raids beginning on August 17, 1943, about 12,000 tons of bombs were dropped on this target – about one-half of one percent of the total tonnage delivered in the air war. In an attack on August 17 by 200 B-17's on Schweinfurt, the plants were severely damaged. Records of the industry taken by the Survey (and supplemented and checked by interrogation) show that production of bearings at this center was reduced sharply – September production was 35 per cent of the pre-raid level. In this attack 36 of the 200 attacking planes were lost. In the famous and much discussed second attack on October 14, 1943, when the plants were again severely damaged, one of the decisive air battles of the war took place. The 228 bombers participating were strongly attacked by German fighters when beyond the range of their fighter escort. Losses to fighters and to flak cost the United States forces 62 planes with another 138 damaged in varying degree, some beyond repair.

The survey went on to say that because the USAAF stopped the attacks, the Germans were able to recover and disperse production, so the overall effect on the war effort was negligible.

Speer:

> We barely escaped a further catastrophic blow on 17 August 1943, only two weeks after the Hamburg bombings [the Bomber Command night attacks]. The American air force launched its first strategic raid. It was directed against Schweinfurt where large factories of the ball-bearing industry were concentrated. Ball bearings had in any case already become a bottleneck in our efforts to increase armaments production ... After this attack the production of ball bearings dropped by 38 per cent.

In the absence of alternative production facilities, or the time to move such key production, the Germans had little option but to make repairs and hope the other sites were not attacked in the same way. The Allies missed an opportunity by not focusing concentrated effort on this crucial area.

Speer:

> In June 1946 the General Staff of the Royal Air Force asked me what would have been the results of concerted attacks on the ball-bearing industry. I replied: Armaments production would have been crucially weakened after two months and after four months would have been brought completely to a standstill ... In those days we anxiously asked ourselves how soon the enemy would realise that he could paralyse the production of thousands of armaments plants merely by destroying five or six relatively small targets.

So, this was indeed, as the planners predicted, a vulnerable target set; however, the Allied strategic failure was that the target set was not prosecuted, and so the Germans were able to recover. When the Americans returned again, on 14 October. Speer was with Hitler when the news came of

> ... a great victory for our defences. I wanted to telephone Schweinfurt myself. But all communications were shattered; I could not reach any of the factories. Finally, by enlisting the police, I managed to talk to the foreman of a ball-bearing factory. All the factories had been hard hit, he informed me. The oil baths for the bearings had caused serious fires in the machinery workshops; the damage was far worse than after the first attack. This time we had lost 67 percent of our ball-bearing production.

So a Luftwaffe tactical 'victory' with the 'countryside strewn with American bombers' remained a strategic defeat or would have been if the Americans had kept going.

> Our reserves had been consumed; efforts to import ball bearings from Sweden and Switzerland had met with only slight success. Nevertheless, we were able to avoid total disaster by substituting slide bearings for ball bearings wherever possible. But what really saved us was the fact that from this time on the enemy to our astonishment once again ceased his attacks on the ball-bearing industry.

It was fortunate for the Germans that the Eighth Air Force had lost so many bombers on the raid that, for now, it was not ready to repeat it.

But to return to the events of 17 August. The fact that American fighters had crossed well into Germany was not lost on the likes of Galland, but when he tried to raise the issue with Göring, the conversation was not productive.

> I witnessed a dramatic scene between Göring and General Galland, who commanded his fighter planes. Galland had reported to Hitler that day that several American fighter planes accompanying the bomber squadrons had been shot down over Aachen. He had added the warning that we were in grave peril if American fighters, thanks to improved fuel capacity, should soon be able to provide escort protection to the fleets of bombers on flights even deeper into Germany. Hitler had just relayed these points to Göring. 'What's the idea of telling the Führer that American fighters have penetrated into the territory of the Reich?' Göring snapped at him. 'Herr Reichsmarschall,' Galland replied with imperturbable calm, 'they will soon be flying even deeper.' Göring spoke even more vehemently: 'That's nonsense, Galland, what gives you such fantasies? That's pure bluff!' Galland shook his head. 'Those are the facts, Herr Reichsmarschall.' As he spoke, he deliberately remained in a casual posture, his cap somewhat askew, a long cigar clamped between his teeth. 'American fighters have been shot down over Aachen. There is no doubt about it!' Göring obstinately held his ground: 'That is simply not true, Galland. It's impossible.' Galland reacted with a touch of mockery: 'You might go and check it yourself, sir; the downed planes are there at Aachen.' Göring tried to smooth matters over: 'Come now, Galland, let me tell you something. I'm an experienced fighter pilot myself. I know what is possible. But I know what isn't, too. Admit you made a mistake.' Galland only shook

his head, until Göring finally declared: 'What must have happened is that they were shot down much farther to the west. I mean, if they were very high when they were shot down, they could have glided quite a distance farther before they crashed. Now then, Herr Galland,' Göring fulminated, trying to put an end to the debate, 'I officially assert that the American fighter planes did not reach Aachen.' The General ventured a last statement: 'But, sir, they were there!' At this point Göring's self-control gave way. 'I herewith give you an official order that they weren't there! Do you understand? The American fighters were not there! Get that! I intend to report that to the Führer.'

The suicide of Chief of Staff General Jeschonnek on 18 August following another tirade from Hitler over the constant failings of the Luftwaffe, this time in reference to the RAF's attack on Peenemünde, was a loss to the Luftwaffe; his role was taken by General Günther Korten, an experienced air fleet commander but by no means the type of leader to reinvigorate the Luftwaffe or stand up to Göring and Hitler. As I have said a number of times, inadequate strategic and tactical leadership was one of the key Luftwaffe failings. In fairness to Korten, he supported Galland in the need for strengthened home defence, and in the face of opposition from combat zone commanders he transferred fighter units, but he was also tied down by the Hitler-driven, and Göring-promised, new offensive capability from the Luftwaffe, based on new aircraft and technology, some of which had just been seriously delayed by the RAF's attack on Peenemünde.

The rest of the summer of 1943 did nothing to ease the fears of those who considered that the daylight offensive was being literally blasted out of the skies. Loss rates had reached a point which would soon become unsustainable and it is remarkable how well morale held up amongst the young men of the bomber groups. Back in 1941, when the air strategy was outlined, USAAF planners had calculated the number of aircraft needed as 7,000 bombers; they suggested that losses of aircraft would mean over 2,100 replacements would be required each month. But they had not calculated the number of replacement aircrew needed or taken into consideration accident rates in the overall loss rates of men and machines. According to one study: 'No mention of air crew attrition rates was discussed and clearly, his only concern was the aircraft attrition rate and not that of the men who flew in them. The impression given by the planners was that the men were an inexhaustible resource to be utilised when necessary.' Accident rates and aircrew losses were the factors that bled the operational force as much as the losses to enemy action.

Data for the Eighth Air Force for 1944 show:

> ... 2,562 aircraft accidents not related to combat, involving 2,835 aircraft, and resulting in the death of 1,692 persons. This amounts to seven accidents and 4.6 fatalities every day of the year. The total number of accidents per month averaged more than 200, ranging from 148 in February to 271 in July, with well over half the accidents occurring during non-operational flights. The B-17 had an accident rate of 110 per 100,000 hours of flight time and the B-24 was experiencing 96 accidents per 100,000 hours of flight time.   (Summary of Aircraft Accidents in the Eighth Air Force [1944])

Nearly 40 per cent of accidents occurred in the landing phase. This meant that most bases were all too familiar with frequent combat and non-combat losses.

The CBO against the German fighter industry and the fighter airfields appeared to be having little effect on the Luftwaffe, although in truth, the German fighter arm was itself reaching a critical period and the seeming success of mid and late 1943 hid many fundamental flaws. In 1943 total Luftwaffe fighter losses were around 10,000 aircraft, with some 8,300 being single-seat fighters. Production that year was just under 14,000 fighters, a major increase, and also a percentage increase (47.6 per cent of total output versus 31.7 per cent the previous year); total production was a major achievement and the greater swing towards fighter production a major change of policy, although they were still the tried and tested but increasingly outdated types. At the August 1943 aircraft production conference the priorities for aircraft production and the types to be developed had been discussed, and Milch came down in favour of numbers rather than new types that might take some time:

> If we put twice as many fighters in the air, the number of successes will be at least twice as high. If we have four times as many fighters, the number of successes will be at least four times as high. But if we shoot down at least four times as many heavy bombers as now, and that is no astronomical figure, about 700 fighters would be required, which is less than one month's output, then I swear the daylight raids would have to stop.

Galland agreed:

> To protect Germany we must have three to four times as many fighters as the enemy bombers. If the enemy escort strength continues to increase, the German side must have an [equal increase in] strength

at least in order first to wage the battle for air superiority as the first condition for combat action against the bombers.

In fact, the Luftwaffe had seen a major increase in fighter strength for Reich defence, with Luftwaffe-Befehlshaber Mitte (soon to be renamed Luftflotte Reich) increasing from an establishment of 512 fighters on 30 June 1943 to an establishment of 1,000 by 30 September, with serviceability figures of 301 and 533 respectively. There are two things to note here: firstly, the poor serviceability rate, which was worse than it had been in 1942 and at around 50 per cent should have been a major cause for concern; secondly, a big increase in numbers put a strain on the command and control system. There was also the factor that those new to the area and role had to learn the tactics and the threats, and how to be successful.

August 1943 saw a flurry of activity not only in the much-needed re-organisation of the Luftwaffe's command and control structure, particularly the zones and areas of responsibilities, but also tactical direction to the fighter units. Galland sent a memo that emphasised instructions from Göring that, when engaging the daylight raids:

- Only bombers in formation are to be attacked, without regard for whether they are inbound or outbound;
- Individual bombers are to be attacked only after the entire formation has been broken up or there is no other possibility of engagement;
- Rocket-equipped aircraft are permitted to attack stragglers after successfully firing their rockets; no other exceptions allowed;
- Formation leaders and pilots who violate these orders are subject to court-martial on the grounds of military disobedience with severe consequences to the security of the Reich.

Evaluation of tactics suggested that head-on attacks remained the most effective, and if well executed led to the break-up of the bomber boxes. It was also noted that, despite undoubted successes, not enough bombers were being knocked down. A conference on 3 September looked at the overall tactical situation and amongst its findings was that a greater concentration of fighters and co-ordinated attacks were needed:

It is critical that a single attack wave is formed, with maximum strength. Attacks must be made by at least two *Gruppen*, led by the *Kommodore* on a single radio frequency. Each unit is primarily to attack one and the same bomber box. If it jettisons its bombs or otherwise splits up, the next formation in sight is to be attacked. The first attack has the goal of splitting up the enemy formation. Attacks are to be made from the most favourable position possible.

There were also some harsh words:

Pilots who without sufficient reason do not approach to the ordered firing distance are to be brought before a court-martial for cowardice before the enemy. Leaders and pilots who violate these instructions are to be brought before a court-martial for insubordination resulting in grave consequences for the security of the Reich.

This accusation of cowardice was to become a theme from the likes of Göring, although this set of notes came from Galland. However, Göring reinforced this view at the October air defence conference when he criticised the fighting spirit and morale of his fighter pilots. He accused them of firing from too far away, whereas if they closed in, they would bring down four times as many bombers, which would help the situation and improve their morale. In a very Stalinist move he also instructed that political officers would supervise units and that recording devices would track pilots' actions. Inevitably all of this had an adverse impact on the morale of the fighter force, which in the face of ever-increasing odds and losses was proving itself on a near daily basis.

Leadership at the top was key and the USAAF had its fair share of problems, too; on 29 August command of VIII Fighter Command transferred from Maj Gen Hunter to Maj Gen William Kepner. The fighter-sweep strategy Hunter used had proved ineffective, but in fairness to him, he had little choice: he had fighters without the range to escort into Germany, and he had to use them in some way, if only to give them theatre and combat experience. Kepner established a reputation as the leader who forged the American fighter weapon, but he took command at a time when the tools, primarily the P-51 and several now experienced and aggressive fighter group and squadron leaders, were almost ready. However, he still had to 'fight' his USAAF colleagues to ensure that his command was given the resources it needed, and to support his subordinates in becoming effective.

Having rested from the August attacks, the Eighth Air Force's next trip to Germany was just as disastrous; a raid on Stuttgart on 6 September cost 45 bombers plus many damaged and some eventually written-off. The mission was the largest to date, 338 B-17s from the newly re-organised 1st and 3rd Bombardment Divisions, but it was ineffective due to poor weather, which also was the root cause of many of the losses (running out of fuel). The Americans still had no effective blind navigation and bombing system and were still learning that European weather was challenging.

But the Americans were also making major changes, three of which would help transform the daylight offensive: effective drop-tanks, the already noted change of commander in VIII Fighter Command, and the introduction of the Merlin-engined P-51B and C versions of the Mustang. Despite the introduction, initially with mixed results, of external droppable fuel tanks for the P-47s, the fighter escort debate still raged. True, the Thunderbolts were taking a toll of German fighters: the 56th FG had a particularly good day on 4 October when they intercepted the Bf 110s of ZG 76 and promptly shot down nine aircraft. However, what was needed was a more effective escort fighter and in larger numbers – and that's what arrived in the shape of the P-51 Mustang. The first Merlin-powered Mustang unit, the 354th FG arrived in the UK (Greenham Common) in October 1943 but had to wait until the following month to receive its P-51Bs. The unit, under Lt Col K. Martin, was allocated to the Ninth Air Force but following pressure from the hard-pressed Eighth, was attached to VIII Fighter Command and moved to Boxted.

Whilst the P-51s were still working up, the bombers over Germany were still suffering. On 8 October the main target was Bremen and just over 300 B-17s were airborne. This was the first time the Luftwaffe employed its new command and control, ensuring the right fighter groups were in the right place, for example by making sure the Bf 110s only appeared outside the fighter escort range. Overall this worked well, and the Americans lost 27 bombers, with a further 205 damaged, as well as three P-47s. The Luftwaffe lost 24 fighters, with 21 pilots killed. The Eighth Air Force commanders had little choice but to persevere with the attacks on Germany; if they did not do so then what was the point of their bomber force?

Bremen was the target again on 25 November, a mission recalled by Ray Matheny, a gunner with 379th Bomb Group:

> When the target was revealed on the map that morning showing our track to Bremen, an audible moan went up from the crews. We had heard that Bremen was a tough target because the shipping area was defended by 236, 30-meter tall, concrete flak towers each mounting two 88 mm anti-aircraft guns . . .
>
> I heard a light slap-slap sound as pieces of exploding shell hit our airplane and spun around in the turret looking for damage. The flak was intense, and it frightened me. The worst thing about it was there was nothing that could be done once the bomb run was under way on the autopilot. I heard a 'crump', 'crump' sound telling me the flak was very close. Then our ship was thrown upward, and a large hole appeared in the right wing. There was a sound of more flak

bursts and more holes appeared. A green burst of flak appeared, and fighters suddenly resumed their attack.

At some point the bombardier, 2nd Lt Melvin Henroid, was wounded:

> We approached Kimbolton airfield with a ship in front of us that was firing red flares into the air indicating wounded on board. . . I fired a red flare through a Very pistol mount in the top of the cockpit, then Eaton slipped in behind the other ship. I suppose that everyone was getting nervous at this time as fuel was quite low. What a relief to get down on the ground, and how good it felt to jump out of the ship and feel the earth beneath my feet. This flight had taken six hours.

The damage to the bomber meant that the starboard wing had to be replaced. Ray found evidence of the bullet that had wounded the bombardier, which suggested it was from a B-17 . . . the intense cross-fire of the bomber boxes was a threat to enemy fighters but was also a danger to the bombers themselves.

The P-51s of the 354th FG flew their first mission on 1 December 1943, with 24 aircraft taking part in a 'familiarisation' flight down the Belgian coast and Pas de Calais, led by the 4th FG's experienced Don Blakeslee, another of the great American fighter leaders. Four days later, the Mustangs undertook their first escort mission, accompanying B-17s to Amiens. However, it was with the third mission that the USAAF began to make full use of the capabilities of its new fighter. Fitted with two 75-gallon drop tanks, the fighters escorted their B-17 charges to Emden on 11 December and two days later undertook the longest mission to date, a 1,000-mile round-trip to Kiel. This was a truly amazing radius of action, making that of the Spitfire and even the P-47 seem minuscule. The P-47 with two external tanks could escort bombers 475 miles, still appreciably more than a Spitfire or a P-47 with no tanks, whereas a P-51 on internal fuel alone had a similar radius. Admittedly, external tanks were initially looked on with disfavour; they altered the performance of the aircraft, would need to be dropped when combat was joined, and were considered a fire risk.

The Eighth Air Force had sent nearly 400 bombers out and only 8 were lost; they had been escorted by 131 P-47s, 31 P-38s, and 39 P-51s, a total of over 200 fighters.

Of note a few days later was the first attack on a target in Germany by bombers of the Fifteenth Air Force from Italy; they had been striking targets in Austria for some time, but this new venture made the attack on the Nazi heartland two-pronged. This also further diluted the efforts of the Reich air defence, as it now had to increase its capability across a wider area.

Despite this, December 1943 was a frustrating month for the P-51s, with technical problems that had to be overcome, mainly caused by the new environment in which the aircraft were operating, with long flight times in sub-zero temperatures. The freezing of oil and lubricants put strain on the engines, ammunition belts also froze or jammed under *g* loading, engines had a habit of overheating and the plugs of fouling up. Most of these issues were readily overcome, but most aircraft losses during December were put down to one or other of the technical problems. Nevertheless, the ability to escort the bombers to the heart of Germany had a great effect on the morale of both the bomber crews and of the enemy fighter pilots.

The Spitfires, P-38s and P-47s had carried out the escort task with determination and they had certainly dented the Luftwaffe's offensive capability. However, it was the arrival, in large numbers, of this more effective fighter that helped tip the balance. Indeed, one author has stated that the P-51 was the 'saviour of the CBO', a claim that does hold an element of truth. Losses in late 1943 had reached such a level that commanders were concerned that the daylight offensive would have to be cancelled or significantly changed.

German problems were intense, too. Galland:

> We have now reached the point where the serious position of our fighter defence makes us call for an aircraft with at least equal performance to enable us to carry on; if possible one with superior performance to outmatch them. We do not know what the enemy is doing in the whole field of aircraft construction, but I consider that we shall be making the greatest mistake if we take too narrow a view in our planning and specify for a fast bomber without any account of the fact that the same aircraft, or some similar aircraft, may in an emergency have to be used as a fast fighter rather than fast bomber.

He also expressed concern that unless the Luftwaffe had jet fighters, they would be vulnerable to the Allied jet fighters that must inevitably be on the way. Both Messerschmitt and Heinkel agreed and said they were ready, the latter stating: 'If we make a start today, we can produce the fighters and the bombers at the same time. I think we must go all out to have 50 or 60 of these bombers or 575 mph fighters by 1944.' Although the second half of 1943 had seen the Luftwaffe seemingly able to provide a robust defence and to cause high loss rates on the daylight offensive, the determination of the Eighth Air Force to press on and reach its targets meant that the Luftwaffe was not actually able to declare itself victorious. For those who were paying attention, it should have been clear that without some drastic solution the situation would rapidly deteriorate, as the American bomber strength and thus destructive capacity grew, and an ever-increasing number of long-range fighters appeared.

As 1944 opened, the balance of fighter advantage remained with the Luftwaffe in terms of numbers over Germany, but those numbers still included large numbers of Bf 109s, which were now outclassed in almost all respects. The Fw 190 was little better, although it was more robust and able to take greater damage. The armament of both was generally inadequate, and when underwing rockets were added to address this they greatly reduced the fighters' performance. The Bf 110 was all but useless now that escort fighters were around, and its replacement, the Me 410, was having troubles of its own and was generally disliked. There was also the issue of risking the Bf 110 night-fighter aircraft and crews on this type of work, with the consequent reduction in the capacity for night-fighter defence. However, morale was still strong as 1944 opened, as it seemed that the defenders were still in good shape.

Meanwhile, the Americans had a new strategy and a new commander; Lt Gen Carl 'Tooey' Spaatz took command of the new US Strategic Air Forces in Europe organisation on 1 January 1944. This took operational control of the strategic bombers in the UK (Eighth AF) and Italy (Fifteenth AF), to provide a more coordinated offensive, one that was also working better with Bomber Command. With his bomber pedigree in the European and Mediterranean theatres, Spaatz was convinced that concerted and concentrated bombing of critical target sets could be devastating. His two air force commanders, General Doolittle (Eighth AF) and General Twining (Fifteenth AF) were likewise experienced and driven officers, but Doolittle had already proven himself something of a maverick thinker and he was not a 'dyed in the wool' bomber man. In consultation with his fighter leader, General Kepner at VIII Fighter Command, he determined that the Pointblank directive to focus on German air power, and especially fighters, was correct but was not effective. It was all very well trying to destroy them whilst in production, but the quickest impact could be made by destroying them in the air and on their airfields. Spaatz was also fortunate in that he now had P-47s and P-51s with the range to make this a reality, but he also had to change the bomber mindset of close escort to one of 'go get them'.

On 21 January Spaatz announced: 'The fighter role of protecting the bomber formations should not be minimised, but our fighter aircraft should be encouraged to meet the enemy and destroy him rather than be content to keep him away.' This of course was just what fighter pilots wanted to hear, but was equally unpopular with the bomber leaders: 'As soon as my decision was announced to the bomb groups, their commanders descended on me . . . to tell me, in polite terms, of course, that I was a "killer" and a "murderer".' This was a very understandable reaction from bomber men who had only just got used to seeing the friendly shape of an American fighter; the fighter might shoot down more enemies a few miles away but if the bomber boys didn't see that and they were still under attack, it seemed they had been abandoned. In fact, as more fighters became available, the Americans ended up with a mix of tactics.

The Eighth Air Force was now regularly sending out more than 500 bombers per day, and the sight of these American air armadas was having an impact on morale in Germany, and the Nazi leadership was under pressure from its local political bosses to do something about it – not that there was much they could actually do! Starting with the 7 January attack on Ludwigshafen, which saw over 1,000 tons of bombs dropped on and around an important chemical site, the escort fighter plan was based on tighter scheduling of the fighters to maximise their range by assigning them a specific time and location to meet up with the bombers. Overall the tactic worked well, although it did risk the escorts missing the bombers and thus leaving the bombers unprotected, as the previous escort would have little ability to extend its cover.

The first official use of the 'freelance fighter' tactic was on 11 January, with the 56th FG sending two groups of P-47s ahead of and on the flanks of the bomber stream to intercept any Luftwaffe moves towards the bombers. One group claimed eleven enemy fighters in the Osnabrück area in what seemed to be an early success for the idea. The targets that day had been a number of industrial centres and over 660 bombers took part, with 159 of those going to Oschersleben, and losing 34 aircraft, one of the highest loss rates recorded. Their colleagues on the mission to Halberstadt fared much better, losing only 8 of the 107 B-17s. Both formations had been from the 1st BD and the escort had been provided by over 220 fighters, still mainly P-47s, which claimed 27 enemy aircraft for the loss of 2, although German records indicate lower losses.

The 303rd Bomb Group was one of a number to be awarded a Distinguished Unit Citation for this mission and it also had two Medal of Honor winners. Vern Moncur was a pilot with the 359th BS on this raid:

> This mission was the toughest mission thus far, and as later events proved, it was the toughest mission we had in the whole combat tour. In the first wave of enemy planes, there were at least one hundred Me 109s, Fw 190s, Ju 88s and a few Me 110s and Ju 87s [*sic*]. The first pass made at our group included thirty to thirty-five Me 109s and Fw 190s. The low group, to our left, had three Forts go down from this first pass. The No. 4 ship, lead ship of our element and on

whose wing we were flying formation, had its No. 1 engine hit. It immediately burst into flames and dropped out of formation. A few minutes later, this plane exploded. Soon afterward, the No. 3 ship ahead of us also caught on fire in the No. 1 engine and peeled out of formation. Lt Purcell was the pilot, and he and his crew didn't have a chance. I then moved my ship up into the No. 3 position, flying on the left wing of the wing leader, General Travis. Several fierce attacks were made on our squadron. We were all really catching hell. We made several evasive maneuvers to get away from the fighters during this time. Our bomb run was made amidst accurate flak bursts and continued fighter attacks. Our target was the factory that produced 45 per cent of the German Fw 190 fighters. From all reports, we did a highly satisfactory job of bombing and destroyed practically all of this plant. Just before we turned on our bombing run, possibly fifteen or twenty minutes before, a Fw 190 made a pass at our lead ship and then came on through the formation towards us. S/Sgt Rosier, top turret gunner shot him down and thereby got his first fighter. The ball turret gunner, Sgt Hein, got a 'very probable' fighter within two or three minutes after Rosier had nailed his fighter. All of us were a very happy and thankful bunch of boys to get our feet on the ground that day.

When a maximum effort mission was mounted, the Eighth Air Force was now able to put up 700–800 bombers and with the increased effectiveness of fighter escort, the loss rate to German fighters fell. The bomber groups were now arranged in combat wings, which in turn belonged to one of three bombardment divisions, two of which were equipped with B-17s.

Late February witnessed 'Big Week', an intensive period of operations with the Eighth's bombers flying over 3,000 sorties. This mini campaign specifically targeted the Luftwaffe, as part of a determined strategy to achieve air superiority. Whilst there was still some way to go before this was achieved, this week could be described as an effective start. And within months the Allies had achieved a marked and usable level of air superiority. For the first few months of 1944 Mustangs were still limited in numbers, for example they averaged only 10 per cent of the escort effort during Big Week, whereas the P-47s accounted for 80 per cent and P-38s the rest. However, in terms of success they were claiming more victories per fighter than the other types; on 25 February, their greatest effort so far in terms of percentage of the escort force, they comprised 15 per cent of the force and claimed 46 per cent of the victories. Big Week had an impact on the German planners; at last they realised the vulnerability of the aircraft industry. Although the

USAAF had suffered heavily, the Luftwaffe had reached a point of near exhaustion.

Speer:

> On 23 February 1944, Milch visited me in my sickroom. He informed me that the American Eighth and Fifteenth Air Forces were concentrating their bombing on the German aircraft industry, with the result that our aircraft production would be reduced to a third of what it had been, at least for the month to come. Milch brought with him a proposal in writing; we needed a 'Fighter Aircraft Staff' which would pool the talents of the two ministries (Air Ministry and Ministry of Armaments) in order to overcome the crisis in aircraft production.

A report on the post-war interrogation of General Frydag stated that he:

> . . . made the point that the heavy attacks on the aircraft industry culminating in the closing days of February 1944, had made it highly unlikely that many of the factories would be able to adhere to their monthly production quotas as laid down in Programme 225. The attacks on the Messerschmitt factory at Augsburg during the winter of 1943/1944 and the attack which took place he believed in February 1944 caused the complete destruction of the shops manufacturing Me 262 jigs. The effect of these raids, which also caused the death of a number of experienced jig-builders, was to retard production of the Me 262.

Just under 200 B-17s of the 1st Bombardment Division were sent against Augsburg's aircraft factories on 25 February, the closing day of 'Big Week'; this was one of a number of co-ordinated attacks on the aircraft industry, with the main target being Regensburg.

Hitler formally approved the creation of a new production organisation, the Fighter Staff, in March; it was quickly established, and due to the close relationship of key players such as Milch and Speer, it was to prove very effective. Established by Speer, and under Karl-Otto Saur, the intention was to use 'dictatorial powers' to shake up the production of aircraft by removing the politics (not much hope of that in Nazi Germany). Saur had no aviation background and, according to Baumbach,

> The men around him came from labour circles and knew nothing of aviation. The decisions of the new men were often based on the information and advice given to them by those who had been failures in the Air Ministry and industry. In other cases, they made up their

minds without concerning themselves with the requirements of air warfare.

Still, the Allies were lucky that this organisation was not in place a year earlier; it had taken the increasing weight of attacks on the German aircraft industry and the increasing fighter loss rates to make a decision that should have been clear long before. The organisation worked miracles, albeit primarily turning out old types, and shortage of fighters was not the main reason for the ultimate defeat of the Luftwaffe. As an indication of its success, average monthly production of fighters in 1943 had been just under 1,400; by April 1944 this had risen to over 2,000 and by September 1944 it had reached over 3,500.

Jet Fighters

Once again it was Hitler who, despite all the tactical mistakes of the Allies, ordained those very moves which helped the enemy air offensive in 1944 achieve its successes. After postponing the development of the jet fighter and later converting it into a light bomber, Hitler now decided to use our big new rockets to retaliate against England. From the end of July 1943 tremendous industrial capacity was diverted to the huge missile later known as the V-2: a rocket forty-six feet long and weighing more than thirteen metric tons. Hitler wanted to have 900 of these produced monthly. The whole notion was absurd. The fleets of enemy bombers in 1944 were dropping an average of 3,000 tons of bombs a day over a span of several months. And Hitler wanted to retaliate with thirty rockets that would have carried twenty-four tons of explosives to England daily. That was equivalent to the bomb load of only twelve Flying Fortresses.   (Albert Speer, *Inside the Third Reich*)

Galland flew the Me 262 and stated: 'The Me 262 represents a very great advance which will assure us an inconceivable advantage if the enemy sticks to piston engines much longer. The aircraft offers completely new tactical possibilities.'

During an armaments meeting at Rechlin in September 1943, Milch confided to Speer that Hitler had ordered a halt to large-scale production of the Me 262. Whilst they conspired to circumvent the order, it was impossible to do much to revise the priority of resources. As was typical of Hitler, he subsequently changed his mind and by January 1944 was urging production of the maximum number in the shortest time.

Speer:

> Hitler indicated that he planned to use the plane, which was built to
> be a fighter, as a fast bomber. The air force specialists were dismayed
> but imagined that their sensible arguments would prevail. What hap-
> pened was just the opposite. Hitler obstinately ordered all weapons
> on board removed so that the aircraft could carry a greater weight of
> bombs. Jet planes did not have to defend themselves, he maintained,
> since with their superior speed they could not be attacked by enemy
> fighters. Deeply mistrustful of this new invention, he wanted it
> employed primarily for straight flight at great heights, to spare its
> wings and engines, and wanted the engineers to gear it to a somewhat
> reduced speed to lessen the strain on the still untried system.

In January 1944, in reference to the Me 262, Hitler told Milch: 'If I get
them in time, I can beat off the invasion and the rest of it. Other things
are important but not so vital.' The fighter versus bomber debate had been
raging since the 262 had first been mooted; with many expecting that it
would be the decisive fighter, a position favoured by Milch and Saur, and
most of the fighter community, even though way back in 1942 it had been
projected as a fast bomber – but back then the fighter situation and the
defence of the Reich were not as critical as they had now become. The lack
of an effective bomber in the German arsenal was one of the reasons Hitler
looked to the Me 262 jet to take on the bomber role, another controversial
(and dumb) decision in the opinion of many historians. Hitler was furious,
declaring 'what I had ordered has not been carried out'. Göring gave way
immediately and issued new directions:

> To exclude any possibility of error, we must not go on calling the
> aircraft a fighter but a fast bomber . . . The Führer's will is that some
> of the prototypes shall be given further trials and developed as
> fighters. The prototypes must suffice for the production of the fighter
> while mass production is as a bomber only. Let there be no mistake,
> the time for discussion and debate of the fundamental question has
> gone by.

The jets were yet to make their appearance in any role, and in the meantime the scale of the American offensive continued to increase, as did its
targeting of the German aircraft and associated industries. There were
some further attacks on ball-bearing works, though the last concerted ones
took place in February 1944, with raids on Schweinfurt, Steyr, Erkner and
Cannstatt, which once again smashed production. Speer later commented
that this devastating series of attacks caused great concern, but then the

Allies stopped such attacks and the Germans were able to restore production and keep the arms industry supplied.

One reason why the Allies gave up was that they believed that the Germans would have dispersed production and that there was less value in hitting the limited number of known major centres. In fact, the Germans had failed miserably to disperse key production facilities, something the British had done even before the war had started.

Speer:

> As early as 19 December 1942, eight months before the first air raid on Schweinfurt, I had sent a directive to the entire armaments industry stating: 'The mounting intensity of the enemy air attacks compels accelerated preparations for shifting manufactures important for armaments production.'

But there was resistance on all sides. The Gauleiters did not want new factories in their districts for fear that the almost peacetime quiet of their small towns would be disturbed. The result was that hardly anything was done.'

From the Allied perspective the failure to prosecute a target allowed the Germans to recover from what could have been a critical loss.

By spring 1944, five more groups within VIII Fighter Command had converted to P-51s as this fighter type began to dominate in the escort role. The air battle was by no means won and the Mustangs had plenty of hard fighting left to do. Bomber losses remained high for much of 1944 but, whilst there were many hurdles yet to jump, the writing was finally on the wall for the Luftwaffe. A change in bombing strategy accelerated that ultimate demise. In a record (to date) the Americans had sent 730 fighters to escort the bombers on 3 March, including the combat debut by yet another Fighter Group, the 364th FG with P-38s. It was also the first time the fighters got close to Berlin. The following day nearly 800 fighters went out, but a record 24 fighters failed to return, as well as 30 bombers. Simply having large numbers of fighters was not a guarantee of success, although it was estimated that 11 of the losses were weather-related and not combat casualties; the Americans still had a great deal to learn and experience to gain.

The Eighth Air Force made its first trip to Berlin on 6 March 1944, with over 700 bombers despatched against industrial targets, along with over 800 escort fighters. This massive air armada must have given the German leadership cause for concern; that concern was alleviated somewhat by the success of the Luftwaffe, with claims for 69 bombers, with the 100th BG alone losing 15 of its B-17s; in addition, 11 American fighters were lost. In return the American fighter pilots claimed 81 victories, and the bomber gunners a similar number. Luftwaffe records suggest an actual loss of 64 aircraft; this was nearly 20 per cent of those engaged, and with very few of the pilots surviving. The Germans had used a new massed head-on tactic, which had contributed both to their successes and their losses. It certainly spelt disaster for the box on which they focused, as happened again on the next Berlin raid two days later. Nearly 900 Allied fighters claimed 77 of their opponents. Interestingly, when Berlin was attacked again on the 9th, there was very little fighter opposition, the Luftwaffe commanders being unwilling to risk the losses, and having accepted that the 'propaganda battle' for Berlin had been lost.

This by no means meant the end of heavy fighting in the air but was indicative of the Luftwaffe's growing need to pick its battles. An Eighth Air Force report following the 29 April attack on Berlin noted how effectively the Germans were using their fighter force, with an estimate that 400 or so fighters had been employed but 'refused to engage unless assured of substantial numerical superiority and rapidly exploited weakness or gaps in the fighter escort. His effort paid high dividends at a relatively low cost.' The attack cost the Americans 38 B-17s and 25 B-24s out of a force of 578 bombers, a terrible loss rate; with 13 out of 814 fighters also lost. The American fighters only downed 11 enemy aircraft and spent most of their time chasing around the sky looking for the enemy.

The Allies were now giving greater focus to hitting the Luftwaffe on the ground, and there was an increase in the number of enemy aircraft destroyed on or near their airfields, which combined with the aerial attrition to sap the Luftwaffe combat capability. Lack of fuel was also becoming a major factor. At the end of April Galland had commented:

> In each of the last ten daylight attacks we have lost on average over 50 aircraft and 40 pilots. In view of the present state of training and the rate of these losses, formations cannot be supplied with fresh pilots. Replacements can be found in a purely numerical sense, but this will not give us organised formations. It must be made clear that performance is at least of equal importance. Even if their numbers are limited, we need high-performance aircraft to restore the feeling of superiority in the Luftwaffe.

He was, of course referring to the Me 262 and he stated he would rather have one Me 262 than five Bf 109s.

Bomber crews, RAF and USAAF, knew the significance of Berlin, but they never liked to see the mission tape head to the 'Big City'. Art Livingston was with the 93rd Bomb Group:

We made it back to base and went into interrogation where the interviewers asked about all phases of the mission. At this time each person told what he had seen, and the number of planes shot down, the type and chutes if any. This is where I learned one of the missing planes was your brother's. All of us were stunned by this news. We left the interrogation and walked back to the hut. All of us were a little shaken and it was eerie walking into that hut and looking down to the other end of it and knowing it would be empty. All of that crew's belongings were just where they left them that morning. All the uniforms hanging in a row, pictures of their families on display, shoes lined up under their bunks, and all the items they enjoyed. The door to our hut opened and three men we didn't know entered and asked where the Helfers crew slept. We pointed out the location and they started to lay out the men's belongings in two piles. One for government issue which would be recycled and the other pile of the men's personal belongings that would be sent home to the families. When all the items were packed, they took off the blankets and mattress cover from each bunk, folded up the mattresses, and left with all the bags.

And these young men went back time and again.

The Oil Target

Allied bombing strategy, especially since the advent of the day–night CBO, had been subject to much internal debate and political pressure regarding where the main effort should be made. However, by spring 1944 there were two main strategic target sets, oil and communications, and advocates and detractors for each. The oil lobby was predicated on the disruption and destruction of the oil production and supply system, primarily to impact air operations but also, of course, ground operations. Communications, especially rail links, were an element in the supply distribution network, but it was the production and storage sites that were the focus of bombing effort. The transport lobby had as its main thrust the disruption of the movement of land forces between operational areas and, with an eye to the Normandy invasion, especially into that area, of which more later.

Germany had recognised in the 1930s that oil was one of its strategic imports, especially for its burgeoning military, and that there was a high risk of supply disruption. With an abundance of coal readily available, the German solution to easing the risk was the development of synthetic oil plants, where coal was used to make petroleum products. Despite massive investment in this, and an increased percentage of requirement being met by such products, it still fell well short of the growing demand, and by 1937 Germany was importing more oil than ever, an indication of the growth in consumption. A year later, the strategic oil reserve was only able to meet 25 per cent of the military's mobilisation requirements, some four months of operations, whilst some specialist areas, such as aviation lubricants, were as low as 6 per cent. There was oil to be had on the open market, but Germany lacked the hard currency to make significant purchases.

Germany had started its synthetic oil expansion in 1936, as part of the four-year plan, with a strategy to be (almost) self-sufficient in liquid fuel supplies by the early 1940s. The total planned output from the plants was to be 700,000 tons a month, of which 150,000 tons would be aviation spirit, these figures being the target for late 1943. With the German expectation of short conflicts that would also give them access to oil supplies, the plan was sound on paper. Actual production was less than expected, and had reached 540,000 tons by early 1944, but a number of plants were not yet at maximum capacity. The Germans had suffered their first 'oil crisis' as early as 1942, with increased demands from the Russian and Mediterranean/ Western Desert theatres, but this had been effectively overcome by a slight reduction of allocations to training and some units, but primarily by an increase in the output from the synthetic oil plants.

> In 1944 things only got worse. The day raids of the Eighth and Fifteenth US Air Forces, accompanied now by their escort fighters, began to get into their stride with their heavy attacks on aircraft production factories and oil. The appearance of the US long-range escort fighters over Berlin took the Germans by surprise. At first, they would not believe it, until the German C-in-C Fighters watching an air battle in his own aircraft was chased. When at last he was convinced, Göring remarked that the war was lost. Every priority was now given to the production of fighters, and the bomber force to all intents and purposes was scrapped. Fighter production was doubled, a big achievement in view of the dispersed state of the industry that our bombing had caused. The pilots, although now poorly trained, showed the greatest determination and fighting spirit. By the end of June 1944, two-thirds of the GAF fighter force was defending the Reich from west, north and south.   (Elmhirst lecture)

The Transport Target

Harris had long accepted that attacks on communication nodes played a major role in disrupting the flow of raw materials and finished products, and thus were important in the overall reduction of German fighting capability. As many of the key nodes were also in the major cities, he argued that the campaign against cities had direct impact against factories (and their workers), the communication network, and civilian morale. However, it was not until late 1943 that the Allies truly looked at a transport strategy, and in part that was influenced by Operation Strangle that had been used in the Italian campaign. The overall German transport system had inland waterway, road and rail elements, and all three were subject to attack; however, it was rail that was the most important in terms of raw material, equipment and mass troop movement. Attacking the rail system had several key elements, such as destruction of key rolling stock, especially locomotives.

The other aspect to target was the infrastructure, the lines themselves and vulnerable points such as bridges and tunnels. Cutting lines tended to be little more than a nuisance and the Germans proved brilliant at making rapid repairs. Destroying bridges was more effective, as they were much more difficult to repair, but they were a far harder target to hit. The main success against bridges was by medium bombers, especially those of Ninth Air Force, and the fighter-bombers, especially the P-47s. Whilst the overall transport strategy played a major role in the success of the invasion, and was largely achieved by air power, it was not contested in any significant way by the Luftwaffe and so falls outside the current study, other than its direct impact, as alluded to in various places, on the effectiveness of the Luftwaffe.

Luftwaffe Pilot Problems Increase

An RAF Air Intelligence report of early 1944 stated:

> As far as I can see the crew position of the GAF can be summarised as follows:
>
> Experienced Crews: These are in extremely short supply and even the night fighters are being milked to provide experienced squadron commanders for the single-engined fighters employed on the strategic defence of Germany.
>
> Pilot Officer Prune Crews: These are being turned out in large numbers by the quick conversion of bomber pilots, transport pilots, etc. to single-engined fighters. As there are plenty of single-engined fighter aircraft the general position is that there is a large single engined fighter force adequately but not very efficiently crewed.
>
> Crews from ab initio Training: The supply of crews from this source will soon be negligible owing to the closing of ab initio training schools due to lack of petrol.

The fighter force at the present time is large, not very efficient and expanding. So long as the supply of aircraft and crews from within the resources of the GAF continues, this force will continue to maintain its strength or even expand. As the resources of convertible pilots from within the GAF are used up, so will the input of crews into the single-engined fighter force decrease and owing to the lack of output from the ab initio training schools eventually cease altogether. Therefore, at some point wastage will overtake crew input and the force will commence to decline. At the present time our bombing policy is the indirect attack on the GAF by destroying its oil resources. This and other factors, such as the loss of Ploesti, have brought about the closure of the ab initio flying training schools and hampered the operations of the strategic fighter force itself. Nevertheless, the force is a formidable one and is becoming increasingly so.

By early 1944 Allied aircrew were claiming large numbers of enemy aircraft destroyed, especially the USAAF fighters and the bomber gunners. Whilst every attempt was made to verify claims, post-war records tend to suggest that the true numbers were around 25 per cent of those claimed. In one period when Allied claims were over 1,500 destroyed, German records suggest a total loss of only 338 in air combat but with a significant number of aircraft being destroyed on the ground, for example 124 in May alone. Interestingly, and part of the overall 'numbers game', the Germans also had 407 non-operational losses in the same period, which is a reflection on the lower quality of pilots and training and the impact of the Allied assault on airfields. However, overall the problem was one of pilot numbers and quality – and the fuel to allow flights to be made.

On 27 April 1944, at a Fighter Staff conference, Galland commented:

The problem which the Americans have set the fighter arm, and I am intentionally only dealing with the problem of the day fighters at this point, is quite simply the problem of air superiority. The numerical ratio in daylight operations Is approximately 1 to 6 or 1 to 8. The enemy's standard of training is astonishingly high. The technical capabilities of his aircraft are so manifest that we are obliged to say that something must be done immediately. In the last four months, well over 1,200 day-fighter pilots have been lost, including of course many of the best unit commanders. We are having great difficulty in closing this gap, not in a numerical sense, but with experienced leaders. In each of the last ten daylight attacks we have lost on average 50 aircraft and 40 pilots, i.e. 500 aircraft and 400 pilots in ten major operations.

Göring, Galland and others took part in a conference on 15–16 May 1944 to look at fighters and fighter personnel, with losses for the month having increased. As to numbers of pilots, Galland outlined the growing crisis with fighter pilots, highlighting losses for April 1944:

Luftflotte Reich	38 per cent
Luftflotte 3	24 per cent
Luftflotte 2	18.2 per cent
Luftflotte 5	12 per cent
Luftflotten 4, 6 & 1	11 per cent

The total loss was 489 pilots, 100 being officers, whilst replacements were only 396 (62 officers), a net reduction of nearly 100. As the percentage figures showed, the situation was particularly bad in the home defence fighter units (principally Luftflotte Reich plus Luftflotte 2 and 3 in Italy and western Europe respectively). Galland suggested as a start that 'all fighter pilots be withdrawn from staff appointments if they are still fit for flying'. It was agreed that the flying schools would release 80–100 instructors, and some night-fighter pilots would be transferred to daylight operations. Göring stressed that great importance should be attached to good training of pilots who are transferred from other commands but the reality was that all these measures could only partially stem the increasingly desperate situation. To boost the numbers in Reich defence it was decided to move two fighter groups from the Eastern Front and to request that all ground-attack pilots with more than five aerial victories should convert to fighters. One of the problems for the training units was the limit on fuel supplies; in the May fighter conference, the request for an increase in the monthly fuel allocation to 60,000 tons was rejected and the allocation was fixed at 50,000 tons, although the actual monthly average availability was only 35,000 tons.

By late March, RAF Intelligence was suggesting that Luftwaffe depots be added to the target list as part of the anti-air campaign:

> Since the bomber offensive against German aircraft production plants and factories has proved so successful, it seems that the time has now come to extend the attacks to those depots and dumps where the main stocks of equipment, apparatus, bombs, ammunition etc., are stored. It is known that many items are in short supply, and if there are difficulties in production nothing can now inflict greater damage to the operational efficiency of the GAF than the destruction of those reserves of essential materials for repair and maintenance, upon which the Air Force must now largely depend. It Is important

that the two programmes, namely attacks on GAF targets and attacks on Army targets, should not be dealt with concurrently, because as soon as one or two targets belonging to the GAF of this type have been attacked, it is probable that rigorous dispersal measures will be taken. In other words, the success of the programme as regards GAF targets depends upon the attacking of all targets within as short a space of time as is reasonably possible.

The first concerted attack on oil took place on 12 May 1944, the main targets being Böhlen, Brüx, Lützkendorf, Merseburg, Zeitz and Zwickau. Over 800 bombers and over 1,000 fighters took part, including 245 provided by RAF Fighter Command, in order to saturate the routes and the target areas. Many of the targets were heavily damaged, and the attackers also claimed 200 German fighters. The Luftwaffe had put up a large number of fighters but in the face of the swarms of American fighters they were overwhelmed. They had successes of course, knocking down several bombers and some fighters, but these were insignificant in terms of the overall air armada, and that armada had caused serious damage to a key asset.

The failure of the Germans to disperse oil production or to move some to underground facilities meant that this target system was vulnerable to the Allied bomber offensive. Some 90 per cent of aviation spirit came from the synthetic oil plants. In May 1944, 150,000 tons was delivered; this dropped to 52,000 tons the following month and was down to 7,000 tons for September. This had a direct impact on stocks, with the OKW reserve dropping from 107,000 tons to 30,000 tons between May and November. The separate 'Führer Reserve' dropped from 207,000 tons to zero. The full severity of the crisis was felt from about August onwards, when drastic measures had to be taken in order to make the necessary economies. 'Operations were adversely influenced, in that night-fighter sorties had to be cut down in order to permit as many daylight operations as possible with the fuel available' (RAF oil report, 1945).

Speer once again foresaw imminent disaster with the drop of production and opined that if attacks had been maintained, it would have kept German war production at below 10 per cent of former levels. The Allied effort moved elsewhere, primarily in support of D-Day, and by mid-July the Germans had restored 40 per cent of production, especially at the key Leuna plant. It was short-lived recovery and air attacks soon dropped production back to below 10 per cent. As the Allies once again cut back on the attacks on the oil plants, the production rate recovered to 39,000 tons in November, but with the reduction in stocks and this still very low production rate, the aviation spirit 'target system' was at breaking point.

On 30 June, Speer sent a personal report to Hitler on the effects of the attacks on the synthetic oil plants.

> Although you, my Führer, are kept continuously informed through the agency of General Keitel of the severity of the attacks and the losses which result from them, yet I feel it my duty to give you an additional review of the losses to the German fuel production since the beginning of May. In May and June, the attacks concentrated on the German aviation spirit production. The enemy succeeded, therefore, by 22 June, in bringing the loss of aviation spirit up to 90 per cent. Only through the most rapid repair of the damaged plant, will it be possible to restore a part of the catastrophic loss of 22 June. Nevertheless, the output of aviation spirit is wholly insufficient at present. As virtually the whole of this type of fuel is produced in Germany, no improvement can be sought from imports.

He went on to detail the production targets and the fuel reduction measures he had implemented but then said:

> The strictest measures must be taken, even today, to reduce flying as far as possible. From now onwards no flight which is not directly needed for battle, training or testing must be carried out. In a couple of months, we may grievously regret every ton of fuel which is now being used up unnecessarily, for already today the increasing fighter programme bears no relation to the falling fuel production.

He closed by proposing increased passive defence (smoke generators) and active measures (more flak and the provision of fighters). Fuel was indeed the weak spot and now that the Allies had the capability of causing critical damage, they should have made even greater efforts to prevent repair work. The ability of the Germans to make repairs in the last year of the war was truly astounding.

Speer:

> I was aghast at the incomprehension of our leadership. On my desk lay reports from my Planning Department on the daily production losses, on plants knocked out, and the time required for starting them up again. But all these projections were made on the clear premise that we would manage to prevent or at least reduce enemy air raids. On 28 July 1944, I implored Hitler in my memorandum to 'reserve a significantly larger part of the fighter plane production for the home front'. I repeatedly asked him in the most urgent terms whether it would not be more useful to give sufficiently high priority

to protecting the home hydrogenation plants by fighter planes so that in August and September at least partial production will be possible, instead of following the previous method which makes it a certainty that in September or October the Luftwaffe both at the front and at home will be unable to operate because of the shortage of fuel. After our Obersalzberg conference at the end of May he had agreed to a plan drawn up by Galland providing that out of our increased production of fighter planes an air fleet would be assembled which would be reserved for defence of the home industry. Göring, for his part, after a major conference at Karinhall where the representatives of the fuel industry had again described the urgency of the situation, had solemnly promised that this 'Reich' air fleet would never be diverted to the front.

May 1944 was the month in which the Me 163 rocket fighter made its appearance, as I./JG 400 now had a few ready for operational use. Major Wolfgang Späte flew the first sortie in a bright red aircraft, which promptly got him posted away from the unit. Production rates were never large, with very small numbers per month from May to September 1944, with figures for the last three months of the year of 64, 95 and 98 respectively, with final assembly and flight testing at Königsberg/Jesau.

As a point-defence fighter, the concept was interesting, as a viable weapon of air war it was pointless, especially when the high casualty rate through accidents was taken into consideration. The same was true of the various other designs that were also in hand for the point defence of key installations. The Me 163 does not, therefore, play an important part in this discussion, unlike its more viable partner, the Me 262. The latter was still in its troubled development phase; the first unit, ErprKdo 262 based at Lechfeld, under the command of Hauptmann Werner Thierfelder had received a few aircraft by this time but in the absence of an operational capability he was sending personnel to the factory at Leipheim both to learn and to push the manufacturer.

The jets were thus yet to make their appearance, and in accordance with a new directive from Hitler when they did so it would be as bombers. Milch and Galland were infuriated, as both believed the jet would enable the Luftwaffe to re-establish air superiority. By the middle of 1944 this was a fantasy.

Pre-invasion Bombing and D-Day

Of all the Allied operations of World War Two, the largest, most complex and most fraught with risk was the assault on 'Fortress Europe' – the landings in Normandy. Air power played a key role in both the preparation and successful execution of this amphibious and airborne assault. The air forces based in the UK, British and American, flew thousands of sorties on reconnaissance, deception, fighter cover, bombing, transport and all the other roles of air power. On 31 March 1944, the CBO was officially suspended, with the assignment of the Eighth Air Force to General Eisenhower's Allied Expeditionary Force as part of the invasion air-support component, although the bombers were allowed to keep their existing strategic role (and targets) as long as the pre-invasion bombing campaign was also executed, to which was soon added the anti V-1 campaign as well.

Staff Sergeant Norman Yarborough was a ball turret gunner with the 566th BS of the 389th BG, and flew his first mission on 28 April 1944, the target being V-weapon sites in the Pas de Calais area; there was no fighter opposition, but flak was assessed as 'medium'. In his diary he recorded his reaction as 'scared'. It was the same target area the following day but his B-24 had to return with engine trouble; he recorded his reaction as 'pissed off as this should have been Mission #2'. His comment on the 8 May mission to Brunswick, a mission of nearly six hours, was 'Badly shaken, fired approx. 500 rounds, got one Fw 190. More Jerries than law allows. Saw 10 B-24s go down. Sure hope I never go on another like this. Me and Fw pilots seemed to be inexperienced but had plenty of guts.' A few missions later his reaction was more along the lines of 'missions feel like routine now' and 'we really had a Sunday tour of Germany'. There were a few more difficult missions, especially Brunswick again, before Norman flew his 30th and last mission on 25 August, the target being Wismar. His reaction was 'Boy, that's it, we've had it.' This very personal diary and experience could stand for many of his colleagues in the Eighth Air Force, although for some the magic 30 never arrived (it had been increased from 25 to 30 by General Doolittle).

By mid-April it was generally accepted by both sides that the Americans had day air superiority in that all parts of the Reich were in their reach and loss rates, although not insignificant, could be kept below unacceptable levels. It was by no means all over, and many young men on both sides still paid the ultimate price, as did many on the ground. But from this point on, the final decision was not in doubt, either in the air or in terms of the overall outcome of the war.

The pre-invasion bombing strategy involved the heavies of the RAF and USAAF attacking a wide range of targets, with emphasis on defence positions and lines of communication, the idea being to help the initial assault and to limit the German ability to move reinforcements. Medium bombers, fighter-bombers and fighters were also heavily involved, and the Luftwaffe was unable to have any impact on the air dominance of the Allies.

Although this was a critical juncture in the overall conduct of the war, it adds little to our overall story of the defeat of the Luftwaffe, although they could still cause heavy losses, as Bomber Command found on the night of 3/4 May, losing 42 of the 362 bombers that attacked the 'easy' target of Mailly-le-Camp. The total USAAF air effort in the build-up phase, 1 April– 5 June, comprised:

	Sorties	Bomb tonnage	Losses	Claims
Ninth AF	53,784	30,657	197	189
VIII Bomber Command	37,804	69,857	763	724
VIII Fighter Command	31,820	647	291	1,488

Between 1 April and 5 June Air defence of Great Britain (ADGB) flew 18,639 sorties in support of the Overlord plan, claiming 111 victories for the loss of 46 fighters. The total Allied air effort in this period was 195,255 sorties with 2,655 claims and 1,987 losses – which puts the ADGB effort into perspective!

As D-Day dawned, total Allied air assets numbered over 10,000 aircraft (British and American) and for the next few days, many of these were to be kept busy around the clock. SHAEF anticipated a major German air reaction but for the fighter squadrons D-Day was hectic though unproductive, as recorded in the Fighter Command intelligence summary:

> No major encounters took place throughout the first day of the launching of the invasion of Normandy. Enemy air activity was negligible. It is estimated that both escorting and protective fighters over the assault areas and defensive fighters over France did not exceed 50 to 70 [enemy] sorties.

The Allied expectation had been somewhat different, the directive issued to the fighter forces stating that:

> The intention of the British and American fighter forces is to attain and maintain an air situation which will assure freedom of action for our forces without effective interference by the German Air Force, and to render maximum air protection to the land and naval forces in the common object of assaulting, securing and developing the bridgehead.

The Luftwaffe was simply unable to deliver any response to the overwhelming Allied air strength. Luftwaffe reports increasingly spoke of problems with constant harassment in the air and on the ground from seemingly endless numbers of Allied fighters, plus issues with fuel, pilots and experience. A report of 30 June stated that: 'There is a particular shortage of personnel with powers of leadership for the fighter units. This will be eased as much as possible by transferring officers from bomber units to fighters.' And the following month, 'The shortage of reliable group and unit commanders for fighters has not yet been entirely remedied in spite of the transfer of experienced officers, particularly from the disbanded bomber units, on account of the extra training required, although the position has improved.' The problem of leadership had been growing throughout 1943 and by mid-1944 had become critical; the lack of combat leadership was a factor in the reduction in Luftwaffe combat capability. The problem had numerous causes, including the high loss rate through continuous operations – every experienced leader lost was almost impossible to replace; there was also no leadership course to prepare selected pilots for the role – just being an effective fighter pilot did not make a man a good fighter leader. Galland must take some blame for this; he had flirted with such a course in late 1943 but it did not last long, and he tended to subscribe to the 'learn on the job' approach. The Allies, and especially the RAF, had a comprehensive programme for developing such leaders.

The Final Slope to Destruction

Allied air power had defeated the Luftwaffe, all that remained as the months dragged on was the destruction of the Luftwaffe. To that end, this section will focus on specific aspects of the last year of the war.

The sheer number of American bombers over Germany meant that any defending fighter than got airborne had a chance of making successful intercepts, but first they had to get through the screen of RAF and American fighters. And the Luftwaffe fighters were increasingly being flown by a small cadre of experienced but worn out pilots and a large number of partly trained pilots. A later RAF summary of a German report of 30 June 1944 noted:

> At the moment, the number of crews is satisfactorily in excess of the number of aircraft. Owing to the aviation fuel shortage which has arisen, the bias of training has been altered to produce the full number of fighter and ground-attack crews and, provisionally, 50 per cent of the night-fighter crews. All other types must subsist for the time being on their present strength or on the remaining output of the final training schools. The resumption of training for these units is dependent on an increase in the fuel allocation.

By 31 August the reports were stating: 'If the allocation of fuel to training is maintained at its present low level it will only be possible to concentrate on the training of fighter pilots.' Lack of fuel not only reduced the amount of training time, it also influenced the type of training, and for the day-fighter pilots there was little attention paid to bad weather and instrument flying, which led to an increased loss rate amongst inexperienced pilots who found themselves in situations where they were unable to operate their aircraft safely.

With the Allies ashore in France, Luftwaffe morale went down.

> Two generals visited us in the heat of those days: the liaison officer between Hitler and the Luftwaffe in the west, and our own Fighter General. We were fallen in in flying kit to greet the visitor when our own Fighter General appeared, as always, a fat cigar stuck out above his small beard [sic, a mistranslation of moustache]. 'Well, chaps, what am I going to say to you? You can see yourselves how things are. It's pretty bloody.' The second general, who spoke a few minutes later, seemed to be rather less frank. He had just come from the Führer's headquarters. We moved away afterwards into a tent, where a heated discussion at once began. The depression of the headquarters general was only too easy to understand. He had to keep Hitler informed of the daily state of serviceable aircraft, had himself to meet every criticism, and defer patiently and continuously to the complaints and abuse of his Commander-in-Chief. Hitler was always working himself up over the fact that on numerous occasions scarcely half of the aircraft reported as serviceable actually took off against the enemy. He had made the effort to come here, to his front-line comrades, so as to go thoroughly into these false allegations. After a good deal of talk our *Kapitän* was at last called on to speak. 'Our aircraft are old and tired out,' he began. 'Maintenance services are insufficient, and both material and workmanship faulty. Petrol and ammunition are lying about on the railways, where they've been bombed, and never get here. The training of our young pilots is inadequate, most of them getting shot down during their first sorties. Bombers and low-flying aircraft are ruining our airfields, after every shower the dispersal areas are under water. The order to take off frequently arrives either when the enemy is right over the airfield or has already passed on. And so,' the *Kapitän* ended his lament, 'when an emergency take-off finally does make an interception, the enemy superiority is too great.' The generals looked at one another. The younger of them, himself one of our best fighter pilots, nodded in agreement. But the other shook his head, apparently unable to

accept it all. 'Yes, *meine Herren*, I know your difficulties. They are mine too. But I can't tell the Führer that. He simply won't listen to this kind of thing.' (Gunther Bloemertz, *Heaven Next Stop*)

German ground forces were under constant air attack, making road and rail movement by day all but impossible. Even the squadrons on fighter escort would, having left their bombers under the care of the return escort, use remaining fuel and ammunition to good effect by attacking targets on the ground on the way home; many pilots of VIII Fighter Command ran up appreciable scores of German aircraft destroyed in this way. Unfortunately the Mustang was particularly prone to damage when strafing, as a percentage of bullets always ricochet and have a fair chance of striking the aircraft; the front section of the Mustang was vulnerable to such hits (unlike the somewhat more rugged P-47) and a number of aircraft were lost as a result.

This was little good to the Germans:

> Day by day our air operations were becoming more difficult, the enemy superiority having risen immeasurably, and our formation returning home seldom without losses, only occasionally would one of us climb smiling from his cockpit. The mechanics stuck as well as ever to their jobs, making good by their efforts the failings of manufacturers or the shortcomings of inadequate supply. The belief these fellows in their black overalls still had in victory and their hope of a miracle weapon which should turn the scales gave them the strength to go on. (Gunther Bloemertz, *Heaven Next Stop*)

Oil targets were the primaries for most of the bombers on 7 July, with 930 bombers from Eighth Air Force attacking targets in central Germany and the Fifteenth attacking oil plants in the south. Both were given very strong escort forces. In total around 2,000 American aircraft were involved, and overall the missions went well, with targets being hit and American fighters making claims for 90 Luftwaffe fighters. Bomber losses were generally light, the Eighth losing 39 aircraft, but once again if a bomber formation became exposed or straggled it was heavily punished. On this occasion the B-24s of the 492nd were the victims, on the receiving end of the 2 cm and 3 cm cannon on the Fw 190s of IV./JG 3. In a short engagement the fighters destroyed 11 of the Group's B-24s. Overall the specialist Fw 190s laid claim to nearly 30 of the lost bombers, proof, if proof were needed, that the Luftwaffe was down but not out and that American fighters had to intervene before such attacks could be set up.

On 8 July 1944 Hitler approved proposals that production should cease on all aircraft which were considered inessential at that stage of the war.

As already noted, however, the German indecision on development of new types, the persistence with numbers over quality, by sticking with the proven Bf 109s and Fw 190s despite their inferiority, contributed to the overall decline of Luftwaffe capability. There were constant meetings and directives on aircraft production, none of which made much sense.

Hitler was now totally unenthusiastic about the Luftwaffe, and Göring was well out of favour; only weapons that could turn the course of the war or inflict revenge were considered important, hence Hitler's decision on the Me 262 as a bomber. The departure of Milch, who had been fired, and the death of General Korten (Chief of Staff) in the bomb blast that failed to kill Hitler on 20 July, contributed to the decline in the Luftwaffe's influence in the highest circles. Nazi politics continued to work in favour of the Allies.

Galland had actually been working behind the scenes to keep a fighter version of the Me 262 going, but they were not able to operate as a unit or to attract attention! However, the Me 163 had gone operational with I./ JG 400 and was established at bases to cover the oil installations in the Leipzig area. They flew their first mission on 28 July when the bombers went after these oil plants, and the bomber crews reported sightings of the new fighter, of which they had already been made aware by intelligence. The rocket fighters got nowhere with the bombers but tangled with P-51s of the 359th FG, with neither side scoring any success, though this did enable the Americans to put together new tactical advice for escort fighters, which in part was also supported by Ultra intercepts.

Speer:

> Around 10 August, Galland, in extreme agitation, asked me to fly with him to headquarters at once. In one of his arbitrary decisions Hitler had issued new orders: The Reich air fleet, whose outfitting with 2,000 fighter planes was nearing completion, was suddenly to be shifted to the western front. There, experience had long since shown us, it would be wiped out within a short time.

When Speer and Galland met Hitler he soon grew agitated.

> . . . he roared out at the top of his lungs. 'Operative measures are my concern! Kindly concern yourself with your armaments! This is none of your business' . . . Abruptly, he terminated the conference, cutting off all further argument. 'I have no more time for you.'

The following day, Hitler was even more furious and demanded an end to all aircraft production; the fighter force was to be disbanded and all production resources transferred to anti-aircraft guns. The order was ignored, and Speer told the Armaments Staff that they must maintain the maximum production of fighter aircraft.

September 1944 saw monthly output of fighters reach over 3,100, which included the first production jet fighters. The figures are impressive, but the fighter types being built were no longer suitable for the combat environment in which they had to operate. Ignoring the Me 262 for now, the other day fighters were the Bf 109 and Fw 190, both of which had been in service for many years and although they had undergone performance and weapon improvements, only so much could be done with an 'old airframe'. One reason for keeping the established designs was that more could be built in a shorter period, but this did nothing to address the core issue. The Allies on the other hand had spent a great deal of time and effort in the development of new fighters to meet combat requirements.

As with the RAF in the Battle of Britain, the bigger German problem was not aircraft, but pilots, and the fuel with which to fly. As the loss of supply bit, the allocation to training fell to 20,000 tons for September. By early 1944 the average pilot leaving training had flown a meagre 100–120 hours. At the same stage of their training his American opponents averaged 325–350 hours, and with a training regime that including tactics. The Luftwaffe, especially in the West, was becoming primarily a home-defence force, with the need for day fighters to counter the ever-growing American offensive, with its strong fighter escorts, being the main concern.

> During the month of October, pilot training declined by 30 per cent owing to the reduction of fuel supplies. The planned strengthening of the Reich defence was, however, made possible by the transfer of complete units [*Verbände*] to the fighter arm. The observers released by the conversion of bomber units to jet-propelled types were transferred to the paratroops, the air gunners were transferred to the railway defence of Luftflotte Reich, while the radio operators transferred to radio control duties with the front-line units.

These were sad paths for many aircrew and a waste of their training time and yet there appears to have been little attempt made to convert some of the experienced non-pilot aircrew to pilots.

There was no shortage of aircrew volunteers, but the quality of those recruits was more of an issue. Early in the war the Luftwaffe had attracted the cream of recruits, but many of the best had been sent to the bomber force, as that was the primary arm of the service, and it was also not considered that the fighter pilot had to have the same level of intelligence and education! This basic philosophy never really changed, although by 1944 the overall calibre of recruit had declined and the Luftwaffe was no longer the attraction that it once was. By the time it had become clear that Germany was fighting an air war for survival, it was no longer possible to put in place the corrective action around selection, pilot training and leadership development that was required. As with many of the problems of the Luftwaffe, the seeds of failure had been sown during the years of success. The strategic mistakes of the Luftwaffe High Command, some of which were driven by political considerations, had started in the pre-war structuring and equipping of the Luftwaffe, were reinforced in the years of victory, were extended by the refusal to learn lessons from their own and enemy operations, such as the RAF's victory in the Battle of Britain, and were ultimately particularly devastating as far as the home-defence fighter force was concerned. All of this became very clear in 1944 when it was too late. 'From the end of September onwards the supplies underwent a catastrophic decline and by the end of the year they had fallen to negligible quantities, so that training came almost to a standstill.'

The first Me 262 group was operational in the first week of October; based at Achmer and with an establishment of forty jets and under the command of the fighter ace Walter Nowotny, great things were expected of the unit, but results were mixed. On 7 October the jets claimed three bombers, but lost four aircraft, two in the area of the airfield, whose location was well known to the Americans. Claims were made by Major Richard Conner of the 78th FG and two by Lt Urban Drew of the 361st FG, both flying P-47s. Whilst the Me 262 might have a performance edge in combat it was a sitting duck near its airfields. The jet was still proving technically troublesome as well, which limited the available numbers each day and led to numerous aborts. Recriminations followed over poor tactics, lack of training, poor design and serviceability, all of which dogged the 'wonder jet' for many months. By the end of the year American fighter pilots had claimed fourteen of the jet fighters.

Every time oil was the target, the Luftwaffe tried to put up a strong defence; the trouble was that the odds were so great that no matter what success they scored it came at too high a cost in aircraft and pilots. Loss rates were frequently in the 25–30 per cent range, and whilst the Americans had the numbers to come back day after day, the Luftwaffe was unable to recover. Indeed, one of the most amazing aspects of this period is that the Luftwaffe was able to keep going at all. Drastic solutions were suggested to try and inflict a catastrophic level of losses, perhaps in the hundreds, on the American bombers, but even if they had succeeded the loss to the defenders would have been so high that it would have been a one-time effort – the Allies would still have been back if not the following day, then a few days later.

Merseburg was the target on 2 November 1944; one attacking group suffered a particularly heavy loss, with 9 aircraft downed and 9 damaged of the 36 sent and 82 aircrew listed as KIA/MIA. The Luftwaffe had made a concerted effort that day and reports suggested some 400 enemy fighters had intercepted the attacking groups, with 40-plus focusing on the 457th, claiming 7 bombers in quick succession. Losses would have been higher but for the intervention of P-51 escorts. After this shock, the group had lower losses than average.

Sergeant Jack Scarborough, top turret gunner on the craft piloted by Lt Ernest T. Salzer, one of the four surviving aircraft of the 751st BS, recalled:

> The assembly and the trip over were as usual and everything looked okay, until we noticed that there was only light flak over the target. You could just sense that trouble was brewing. On the bomb run everything went well and our fighter escort was with us. Just after bombs away, enemy jet-propelled planes appeared in a big group at nine o'clock high. At that time, enemy fighters were called out at eight o'clock level and high, sliding toward the tail. I was watching the dog fight at nine o'clock. Then as the jets led our escorts away, I glanced towards the tail and saw about 15 to 20 enemy planes coming in high from about 5 to 7 o'clock, with another front just behind them about level. I picked one out at five o'clock high, the tail gunner had picked one for himself at about six o'clock and the ball turret picked one out of the third wave, the only wave in his view.
>
> The first two waves came in wiping out most of our box, but most of them were also wiped out. The plane I was shooting at went over our tail and tore off his left wing on the vertical stabilizer of our left wingman. I swung my guns back to five o'clock again as the pilot, using evasive action, dropped the plane about 25 to 50 feet, leaving the Fw 190s shooting over us at the spot that we had just vacated. Our low box now consisted of only two Forts. The rest were scattered all over the sky. I started firing at the one at five, and the radio gunner was also firing at him. He started to smoke as he fell off our right wing, and down under our belly he burst into flames. The other one lost his prop and blew up about 25 feet from our tail. It was over! What had seemed like hours, had been only between 3 and 5 minutes. Nine of our Forts did not come back, but we took our toll of the Fw 190s.

The German aircrew position on 30 November was grim:

The output of aircrew personnel has fallen further owing to the small quantities of aircraft fuel available for training. Only through selecting advanced pupils and taking in instructors released by the reduction of training facilities, as well as the transfer of bomber crews to fighters, has it been possible to prevent the number of available aircraft from exceeding that of crews. When these reserves of flying personnel have been used up it will be some time before pupils who are now in the preliminary stages of training can become available. In night fighters the critical point has already been reached, that is the number of aircraft, including Luftflotte reserves, but excluding pools [*Leitstellen*] exceeds by 294 the number of crews available.

In a post-war interrogation, Göring spoke to General Spaatz, who asked him if the Allied attacks affected the training programme, to which Göring replied 'Yes, for instance the attacks on oil retarded the training because our new pilots could not get sufficient training before they were put in the air where they were no match for your fliers.' However, he also said that the jet programme remained a hope to the very last stages of the war: 'The transition to jets was very easy in training. The jet pilot output was always ahead of the jet aircraft production.'

By November 1944 the Eighth was able to send almost 1,500 heavies against targets in Germany – along with an escort of 1,000-plus fighters. In response it was unusual for the Germans to be able to mount more than 200–300 sorties, most of which were unable to penetrate the American fighter screen. Many Germans looked up at the countless condensation trails that criss-crossed the sky, an indication of the Allies' total mastery of the air.

No one was talking in the control-room; everyone waiting for a word from the Fighter-General who was now sitting on a wooden bench among us. He seemed to have aged since his previous visit, although he was still only about thirty. As always, he held a cigar between half-open lips below his small moustache. We loved him: he was ours. He had risen from our ranks, been decorated with the highest orders and been made the youngest general. But his courage, experience and intelligence had not been given full scope, they would listen in high places to his advice and then not follow it. Build fighters, fighters and still more fighters, he had said, but it was never done. And now, with enemy bombers flying undisturbed in their thousands over our country and reducing our towns to rubble our general had been made responsible for the air defence of the Reich. But now, of course, they were asking the impossible. His hand supporting his head, he was looking gloomily in front of him. At last he raised his eyes. 'Well, boys, I just don't know what to do. My influence up there is exhausted and I shall soon be gone.'

(Gunther Bloemertz, *Heaven Next Stop*)

The German ground counter-stroke in the Ardennes was launched on 16 December to take advantage of a period of bad weather that would severely handicap Allied air power. The initial successes were stunning and although some Allied recce and fighter-bomber missions were flown, it was only after the weather cleared that the Germans were literally bombed and strafed into retreat. From the air perspective, there was never any doubt as to who ruled the skies. Likewise, the days of even moderate success against the bombers had gone. The biggest danger to the Americans was mid-air collisions as they tried to get at the increasingly small numbers of Luftwaffe fighters, that and losses when strafing airfields, where flak presented a high risk.

The Final Period – Air Supremacy and Massive Destruction

New Year's Day 1945 saw Operation Bodenplatte, the last great throw of the dice by the Luftwaffe. In an attempt to destroy large numbers of Allied aircraft on the ground, the Luftwaffe threw over 900 aircraft at enemy airfields in the Low Countries. It was futile and idiotic. Although Allied anti-aircraft defences were never as good as German ones, airfields were still heavily defended, and once attacked a swarm of fighters would rise up from there and nearby airfields. Furthermore, strafing was not a role that the Luftwaffe had performed for some time, so most pilots were ineffective. One third, some 300 fighters, failed to return, and amongst the 200-plus lost aircrew were 19 experienced leaders. It might have made good headlines at home, if the losses could have been hidden; it might even have made some Allied personnel wonder where all these enemy aircraft came from, but the only lasting effect of the attack was the final curtain of the Luftwaffe's fighter force. Galland was dismissed and General Peltz, a bomber man, put in charge of the fighter force. The so-called 'Fighter Pilots' Mutiny' in January 1945 underlined the crisis that had settled on the Luftwaffe.

A memo from General Spaatz to the Combined Chiefs of Staff on 5 January showed that the Americans still had concerns over Luftwaffe capability, in part because of the shock caused by Bodenplatte; it was not until after the war that the abject failure of this operation was understood. Spaatz listed all the reasons why the Allies were winning, with comments such as 'the steady deterioration of the flying abilities of the German fighter crews as a result of their losses' but then went on to raise concerns:

Since the German aircraft industry has been shifted to places which are less susceptible to Allied bombing, it has been possible to keep the production on such a level as to enable the Luftwaffe to appear with a superior number of planes over certain salients of the front. Moreover, there must be taken into account the steadily growing number of jet-planes which, by reason of their superiority, form a considerable menace to the American assembly.

There would have been many in the Luftwaffe who would have been heartened to read this.

By now four US air forces were in place: the Eighth continued its strategic bombing from England with increasing success and lowering loss rates; the Ninth moved to France and followed the advancing ground forces, its bombers, fighters and fighter-bombers making life all but impossible for the German ground forces. In Italy, the Twelfth performed a similar task as the Allies fought their way north, whilst the Fifteenth hammered German industry in the two-pronged strategic offensive. Such was the reduced level of air threat that Bomber Command was able to undertake daylight missions in addition to its sixth year of night operations. In regard to the overall story, there is nothing really to add for the months of 1945. The Luftwaffe fighter pilots continued their vain defence in a sky full of enemy aircraft; losses were high, and it is a mark of their courage and discipline that they fought to the end.

The final RAF Bomber Command main force operations against Germany took place by day on 25 April 1945, the targets being Wangerooge and Berchtesgaden. The attack on Wangerooge was made by 482 bombers, over 300 of which were Halifaxes, for the loss of seven aircraft (six of these in mid-air collisions). The Command's final operational bombing mission took place on 2/3 May after a break without operations of almost a week. This was an all-Mosquito affair against Kiel to destroy shipping in the harbour. A total of 126 Mosquitoes attacked in two waves, with a further 53 Mosquitoes flying support, primarily airfield intruder missions, in the Kiel area. Only one Mosquito, from 169 Squadron, was lost. The only heavies airborne were 89 aircraft from No. 100 Group flying RCM support and tragically two of these were lost, probably in a mid-air collision. These three aircraft, from which only three of the Halifax crewmen survived, were the last operational losses suffered by Bomber Command. For RAF Bomber Command its six-year offensive was over; it had started with ineffective daylight bombing by small numbers of bombers and had then gone through years of night bombing with heavy losses and mixed results until it grew into an effective and devastating force.

For the American bombers of the Eighth Air Force the last sorties were flown on 25 April, the targets being the Skoda works at Pilsen and Hitler's complex at Berchtesgaden. The Ninth, Twelfth and Fifteenth Air Forces continued operating into May, and fighter sweeps continued over Germany. The last fighter combat took place on 8 May, Victory in Europe Day.

The Luftwaffe, and much of Germany had been destroyed.

Index

General subjects such as Fighter Command, Bomber Command, Luftwaffe, USAAF are not noted in the index. Many of the core themes, such as strategy, aircraft production, tactics, etc. appear throughout the text, so only major references to them are recorded in this index.

General index

Aircraft: Allied

Aircraft: Luftwaffe

Aifields: Allied

Aifields: Luftwaffe

Personalities: Allied

Personalities: Luftwaffe

Targets: UK

Personalities: Luftwaffe

Targets: UK